Inventing S

Studies
Hegemo
Patriarch
and Colon.allsm

Inventing Subjects

Studies in
Hegemony,
Patriarchy
and Colonialism

Himani Bannerji

Anthem Press
London

Anthem Press is an imprint of
Wimbledon Publishing Company
PO Box 9779
London SW19 7QA

This edition first published by Wimbledon Publishing Company 2002

First published by Tulika, India 2001

British Library Cataloguing in Publication Data
Data available

ISBN
1 84331 072 4 (hbk)
1 84331 073 2 (pbk)

1 3 5 7 9 10 8 6 4 2

Printed by Newton Printing Ltd, London, UK.   www.newtonprinting.com

Contents

For my mother
BINDUBASINI DEBI

In loving memory

Acknowledgements

I want to thank Abhijit Sen of the School of Women's Studies, Jadavpur University, Calcutta, for the help he gave me by hand-copying articles from old Bengali magazines which are literally on the verge of extinction. Thanks are due to Stephan Dobson, who was more than an editor for this volume, and who took much trouble over Bengali transcriptions. I also want to thank my partner, Michael Kuttner, whom it is impossible to thank enough, for all of his help in elaborating the ideas in these essays, entering many of them into the computer, and giving editorial suggestions. I want to thank Ratnabali Chattopadhyay, Jasodhara Bagchi, Uma Chakravarti, Maitreyee Krishnaraj, Judy Whitehead, Shibaji Bandyopadhyay, Manabendra Bandyopadhyay, Sourin Bhattacharya, Ana Davin, Dorothy Smith, Mariana Valverde and Karen Anderson for the many discussions I had with them on these issues and themes. Thanks are also due to Adam Givertz and Jennifer Steele for their interest in developing my critique of ideology in the first two essays. Since research and writing involve more than intellectual support and stimulation, such as housing the body of the scholar, her meals and health, the creation of a pleasant work environment, I want to thank my sister-in-law, Chua Chakravarty, as well as Karuna Chakravarti and Sarbani Goswami of the School of Women's Studies, Jadavpur University. I also want to thank the Social Science and Humanities Research Council of Canada for the financial support they gave me.

Foreword

It is with considerable pride that I write this small foreword. A one-time pupil and, by now, almost a member of my family, Himani is a fellow fighter against the current global onslaught. I recall with pleasure the helping hand that she extended in seeing the School of Women's Studies, Jadavpur University, through its birthing process. The clarity of conceptualization and the warm hospitality of articulation with which she delivered her lecture series, entitled 'Feminism and Method', kicked us off to a start and we never looked back.

Most of the essays in this volume grew out of Himani's project on 'Reform and Hegemony', which she did as a long-term affiliate of the School of Women's Studies. Her interest in tracing the formation of a gendered class subjectivity with colonial compulsion meshed with our own project of retrieving women's writings from the heyday of colonialism to the threshold of India's independence. Throughout the period of intense interchange, Himani was one of us, bringing a critical input from her understanding born of living in an advanced capitalist society. Her critique of colonial class subjectivity was not the product of a 'postcolonial' perspective derived from a reified form institutionalized in North America. As a participant in the Indian women's movement, her exploration of class and gender struggles in colonial Bengal had a political cutting edge. Understandably, these analyses found an urgent context within India. She has acknowledged that her work linked up with several feminist scholars in India who were working on related themes of reform, nationalism, gender and class under colonialism.

The entire range of Himani's lived experience that straddles 'development' and 'underdevelopment' has made her use Marx, Gramsci, Dorothy Smith and Sumit Sarkar very creatively. The solidarity of a resistant politics that the School of Women's Studies at Jadavpur University stands for has been vindicated by this volume. I thank her for it.

April 2001   JASODHARA BAGCHI
Founder-Director
School of Women's Studies
Jadavpur University

Inventing Subjects

An Introduction

Men make their own history, but they do not make it just as they please; they do not make it under circumstances chosen by themselves, but under circumstances directly encountered, given and transmitted from the past.

Karl Marx, *The Eighteenth Brumaire of Louis Bonaparte*

A social group dominates antagonistic groups, which it tends to 'liquidate', or to subjugate perhaps even by armed force; it leads kindred and allied groups. A social group can, and indeed must, already exercise 'leadership' before winning governmental power (this indeed is one of the principal conditions for the winning of such power); it subsequently becomes dominant when it exercises power, but even if it holds it firmly in its grasp, it must continue to lead as well.

Antonio Gramsci, *Selections from The Prison Notebooks*

The essays collected in this volume were written over a period, between 1989 and 1995. When I began my research and started on the first pieces they were quite new in their themes and theoretical preoccupations, especially in relation to elaborating the field of feminist historical sociology and with respect to India. But as the years went by and these articles appeared sporadically as a part of a much larger project, there emerged an extensive body of literature which also dealt with many of the themes or issues with which these essays grapple. We need only to remember the many feminist historians, cultural theorists and scholars in postcolonial studies in India, the UK and the US who have written during the last decade on social and cultural construction, representation and moral regulation of patriarchally inscribed social subjectivities or cultural identities and their ideological and political agencies and implications.[1] They have also shown how these constructions, representations and regulations were produced through colonial, nationalist and reformist discourses. Some of these scholars have taken the issue of class into consideration and written on gendered or patriarchal aspects of class formation and politics. Thus my essays, as their bibliographies and citations indicate, gradually developed a larger set of companions and sources of reference, and issues and themes which were novel in the 1980s are no longer wholly so, though they continue to hold the interest of researchers as their exploration is by no means complete. But the interest of these essays lies only partially in their themes and issues, and more in the theoretical complexity and depth of exploration with which they are treated. Both these reasons have together prompted me to publish a collection of these essays, which are thematically and thoretically connected to each other even though separated by their time of writing and publication. It is my hope that this introduction will speak of their relevance to our present-day scholarly endeavours and mitigate impressions of disconnectedness which might arise if each piece is read in isolation. It should display the logic of the organization of the volume and the coherence of the theoretical preoccupations of the essays. Their current relevance should be particularly noted with regard to socio-cultural and political theorizations, both in the context of India and for the project of building a feminist anti-racist or anti-colonial Marxist historical sociology. A discussion is in order, therefore, regarding the location of these essays within a larger critical epistemological framework. They are, after all, meant to offer ways for thinking through specific or empirical projects of feminist historical and cultural sociology, as well as those of anti-colonial and anti-capitalist political theory in a broadly theoretical manner. It is hoped that the critical approaches developed in these essays and their application to socio-cultural and ideological–political formations in Bengal/ India will attract serious consideration and it will become apparent to the reader how they are bound to each other within the overarching theme of 'inventing subjects'—the title of the volume.

The notion of inventing subjects, read in a nuanced way, contains a double meaning. It speaks to social subjectivity as being both inventing and invented. Through this formulation social subjects can be considered as cultural and ideological objects of others' invention while pointing to the possibility of inventing themselves as subjects within a given socio-historical context. This recognition confers upon them ideological and political agencies in which they can be considered and shown functioning both as existing social subjects and ideological topics. As such neither social subjectivity nor ideological or political agencies can be treated as spontaneous or found objects on the ground of ontology, nor are they to be seen only as functions of discourses. Instead, these essays insist that they be seen as dynamic, and sometimes purposive, constellations of both unconscious and conscious forms of cultural and ideological constructions which are connected to history, social organization, social relations and social locations of these subjects. Thus among the 'invented' and 'inventing' subjects of these essays we encounter different types of socio-cultural entities or identities whose ideological stances or elaborations and political agencies vary as well as overlap.

The volume opens with two essays, "Writing 'India', Doing 'Ideology': William Jones' Construction of India as an Ideological Category" and "Beyond the Ruling Category to What Actually Happens: Notes on James Mill's Historiography in *The History of British India*", which address two grand colonial constructive designs whereby the very notion of 'India' becomes a composite ideological category central to the project of inventing appropriate social subjectivities and agencies for colonial rule of the local peoples and cultures. This categorical 'India' consists of a bundle of racially ethnicized cultural identities, inset within a mythicized history, which are constructed within specific European colonial discourses relevant to the particular enterprise of dominating India. The contents of these constructive designs for projecting colonial identities are not uniform, as they are both orientalist and utilitarian with a christian inflection. Seemingly contradictory at times and coherent at others, and reconciled at the level of ruling, these ideological identities provide a cultural content and sociological framework in relation to which other inventions of social subjectivities or forms of representation produced by the indigenous peoples need to be situated. These latter inventions are not necessarily in agreement with the colonial attempts, but always in response or reference to them.

The next two essays, namely "Age of Consent and Hegemonic Social Reform" and "Attired in Virtue: Discourse on Shame (*lajja*) and Clothing of the Gentlewoman (*bhadramahila*) in Colonial Bengal", offer us two other instances of invention of social subjectivities and moral identities, in which we encounter constructive and interpretive attempts where Bengali/Indian women are subject–objects of both colonial and indigenous hegemonic enterprises. The first relates solely to colonial discourse, showing what the colonial ideological category of 'India' spells out into when its civilizational judgment and representational construction are applied to Indian women. This essay brings to our attention how deeply and necessarily patriarchal ruling enterprises need to be, and also how racist are these constructed ethnic identities in a colonial context. This necessarily patriarchal and racist colonial discourse which organizes the everyday ruling moral constructions and regulations as well as the legal apparatus of the state, is shown to be deployed by both white (English/European) administrators as well as a section of the indigenous male elite. "Attired in Virtue", based on the creation of the typology of Bengali *bhadramahila* or the gentlewoman, a term pertaining to the new middle-class woman through designing her clothing, treats this notion as a complex sign with a concrete significational and practical content. Here the project of creating an ideal genteel feminine identity is one of creating a difference, of creating a sartorial–moral appearance or form which will be distinct from the type of ideal identity for Bengali/Indian women projected either by colonial discourse or by an unreconstructed traditional/feudal one. The woman here, unlike in "Age of Consent", is an upper-class/caste woman with more than a physical function. Thus she is not just a tropical body, a combination of animal sex and fecundity, but rather the object–subject of a moral constellation which signifies transcendence. It is her chaste sexual morality, the minimization of her physicality, her 'decency', that is the goal of the sartorial projects. These sartorial signs of the *bhadramahila*, then, throw up a challenge to colonial discourse even when picking up both moral and visual elements from it. Thus the matter of clothing, of even fashion design, can become one of nationalism—of a consciously hegemonic aspiration. The process is one where the indigenous male elite are the initial designers of this cultural–ideological subject-inventing process centred on women, but soon enough they are superseded by women of the same upper classes who take up the project. As such, Bengali/Indian women themselves end up as the agents and subjects of their own invention. But of course, though some introduce into their discursive dressing a critical awareness of patriarchy and create in their new signs and proposals a visual and moral tension, they also fall back at times upon both brahminical patriarchal indigenous as well as western racialized patriarchal and puritanical, namely so-called 'Victorian', visual discursive forms and moralities.

In these essays I have tried to show the making of a colonial and Bengali middle-class consciousness at work. No matter done by whom, either elite or colonial men or women, these identity designs with their conduct prescriptions and judgments are discursive/ideological staples of what emerges as the complex and contradictory self-consciousness of the Bengali middle classes or the more monolithic colonial stereotypes. This point, particularly about middle-class consciousness, comes out more directly in the essay "Fashioning a Self: Educational Proposals for and by Women in Popular Magazines in Colonial Bengal". Here Bengali middle-class women themselves are the primary or direct agents for the invention of ideal feminine subjectivities—of their moral conduct and political agencies. In their formulations and demands these women often do offer powerful challenges to gender inequalities prevalent within the social space of their own classes, and they often do so in what might have evolved today into 'feminist' discourse. But again they do not make themselves just as they please, but with what discourses and circumstances, goals and realities, they inherit or find around. This of course entails both a negative and a positive relationship to patriarchal colonial and indigenous elite discourses, as well as being determined by their social locations as members of well-to-do upper-caste/class families. As their magazine articles show, they perform through their new moral

figurations a double movement, which simultaneously invents their
own substantive social subjectivities as individuals or persons while
creating a moral–cultural physiognomy which seeks to be influential or hegemonic among different sections of the Bengali middle
classes. These worthy *bhadramahilas* are the counterparts of the
worthy *bhadraloks*, both seeking to create right moral conduct for
the elite. The last essay, "Re-generation: Mothers and Daughters in
Bengal's Literary Space", built on literary material from a much
later time, presents us both with a continuity with the earlier problematics as well as a different one. Here, in spite of a lived familiarity with ideas and practices of the Bengali middle classes, there
is an attempt to go beyond the moral signs or representational figures of the *bhadramahila* and her gendered elite consciousness at
the service of her caste/class. The feminism of the novels considered
here is less compromised and the legitimacy of the ideological practices, namely, the hegemony of the properted classes evolved from
the nineteenth century on, stands a chance of inquiry and disman-
tling by the women protagonists. In fact, the narrative development
of the protagonists consists of just such attempts and challenges.
Though not entirely free from the hegemonic world of *bhadralok/
bhadramahila* or that of a modified colonial discourse, the imagined subjectivities and agencies for middle-class women in these
novels break certain established boundaries.

All of these essays on 'inventing subjects', then, contain
related themes and issues and also overlap with each other, revealing to us that the designs or making of 'selves' and 'others', and
being made by 'others', can often break their significational and
figural boundaries and blur into each other. My interest was more
arrested by these dynamic and interconstitutive significational
practices and moral proposals for making of subjects and agents in
the colonial context than by the all-pervasive concern with colonial
discourse displayed by the relatively new field of postcolonial
studies. These I found to be both derivative and substantive proposals and practices, elaborated within the colonial ideological
apparatus of ruling or in colonial Bengal's upper-class/caste terrain.
They encoded the complex consciousness of the various strands of
the middle classes, but also of variations in colonial discourse. I
was aware of the double-headedness of Bengali middle classes as

being subjects who are ruled and ruling, of the urban and rural, feudal and colonial social bases of the norms and forms of their consciousness. It was obvious that the indigenous male elite both absorbed and resisted colonial discourse, but with little difference of opinion with colonial patriarchy, and that middle-class Bengali women themselves absorbed patriarchal discourses of both varieties while also challenging them in gender terms. At the same time women also disagreed with each other while agreeing with their male counterparts.

Having spoken so far to the theoretical and thematic logic of these texts and the organization of the volume itself, I need to ground the essays in my wider critical and epistemological interest. This is necessary to give my notion of 'inventing subjects' its full theoretical scope. It is important to note, therefore, that my theoretical excursion began from an anti-racist Marxist feminist standpoint. This is still my critical perspective or theoretical position, and then as now, my interest in concepts of social organization and social relations, in class, ideology and hegemony, impels me to explore and elaborate on social theories of Marx and Gramsci, and to apply them to a practical reading of historical sociology of class formation and politics in India. Though concentrated on discourse-based material, the essays in this volume are primarily Marxist from beginning to end, but it is a kind of Marxist social analysis which is refracted through a particular reading of Gramsci which allows me to explore aspects of class as social and ideological formation, thus presenting class consciousness in historical materialist terms. Seen in this way, any reading of class formation or struggle needs the concept of ideology as well as those of hegemony and common sense, which allows us to politicize culture.

Marx and Gramsci both offer theoretical spaces which most effectively implicate questions of social subjectivities, agencies and ideology with those of class struggle and the making of history. As Marx, in particular, was my point of departure, I should mention the two texts which specially intrigued me, namely, *The Communist Manifesto* (1984) and *The Eighteenth Brumaire of Louis Bonaparte* (1963). Even though they had been read and used a lot in different ways, I felt that they could be still reworked by a Marxist feminist historical sociologist for analytical purposes. But this required a fresh exploration and expansion of certain turns of phrase, problematics and concepts within these texts. This I felt should be done through a more complex theorization, as well as empirical sociological research within a historical context. As I was especially interested in the concept of class, I wanted to explore what Marx meant by class and class struggle in the *Manifesto* when he spoke not only of 'open' but also of 'hidden' forms of class struggles. Since the notion of 'hidden' forms is by definition not obvious or spoken of generally, I felt that the problems and problematic of class consciousness needed to be thought through more extensively than was done conventionally. Particularly, as this type of consciousness could be both non-apparent as such as well as a matter of conscious political and ideological project. An 'unconscious' class consciousness, though it may sound paradoxical, is not really so, and in texts such as *The Eighteenth Brumaire* Marx explored this in terms of displaced ideological formations implicated in 'hidden' struggles of classes. The failure of the French revolution to produce a truly equal society is presented here by Marx as disguised moments of class struggle. Here class agents and ideologies were considered in terms of pageants and drama, with actors donning various masks of class. Displacements of class politics were necessarily indistinguishable from culture. Both these texts of Marx provided me with a powerful incentive and a method to read everyday life, that is, culture and social relations, as essentially political spaces and practices. As I have said elsewhere:

> To redefine class as social rather than as solely economic relations is also to realize that not only is that political which claims to be so. Only by taking such a stance can we implant the cultural process within the political process. This enables us to go behind and beyond what is conventionally called political, so that we can begin to realize the full import of direct and indirect forms of politics. Seen thus, sites and forms of class struggle become complex and manifold. Social forms which are elaborated from the social being of classes, which are relatively passive, and others which are, though highly mediated, articulatedly ideological, all become political forms. (Bannerji 1998: 161)

Nothing that is social could fall outside of the purview of class, nor could class be seen as apart from it. I felt that this method of under-standing the social as an integrated formation is one that we must muster if we are to understand what forces create socio-political subjectivities and agencies and impede or facilitate social emanci-pation. What roles social subjectivities or cultural identities play in hegemonic bids by different classes or political systems can not be uncovered without this. This method is something that the rela-tively uncomplicated Marxism of our youth did not have. It meant rethinking Marxism in terms of the social, through a non-binary, non-dualistic formulation of the relationship between political economy and culture.

It is in the quest to understand the social rather than accepting an ascribed economistic interpretation of Marx's views on class struggle and the making of history, of the active roles he assigns to social subjects, that I turned to Antonio Gramsci's *Selections from The Prison Notebooks* (1971). I felt that if I linked Marx's concept of class in its fullness as a complex social forma-tion implying culture, ideology and politics, to that of hegemony, civil society, common sense and different types of political manoeu-vres as elaborated by Gramsci, I would get a better sociological understanding of the ramifications of Marx's method. Gramsci's notion of common sense and concepts such as 'war of position', 'war of manoeuvre' and transformism—all meant to explore the making of historical subjectivities and actions—bonded well with Marx's conceptions of ideology, 'open' and 'hidden' dimensions of class struggle, with attempts to make history. This wide and theo-retical frame allowed me to draw on current epistemological and cultural critiques, for example feminist and anti-racist critiques or critiques of colonial discourse. This meant being able to include various relations of power expressed in terms of 'otherization' and construction of difference. This, I felt, rather than being idio-syncratic, returned Marx's and Gramsci's political enunciations to their fuller value. And most importantly, as a Marxist feminist historical sociologist, I felt the importance of overcoming a binary and inverse relationship between 'class' and 'culture', or 'discourse' and 'social relations', structure and forms of consciousness, which seems to pervade our intellectual world.

Since a historical sociologist necessarily rests her work on

the concept of a historically located 'social'—a concept that illumi-
nates the entire opus of Marx—we can deepen our understanding
of this by turning to Gramsci's use of the concept of 'civil society',
which seeks to delve into the social ground. In the way that he formulates this concept Gramsci allows us a two-way movement to
politicize 'culture' and to find a cultural dimension to politics. He
shows how everyday practices and discourses which are coded as
'culture' and often presented as unconnected to structural social
relations, are actually deeply imbedded in them and are material in
nature. Read thus, 'civil society' becomes the home of political
overdetermination or hegemony, the 'pillbox' that holds up the
state, which expresses the shifting equilibrium of classes. The
norms and forms of the seemingly 'private' spaces of our lives, the
realm of personal experiences, he shows are in the realm of 'class',
inasmuch as class is the social world of 'civil society'. Class here, as
an ensemble of social relations and significational practices, is then
not only an economic but a social form. It indicates how social
spaces of lived relations, valorized practices and experiences are
implicated in relations and moralities of property and labour relations. Thus class consciousness, when elaborated within these
social rather than only *economic* relations, is one with the civil
society. Civil society, therefore, becomes another name for a class
society which houses competing projects of hegemony. So when a
society carries on creating and debating social subjectivities or cultural practices encoding complementary and contradictory moral
constructions and regulations, for example of masculinity and
femininity or of motherhood, it is engaged in creating complementary and competitive forms of hegemonic class consciousness.
Thus social moralities are inseparable from class practices and class
politics. It is this kind of formulation which allows us to comprehend and expand Marx's idea of 'hidden' struggles of class.

      Class politics, we need to remember in this context, always
aims to be hegemonic, and this is not only regarding the other, that
is, the contending classes, but also introvertively. There are, obviously, contending ideological and relational fractions or fragments
within classes themselves. The bourgeoisie are, for example, not a
monolithic formation. The construction and evolution of social
subjectivities and agencies also express this fractional formation of

classes. As such there have to be cultural–moral ideologies and practices which compete and emerge as victorious, rendering others partial or sectoral, to mount a project of hegemony.

Considering class as an ensemble of social relations with their mediating and expressive forms of consciousness brings out not only the point that class consciousness is multifaceted and contradictory, where non-bourgeois and differential bourgeois values and practices collide and converge, but that they all legitimate private property. This also brings us to the realization that groups holding the same relation to the means of production, whether owners or non-owners, do not produce a uniform type of social and political consciousness. This is why we do not have *one* ideology per class—a standardized bourgeois, proletarian or peasant ideology—but rather there are constant attempts by different class fractions, drawing their cultural resources from different places, to create particular social subjectivities and agencies and to influence and overwhelm those put forward by other groups. Social subjectivities and political agencies, various identity enterprises of different classes, therefore, are neither inevitable in their content nor always already there as natural emanations of social ontology. They are constantly elaborated, invented, evolved and waged for as a part of class formation and class struggle. These aspects of class and class struggle become apparent if we scrutinize the so-called public–private divide or bring the notions of power and politics to the seemingly non-political space of civil society, which holds a constitutive relationship with the economic, juridical and political aspects of society.

It should be obvious from what I have said so far that exploring social subjectivities, identities and agencies, or social order/organization and change, is impossible without the concept of ideology. As Raymond Williams (1979) points out, there are different meanings ascribed to this concept, ranging from a neutral and systematic organization of ideas, through the notion of 'false consciousness', to that of an epistemology for producing these 'false' ideas as well as erasures and occlusions of social reality. This last meaning of ideology, which is critical about knowledge production, is central to Marx's use of the concept in *The German Ideology* (1973). My use of it, which has an epistemological thrust, remains very close to his. As such I am concerned with knowledge production not just in terms of the content of particular ideas which are generated, but also with the epistemological devices employed in the process. Furthermore, I try to connect their integrity with subjective aspects of class—namely, those of class consciousness and class struggle. As I mentioned before, this is where I find an opening not only for bringing Gramscian concepts into those of Marx, but also for an overall epistemological social critique. If a certain *content* or particular ideas provide class subjects with their sense of selves, ways to organize and interpret their world and the ideological hegemony of their classes, then we need to explore the knowledge producing devices that allow them to come to life. If ruling or exploitation is accomplished through these devices and ideas which produce consent, absorption or cooptation, or create absences and occlusions of social realities, we may say that both ideological practices and their ideational content are themselves social relations of exploitation. It is from this point of view of speaking of knowledge as a productive form, as modes of mediation of the ruling relations and their apparatuses, that dominating ideological contents as culture or discourses interest me. In the first two essays on inventing 'India' we see how a specific set of civilizational identity inventions and ascriptions, implying or producing significant gaps and absences of a material universe and history of India, function as intrinsic relations of ruling. As such, constructions of orientalists and utilitarians, such as William Jones or James Mill, are not just neutral forms of representation, but rather ideological practices and power/knowledge content which are instituted as modes of ruling. It is perhaps an important aside to mention that through such a dehistoricizing and socially occlusive form of knowledge production established materialist or Marxist categories can become ruling categories. An economistic rather than a fully socialized use of the category 'class', or a use of the category 'woman' which occludes class and other social relations of power, becomes such an ideological or ruling category critiqued by Marx in *The German Ideology*. The same can be said of notions such as that of 'nation' when conceived outside the context of capital, class, patriarchy and imperialism. The essay "Age of Consent" shows how the cultural categories of the 'tropical' and the 'hindu' woman serve as such ideological categories for colonial rule, while in "Fashioning a Self" I explore how a non-adjectivized notion of 'woman' serves the same purpose in instituting the middle-class Bengali woman as a universal, that is, hegemonic identity for women in all other social locations.

Ideology, then, both as form and content, cannot be comprehended without its visceral connection with historical social relations and moral codes of power which texture the everyday life of any civil society and culture. Neither 'open' nor 'hidden' formations and struggles of class can happen without their formative mediation. As such, social organization and relations of gender or patriarchy, with their implied sexual and social division of labour and moral construction and regulation, are indispensable to the workings of ideology. Any critique must be cognizant of that. If the notion of 'class' is a code for social relations of property, and if this property consists of both productive and reproductive labour, then it necessarily entails gender or patriarchy in all senses. Male social control of differentiated bodies and power relations between them, both in terms of activities and meanings, are essential, not peripheral, factors of this. Thus characteristics of property both in the private sphere, that is, the family, and the public, that is, the economic and political sphere, must come together in any study of class. These essays, as a study of engendering of classes and classifying of gender, are meant to provide us with this window of insight.

My account of reading Marx and Gramsci with a feminist sociologist's eye and arriving to this position from the standpoint of feminist Marxism is incomplete without mentioning the influence of Dorothy E. Smith. Smith's feminist sociology, which rests on the ground of critical epistemology directed towards discovery of the social, or what actually happens, taught me to read Marx's concept of ideology as I have done. That knowledge is a matter of social organization and serves a social relation, rather than being an exercise in transcendental truth, and as such helps both in occlusion and revelation of the world in which we live and our formative subjective relations to it, is a key position from which these essays are written. Similarly, I must acknowledge Smith's help in the way in which I have constituted the class–culture problematic in some of my essays to be a problematic of the everyday world, and how gender/patriarchy texture this problematic. Two of Smith's texts, *The Everyday World as Problematic* (1987) and *The Conceptual Practices of Power* (1990), are repeatedly drawn upon in constituting the theoretical frameworks for the essays here.

This introduction would also remain incomplete if I stayed only at a theoretical level and did not provide a practical and an immediately political context for the essays in this volume. I should begin by speaking of my long association with the development of feminist politics and perspectives in India, including the development of women's studies, especially in West Bengal. In particular this means acknowledging my debt to Sachetana, a Calcutta-based feminist women's group, and to Professor Jasodhara Bagchi who, mobilizing help from many, including myself, created the School of Women's Studies in Jadavpur University. Sachetana, with which I was associated from its inception, not only became a place for me to learn about Indian feminist perspectives, especially in the 1980s, but also inspired my commitment in finding out the physiognomy of patriarchy and the gender evolution of my own class. What, I thought, as a Bengali *bhadramahila* myself, went into our making as class subjects? What are the historical and sociological bases to how we define and occupy our place as feminist women who are members of propertied classes? Discussions with Professor Bagchi, as well as with Professor Ratnabali Chattopadhyay of Calcutta University's history department, helped me to develop these questions. I decided to conduct my research through the School of Women's Studies at Jadavpur University. Professor Bagchi in particular shared my interest in the theme of engendering of class and classifying of women. Under a project entitled 'Reform and Hegemony' I became an honorary fellow of the School and entered into exploring and analysing a large body of textual material on women and family which was primarily generated in nineteenth-century urban Bengal. The old problematic of social reform versus hindu cultural revival with regard to these themes served as a good enough launching pad for formulation, while a post-doctoral award from the Social Science and Humanities Research Council of Canada enabled me financially to conduct this research in the first phase.

In terms of the Indian aspect of this research there were

and are other Indian influences that I must mention. When I was beginning to rethink Marx and Gramsci I came across Sumit Sarkar's *A Critique of Colonial India* (1985a). In one of the essays in this volume Sarkar remarks upon an overwhelming body of literature on women, family and associated social morality in nineteenth-century Bengal. He suggests that this literature be treated as pivotal to the innovation and elaboration of nineteenth-century Bengali social and political thought. I had also noticed this phenomenon myself while doing research for my doctoral dissertation, which involved an inquiry into social formation and class politics in nineteenth and twentieth-century Bengal. While this material had helped me to flesh out the social dimensions of class for my dissertation, I had not explored it in any depth. I was familiar as well with literature on women and social reform in the context of debates on Bengal renaissance. I had also noticed that this interest in women and family receded to the background as the nationalist project became stronger in Bengal. What I had not considered was why so little had been done even in later writings on social and political thought in Bengal to give a central location to this obsessive preoccupation with women's or family conduct on the part of both the male and female intelligentsia. Though Sarkar gave them much importance and suggested that they be examined in terms of creating class and national identity, he had not yet shown us in any detail how this was the case. This 'how' got addressed in exciting ways by Indian feminists, in *Recasting Women: Essays in Colonial History* (Sangari and Vaid 1990), and by what I heard in conferences on women organized in different parts of India. Papers presented in one of these conferences, held in Jadavpur University [subsequently anthologized in *Indian Women: Myth and Reality* (Bagchi 1995)], were especially illuminating. In particular, four Indian scholars interested me tremendously— Kumkum Sangari, Tanika Sarkar, Uma Chakravarti and Jasodhara Bagchi. In their work everyday life pertaining to women and the family lost its unimportance or taken-for-granted status and became charged with deep social significance, ideologies and active practices. Gendered aspects of class, politics of motherhood, conjugality and sexuality were discussed in a multidisciplinary manner. Essays on women, gender and class in this volume build on their work. It is with this feminist scholarship that a proper social history of Bengal came to life. I could now see and show how the humble, everyday life of women, relegated to the private sphere, was the home of hegemony for both dominant and oppressed classes.

I wanted to join my own work to this type of scholarship, and found much to learn from it in terms of both theorization and empirical research. I interjected some of the themes and issues of Indian feminists into my own interest in bridging the gap between feminist social history, cultural critique and historical sociology. Unlike *The Great Arch: English State Formation as Cultural Revolution* (Corrigan and Sayer 1985), that superb book of historical sociology to which I remain indebted for understanding the connection between moral regulation, hegemony and the state, I touched upon the state only limitedly. The subjective aspects of class formation and consciousness of the Bengali middle classes, with a special emphasis on women as both objects and subjects of these projects of self-making of classes, and their political implications, remained my primary focus, though the discursive project of the colonial state served as the 'great arch' for my work. I wanted to show that these invented subjects of the essays are pre- and/or sub-texts of hegemony and that they are by no means empty or floating signifiers amenable to arbitrary interpretations, but rather embedded in their own socio-historical grounds. They are ideological or discursive forms which are constitutive of and constituted by colonial capitalism as transplanted in variously developed precapitalist societies. What is more, these constructive enterprises are tense and contested affairs.

I want to conclude by acknowledging the impact of especially English social historians on my project. I could never have thought of or elaborated my own theoretical/critical stance if I had not read the works of E.P. Thompson or Christopher Hill. Thompson's *The Making of the English Working Class* (1966), in particular, still holds me in fascination. In retrospect, I realize that my ambition was to produce a work which would do for the colonial Bengali middle classes what Thompson's work did for the English working classes. But I wanted to go beyond Thompson by expanding the notion of class to hold a fuller social scope. This meant, for me, complicating the relationship of class and culture by introducing a feminist and an anti-racist perspective. I was surprised and disappointed by the absence of gender or patriarchy in Thompson's understanding of class consciousness. Joan Scott, in her *Gender and the Politics of History* (1988), wrote of this absence eloquently. The absence of empire, colonies or "race" as a formative part of English working-class consciousness was also disturbing. Stuart Hall (1992), among others, helped me to think clearly of this lack. My intellectual and political debt extends to other Anglo–American feminist historians who have written in the last three decades. The imaginative portrayal of the mental–social universe of the English middle classes found in Leonora Davidoff and Catherine Hall's *Family Fortunes: Men and Women of the English Middle Class, 1780–1950* (1987) must be mentioned. They succeeded in doing much of what I wanted to do for the Bengali middle classes. I also learned about gendered or patriarchal inflections in class formation and politics, and of patriarchal morality of national and colonial projects, from authors such as Ana Davin, Ann McClintock, Judith Walkowitz, Antoinette Burton and Lata Mani, among others.

I am still quite a way from realizing my highly ambitious project of writing a book on the making of the Bengali middle classes, but all work is work in process, and these essays are small sketches or road maps of the direction in which I have travelled and mean to go. I want to end by saying that I hope that these essays will offer an integrated insight, rather than random thoughts, into the making of the social, where both dominating and liberating forms of consciousness are inseparable from historical social relations and where determined and determining social subjectivities and agencies make history move.

Note

[1] Many of these authors are referenced in the essays in this volume, therefore I do not cite them separately here.

Writing 'India', Doing 'Ideology'

William Jones' Construction of India
as an Ideological Category

> Our knowledge of [contemporary] society is to a large extent
> mediated to us by texts of various kinds. The result, an objecti-
> fied world-in-common vested in texts, coordinates the acts, deci-
> sions, policies, and plans of actual subjects as the acts, decisions,
> policies, plans of large-scale organizations.
>
> D.E. Smith, *The Conceptual Practices of Power* (1990)

Introduction: A New Historiography as a Critique

The objectives and representational efforts of European
history have come up for interrogation from some quarters in the
last two decades. The reasons for this lie in a wide recognition of a
constructive relationship between knowledge and power. This critical impetus seems to have come more from Foucault's 'power/
knowledge' formulation and other associated attempts than from
an extension of Marx's theory of ideology which was until then the
primary critical tool for establishing relations between ideas and
exercises of class power with class understood mainly as an economic form. Interest in Marx's notion of ideology dropped consi-
derably in the Anglo–American academic world after the entrance
of Michel Foucault's and Antonio Gramsci's works in translation,
while social movements with no direct connection with class as
defined by Laclau and Mouffe gained momentum. Political economy receded into the background and cultural theories became
highly prominent in studying politics. Whereas attempts at work-

This essay was first published in *Left History*, Vol. 2, No. 2, 1994, pp. 5–36.

ing in Marx with Foucault and Gramsci were rarer, there was a greater success in blending Foucault with Gramsci. This was achieved particularly through a manipulation of the categories 'hegemony' and 'common sense' in culturalist terms. An important moment of this success, at least in the English-speaking world, was Edward Said's *Orientalism* (1978). But *Orientalism* was only the tip of the iceberg of critiques which addressed the power/knowledge relations of the conventional academic disciplines. History writing in particular came in for a trenchant criticism from those who sought to create new interdisciplinary histories, epistemologies and new forms of narratives—sensitive to discursive inscriptions of power or power as discourse. Other disciplines were also affected; Philip Abrams' *Historical Sociology* (1982) and the writings of Philip Corrigan, Derek Sayer and Joan Scott, among others, may be remembered in this context. These were radical, Marxist or even anti-Marxist efforts, drawing upon classical European philosophy, literary and cultural theories. Criticisms of metaphysics and foundationalism offered by Jacques Derrida or Richard Rorty, for example, provided the theoretical bases for many, in combination with Foucault's discursive structuralism.

The new schools produced important critiques, especially thematized around 'difference' and 'representation'. They uncovered significational forms of domination in culture, showing how culture was textured with colonialism, racism, sexism and heterosexism. Of these attempts a very important one was the critique of colonial discourse (popularized by Edward Said) which centred on the relationship between reification and domination in the colonial representation (i.e. construction) of Europe's 'others'. Among the representations of these colonized 'others', cultural construction of India became a central area of critique. Perhaps the most extensive of these is Ronald Inden's *Imagining India* (1990). Here Inden takes history (his own discipline) to task for "imagining" (i.e. representing cum constructing) India through the epistemological lens of colonialism:

> I criticize the knowledge of 'Others' that Europeans and Americans have created during the periods of their world ascendancy. The specific object of my critique is the Indological branch of

> 'orientalist discourse' and the accounts of India that it has pro-
> duced since the Enlightenment, but it also takes on the other
> disciplines that have had a major part in making these constructs
> of India—the history of religions, anthropology, economics and
> political philosophy. (1990: 1)

It does not take much perspicacity to realize that Inden's orientation is sensitized by Said's *Orientalism*, though his critique of
indology, mainly based on the philosophy of R.G. Collingwood
(1889–1943), takes him to a somewhat different political conclusion than Said's critique of orientalism.

   While we need not detain ourselves with an examination
of *Imagining India*, it is clear that this re-reading of Indian history
derives from a general attempt to establish *representation* as a key
theme in historiography. It expands 'history' to include various
narrative forms, among them translation. Interpretive deconstruction becomes the current method of history writing and replaces
more conventional tasks of archival retrieval, documentation and
so on, with their explanatory or 'truth' claims.[1] As a representational effort history becomes a cultural–political project. It is read
as a repository of constructed content, of an accretional body of
concepts and images, regarding and standing in for the object/sub-
ject under representation. This representational content is read as a
gesture of power/knowledge, with embedded moral regulations
and political imperatives, for all of which the word ideology, albeit
in a non-Marxist sense, is sometimes loosely used. A pattern of circulation is also detected within this representational content travelling through the arteries of discursivities and intertextualities. A
gathering body of themes, images, icons and narrative forms, such
as travelogues or translations for example, are explored to determine what the representational terms are and how they constellate
as discursive apparatuses decisive for constructing the 'other'.[2]

   This discursive generation and movement of content has
come to be considered problematic in that it allows a historically
specific content to take on the status of a stable, and even an essential and transcendental, form of knowledge. It has been noted that
through this process there developed, over a period of time, a "conceptual economy" (Niranjana 1990: 773) which has provided a

foundation for the proliferation of power/knowledge projects. In an essay on "Translation, Colonialism and the Rise of English", Tejaswini Niranjana points out crucial aspects of this incremental, circulatory and ideologically informing nature of colonial knowledge production in the orientalist context of translation of Indian texts. According to her:

> In the colonial context, a certain conceptual economy is created by the set of related questions which is the problematic of translation. Conventionally, translation depends on the Western philosophical notions of reality, representation and knowledge. Reality is seen as something unproblematic, 'out there'; knowledge involves a representation of this reality; and representation provides direct, unmediated access to a transparent reality. These concepts render invisible what Jacques Derrida calls the logocentric metaphysics by which they are constituted. (Niranjana 1990: 773)

For Niranjana, the problem with this "conceptual economy" is its unproblematic assertion of correspondence between reality and its representation. This transparency and an "out-thereness" of the representational content allows it to stand in for reality. Following Jacques Derrida, she connects this "conceptual economy" to a "logocentric metaphysics" which erases the foundational dependence of putatively transcendental disciplines (such as philosophy) on mundane, historical/temporal power-informed representational practices and forms.

Assuming Derrida's critique of metaphysics as her point of departure, Niranjana phrases this problem of power/knowledge in philosophy, history and translation in the following way:

> Here I should point out that classical philosophical discourse does not merely engender a practice of translation that is then employed for the purposes of colonial domination; I contend that, simultaneously, translation in the colonial context creates and supports a conceptual economy which works into Western philosophy to function as a philosopheme, a congealed base unit which does not require further breaking down through analysis. As Derrida suggests, the concepts of 'Western metaphysics' are

not bound by or produced solely within the 'field' of philosophy. Rather, they come out of and circulate through various discourses at different levels and in different ways, providing thereby 'a conceptual network in which philosophy *itself* has been constituted'. (1990: 773)

If we adopt this idea of a conceptual economy of knowledge, then an interconceptual and intertextual nature of knowledge production becomes visible. In addition, it becomes difficult to speak in isolated disciplinarian terms, or solely in terms of synchronicity of representational content or modes. We can and need to speak of a whole intellectual culture, containing a foundational body of "philosophemes" as "conceptual naturals" which are unexamined as such. But these "philosophemes" regularly serve as epistemes which are axiomatic as interpretive devices for further knowledge. Attention is drawn to this by Dorothy E. Smith, for example, in the epigram to this paper, who calls them our "terms of knowledge", or "the lineaments of what we already know" in our new knowledge. They provide the anchor or meaning connection between our old and new learning.[3] Niranjana's article shows how such a "conceptual economy" with its elementary "epistemes" is provided by the orientalist William Jones' translations of classical Indian texts, and how it structures representation of India for the west. She demonstrates how this content persists through this process of intertextual naturalization underwriting a diverse body of European writings on India. She convincingly argues that this content functions as a sort of code of power or ideology, embodying the political hermeneutics of colonialism.

Niranjana equates ideology with the representational *content* captured in their distorted and reified forms. This is also Inden's or Said's position, as well as that of others writing on colonial discourse. Their work uncovers the existence of ideological–representational epistemes and their "economy". Stereotypes or hypostatized negative and otherizing differences, captured in images and concepts, are deconstructively uncovered, disclosing patterns of connected discursivities. But there seems to be little attention given to the fact that in understanding misrepresentations which are constructions of power, there is an equally urgent need to inquire into the epistemological method of their production. It is only through combining criticism of ideology as content with an inquiry into its method of production that we can offer a fuller critique of domination with regard to representation and ideology. It is only then that we can properly historicize or contextualize, and deconstruct the social relations which structure these congealed discursive/cultural forms of power—which Said calls "Orientalism" or Inden "the symbolic cultural constitution" of an imagined India. What is missing therefore in this alternative (to Marxist analysis) critical deconstruction of representation is a sustained inquiry into epistemology which results in the production of otherizing forms of knowledge.

Expanding the equation of ideology as content into an enquiry of an epistemological method is possible only in terms of Marx's own conception and criticism of ideology as explicitly stated in *The German Ideology* (Marx and Engels 1973) and implied and referred to in his other texts. This is elaborately discussed by D.E. Smith whose own feminist theorization treats ideology as fundamentally a problem of epistemological method rather than as a body of 'false' or distorted ideas (concepts, categories or images).[4] This type of Marxist critique of ideology shows how a critique of culture primarily based on the content of representation suffers from the danger of degenerating into a descriptive compendium rather than a critical enquiry into a problem of meaning and knowledge in the context of social relations of power. Thus the possibility of developing a non-reifying, truly deconstructive analytical, that is, altogether non-ideological knowledge, remains inarticulate.

A thoroughgoing critical suggestion, therefore, consists of a proposal for a critique which has two distinct yet ineluctably constitutive aspects: one of *content*, identified as a body of particular conceptual/imagistic re-presentations, and the other, the "conceptual practice" or an epistemological *method of generation* of this content. This entails not only the task of replacing a 'false' content with a 'true' one, or casting a general suspicion upon it, but also of shifting our gaze to the social relations of its production, until knowledge itself can be seen as a form of social relation. This amounts to devising a critical method which reveals any form of representation to be an imaged or coded, interpreted and conceptualized formal–cultural articulation of a definite set of sociohistorical relations.

This inquiry, which attempts to situate the representational content, rests on reflexivity. It involves a query into how visibilities and invisibilities, silences and occlusions, inclusions and exclusions are intrinsic to certain modes of knowing, and how these modes or 'conceptual practices' are encoded in substantive representational forms. This reflexivity is essential for disclosing the implicit social relations which are embedded in representations since a decontextualized knowledge-object behaves pretty much like any independent objectified construction, for example a car, which does not exhibit in its bounded being the social relations of its production; or that of capital—particularly as it enters into a relation of circulation and consumption, away from the process of its production.

This comparison between a car and a reified cultural form, such as an orientalist one, is not so unusual. It can be understood by paying heed to the unproblematized and transparent representation of the colonial creators who supply the conceptual–imagistic content regarding the colonized 'others', particularly aimed at a western audience and readers. The 'philosophemes' or social assumptions that vitiate this body of knowledge are, after all, not generated within the content which they inform or structure. Any criticism of this discourse needs to situate its content into its historical–social relations and uncover its epistemological method whereby it incorporates particular social relations into a cultural form and concepts. The very characteristics of this knowledge form must thus be accounted for. Otherwise we can only critique this or that construction/representational content with regard to its truth claim, or its stand-in effect for the moments of the social. A simple cultural critique locks us, in the last instance, into a series of representational recursivities. There is actually no exit from these mirroring representational constructs, since one is always expecting to come up with one which is 'true', forgetting that the social (that is, 'reality' in a non-metaphysical sense) is always more intensive and extensive than its re-presentation or discursive form even in the most nuanced form of telling.

So far, the cultural critiques of various forms of othering, difference and so on have treated the problem of relation between the social and its re-presentation more or less as one of content. Less sophisticated talk about 'stereotypes' and more complex or refined talk about 'inscriptions', 'discursivities' and 'differences' have this same accent in common. Even when the critics name history, it remains as an assumption, somewhere out there, as a frame to the text under consideration. Since history is mainly entered into the production of consciousness as an accretion of images and ideas, we cannot, therefore, see it as an organization and mediation of social relations as forms of thought. Thus orientalism or indology is treated by Said or Inden mainly as a problem of cultural hegemony cradled within history or a temporal space marked by power. In promising a thoroughgoing critique of hegemony, or 'ideology', cultural critique of colonial discourse has mostly remained at the level of collections of cultural constructs. Criticism has revealed highly sensitive aspects of the content and of hermeneutic relations among them, displaying instability and unreliability on the basis of gaps, fissures and inconsistencies. As such, they decode an attribution of meanings to India or West Asia, revealing imagined geographies of power. This also translates into presentations of peoples of these regions as passive and reified subjects and agents. Lata Mani's acute observations on English representation of *sati* as a nodule of patriarchal–colonial imagination, and thus a form of displaced violence, help to throw light on this:

> Within the discourse on *sati*, women are represented in two mutually exclusive ways: either as heroines able to withstand the raging blaze of the funeral pyre, or else as pathetic victims coerced against their will into the flames. These poles preclude the possibility of a female subjectivity that is shifting, contradictory, inconsistent. Such a constrained and reductive notion of agency discursively positions women as objects to be saved—never as subjects who act, even if within extremely constraining social conditions. This representation of Indian women has been fertile ground for the elaboration of discourses of salvation, in the context of colonialism, nationalism, and, more recently, Western feminism. For the most part, all three have constructed the Indian

woman not as someone who acts, but as someone to be acted
upon. (Mani 1992: 397)

There cannot be any doubt about the political nature of these constructions and the value of having a cultural critique of them. The
direction of the predicative role of the cultural–moral construction
of 'India' as a category for ruling can never be underestimated,
especially with regard to mediating knowledge relationships
between the knower and the known.

But to go beyond the ideological circle and the politics of
representation in ways that offer other epistemological possibilities
needs an anti-ideological "conceptual practice" of power[5] which
entails criticizing particular established representations with regard
to a theory of reification. In other words, the cultural critique of
knowledge as content must also rest upon an epistemological critique of the method of production of knowledge. My suggestion,
therefore, is not to abandon a cultural critique of content, leaving
Foucault and others behind, but to augment this critique with
Marx's own methodological critique. This calls for a different reading of Marx than that provided by many western Marxists or by
the Soviet Academy of Social Sciences through a sloganlike use of
sentences from *The German Ideology*, such as the "ruling ideas of
any age are the ideas of the ruling class". Displaying a more crude
form of content orientation than cultural criticism, this approach
obscures the fact that Marx's debate with Feuerbach hardly centred
itself in a demand for a content substitution, for 'true' or 'authentic' as opposed to 'false' ideas about social reality.

In fact, what disturbs Marx is what Feuerbach *had* done in
that direction by substituting Hegel's notion of the Idea (or christian notion of 'God') with that of 'Man' and 'human essence'. This
was considered by Feuerbach and the Young Hegelians (early Marx
included) as a paradigm shift. However, Marx subsequently dispu-
ted this revolutionary claim in *The German Ideology* where he
argued against the very epistemology at work in Feuerbach *and*
Hegel, rather than the content that resulted from it. He elaborated
a counter-method to the "speculative rationalism" of Hegel and
other more disguised speculative philosophers (metaphysicians)
such as Feuerbach. Focussing on the central problematic of a con-

structive relationship between particular and general, concrete and abstract, experience and analysis, Marx went on to formulate a reflexive critical method. His foremost concern is thus not content or closed, discursive structures, what he calls "interpretive categories" to "trim off epochs of history" with (Marx and Engels 1973). In its place he formulates an exercise in practical philosophy by discerning the main epistemological procedures or "three tricks" of "speculative philosophy" (or metaphysics). This he claims to be the working apparatus of ideology. Equating "philosophy" (metaphysics) with ideology, he calls for a materialist knowledge or a form of knowing which allows for social change. Ideology, on the other hand, is marked out by Marx as the characteristic job of intellectual disciplinarians—whose specialization and expertise consist of practices, relations and discursivities of a mental labour, decapitated from manual and physical labour. Intellect thus severed and spherized, not surprisingly, seeks 'transcendence' from the mundane, from history and everyday life, aspiring to a claim of absolute, universal, essential, once-for-all knowledge.

Marx's critical method is something of a back calculation which picks up a construction or a reified content—a "ruling idea", so to speak—and regrounds it in actual social relations. Considering knowledge as a form of social organization (as forms of intelligibility, mediation and expression), identifying the relationship between manual and mental division of labour with property and class (as an organizational rather than a solely brutal control over labour of others), he challenges the universalist/essential claims of "ruling ideas" of the ruling classes represented as the single rational, universally valid ones (Marx and Engels 1973). Ideology is put forward as not only what is believed in but as a form of *doing* a certain kind of thought or belief, an active epistemological gesture, whose method of production is uncovered by the "three tricks":

> Trick 1: Separate what people say they think from the actual circumstances in which it is said, from the actual empirical conditions of their lives, and from the actual individuals who said it.
>
> Trick 2: Having detached the ideas, arrange them to demonstrate an order among them that accounts for what is observed. (Marx

and Engels describe this as making 'mystical connections'.)

Trick 3: Then change the ideas into a 'person'; that is, set them up as distinct entities (for example, a value pattern, norm, belief system and so forth) to which agency (or possible causal efficacy) may be attributed. And redistribute them to 'reality' by attributing them to actors who can now be treated as representing the ideas.[6]

Marx's critique of ideology puts forward the methodology for a practical knowledge or "praxis". It consists of uncovering *systematically* how a dissociation is produced between history/ society and forms of consciousness. It directs us to look out from a representational construct, rather than look at it. Concrete social relations congealed within the constructed form are treated as a formalized mutuality of consciousness and the social.

Accepting the position that reifying forms of knowing which privileges *any* content as universal and essential will result in a reified content stops us from searching for a more 'authentic' content. When candidates for this 'authenticity' are paced through the anti-ideological critique it becomes a non-issue to discuss what an Arab or a hindu actually 'is'. Our attempts go beyond any homogenization or essentializing, and we recognize the diversity, the historicity and social nature of the content. We treat content as formalized and conceptualized expressions of their constitutive social relations of power, situated within forms of ruling and certain ways of knowing and representing. Thus knowledge exceeds the cultural end product—either of concepts or images—to be stored eventually in textual hold-alls. The issue of 'truth' is expanded from content, or *what* is produced, to that of its process and relations, to the *how* and *why* of its production. This Marxist anti-ideological knowledge, conventionally known as historical materialism, provides a grounded critique of idealism, or metaphysics, reaching deeper than the Derridian counter-discursivity, a particular spin-off from his version of criticism of metaphysics.[7] A fuller critique of colonial discourse cannot be achieved solely through Derrida or other cultural critiques which have not been able to move out into a social and historical space outside the labyrinth of language and conceptualization.

So an anti-ideological analysis, rather than a cultural critique of representation, involves a thorough criticism of the twofold dimension of ideology—as a 'conceptual practice' and a particular content. The concreteness of the content is crucial for
determining the specificity of the ideological excursion under consideration. To challenge any domination, for example, the resistance must be addressed practically and specifically. This implies
definite references to terms, of time, space and cultural forms. It is
this which points out how abstraction or erasures of these elements
are basic to any relations of ruling—for example, of colonialism. Attention to content also allows us to make distinctions between different moments of ruling. Thus content, understood as
intertextuality, or a "conceptual economy" based on "philosophemes", creates not only the recognized veins of intellectual disciplines, but also crumbles into a cultural common sense which sub-
sists as the political unconscious of any society. But having said so,
one has to be equally mindful of ruling as an epistemological
procedure which organizes social relations of domination. This
procedure, involving how thinking is done at all, is also implied in
all situations of domination without partiality to this or that project. As the content of ideology travels through various transcrip-
tive modes through time and space, so does its method as *the
method* for producing knowledge, and elaborates itself in finer and
finer forms of rationalization, or technology, of production of ideas
and images. Thus the relationship between content and form,
between the social and the cultural, the intellectual and the political, can never be torn apart into separate realities. Niranjana's quotation of Derrida's remark about the circularity of "logocentric
metaphysics" expresses partially what Marx meant by ideology.[8] In
a manner of speaking, a critique of ideology is a critique of metaphysics. It also reveals a constructive relationship between empiri-
cism and metaphysics. A stereotype, or an otherizing cultural construct, can thus be seen as a particularist essentialism or
universalization—whereby this or that feature of the empirical is
fuelled with a transcending idealist drive which sends it out of the
orbit of time as lived history. Thus constructs of power, even of
indology or orientalism, are not necessarily 'inventions' or 'lies'
within their own scope of telling, but rather an illicit expansion and

universalization of lived and observed particulars. Thus the idealist/essentializing method of metaphysics dignifies an empirical bit of the concrete into a timeless verity.

According to one version of anti-ideological critique, the question of cultural representation of India has a wider problematic than offered by critics such as Inden. A methodological critique now integrates with a cultural critique. The empirical fact that colonial history and thus the representation of India were in the main produced by Europeans of a certain political and moral persuasion, at a certain juncture in history, is here combined with an epistemological critique. While recognizing that idealist or metaphysical epistemology—that is, ideological method—that produces reified knowledge is not a European monopoly, we also attend to the European colonial context of the texts so produced, which hold a content appropriate to the time and design of that colonialism. We recognize that an 'imagined', 'translated', orientalist 'India' was born through an intellectual process which was implicated in a particular set of socio-cultural relations existing at that time. This content, or an attribution to India, produced through and as ruling independently of Indian agency, entered into European circulation both transcendentally as 'knowledge' and practically as categories for administration (Smith 1990: 61–65, 83–88). Just as 'the Orient', 'Africa', 'the dark continent' contributed to the colonial significational and administrative–exploitive system (Dirks 1992: 1–25),[9] so did this 'India'. This 'India' is therefore more than "imagined", it is rather both an epistemic and a practical form of exploitation and violence.[10]

We can now begin to explore certain representative colonial texts to make our understanding more concrete. Keeping an eye on particular knowledge procedures, their inscriptions and transcriptions, their intertextual travelling paths and 'conceptual economy', we can go beyond Said and other critics of colonial discourse. We integrate a Marxist theory of ideology with specific semiotic content. More than gesturing towards a power/knowledge relation as always already there, we concentrate on the historical dimension and its social organization and relations of knowledge. This allows for more than an exhaustive study of the metamor-

phosis of cultural content. We become alert to the dangers of reified knowledge *per se* which is not provided by a simpler cultural
critique of representation. It becomes apparent that not only in the
context of colonialism, but in creating *all* negative 'others' (internal and external to *any* society), fixed, transcendental, homogeneous and essential verities are crafted by welding together bits of
empirical observables with the method of metaphysics. The fuller
critique thus advances beyond the relatively well-mapped realm of
images, categories or constructs of power, and begins to consider
knowledge in terms of *social relations* and modes of mediation also
between the knower and the known. If 'knowing' consists of 'a
relation between the knower and the known',[11] then it follows that
the *content* of that knowing is deeply informed by that relation
which also dictates and reflects the 'terms' of understanding which
are embedded in it. They constitute the knower's historical and
social knowledge apparatus.

Clear distinctions therefore have to be made between ideology, which erases and occludes by degrounding ideas from history
and society, and knowledge procedures which allow for relational
disclosures. The acknowledgment that some forms of knowing
contain disclosive dimensions, and others block them, renders spu-
rious any questions regarding the fallible nature of perception
while retaining the knowledge relevance of history. If we concentrate on the methodological critique, we can implicate the knower
and 'what' she comes up with (as content) in the very method that
is employed in producing knowledge. We can not only 'show' the
content as facts, description or information, but also unravel the
knowledge-organizing social relation and cultural practices of the
knower impacting on the known. Thus, rather than being only an
end product, knowledge becomes material to, and a form of, social,
conceptual and finally political relations and organization. This
approach to knowledge spells an open-endedness of content in that
it is always dynamic and incomplete, but persistently reflexive. It
should be contrasted to an ideological approach which produces
seamless conceptual or image objects that bind loose ends, erase
contradictions which are a part and parcel of social relations and
locations of the knower and the known. Fixed facts, concepts and

239

images of India or of Europe, whose claim to verity relies on metaphysical notions such as 'essential', 'typical', 'objective' and 'universal', are seen in the end to be ideology.

What then are some of the particular knowledge-producing procedures and content which constructed 'India' for the west? How are we to understand this 'India' from an anti-ideological perspective? What follows is my example of a fuller exploration of the work of one of the earliest English writers on India, who is a scholar in his own right as well as an administrator. He represented India to the west from his vantagepoint within colonial relations, and these representations took root and branched out as 'philosophemes' of further European knowledge of India and provided the categorical bases for forms of ruling. The writer in question is William Jones, Chief Justice of the Supreme Court of Bengal, and a co-founder with Warren Hastings of the Royal Asiatic Society (1784), a scholar of classical European and Indian languages and a translator of Sanskrit legal texts. I chose to study this author and his authoritative text rather than an overall cultural compendium of images, opinions and descriptions as the basic element of 'India' because 'India' as constructed by him occupies foundational textual and administrative spaces. His 'India' is truly a 'ruling' category in so far as it directs other texts both in terms of knowledge production and in the work of administering the East India Company and the colonial empire. His texts thus hold an inscriptional status and confer the seal of truth upon others which were reproduced through their ideological prescriptions. This author, in short, is crucial in leaving an imprimatur on what Europe and the west came to know as India.

Contexting the Text

When I was at sea last August, on my voyage to this country [India], which I had so long and ardently desired to visit, I found one evening, on inspecting the observations of the day, that *India* lay before us, and *Persia* on our left, whilst a breeze from *Arabia* blew nearly on our stern. . . . It gave me inexpressible pleasure to find myself in the midst of so noble an amphitheatre, almost encircled by the vast regions of *Asia*, which has ever been esteemed the nurse of sciences, the inventress of delightful and useful arts, the scene of glorious actions, fertile in the production of human genius, abounding in natural wonders, and infinitely diversified in the forms of religion and government, in the laws, manners, customs and languages, as well as in features and complexions of men. I could not help remarking, how important and extensive a field was yet unexplored, and how many solid advantages un-improved. . . .

> *A Discourse on the Institution of a Society,*
> *for inquiring into the History, Civil and Natural,*
> *the Antiquities, Arts, Sciences and Literature of Asia,*
> *by The President* [William Jones], (24 Feb. 1784)
> (Jones 1799: [I])

The ideological concerns and construction of 'India' as produced by William Jones and other orientalists requires a simultaneous probing of method and content in order to determine its ideological status. This means situating the knower, William Jones, on the deck of a ship, arriving at Calcutta not just as a visitor, but as the head of the colonial justice system and an aspiring explorer of India bent on "improving solid advantages". It also means observing how India the known becomes Jones' 'India', a knowledge object for colonial ruling. Thus the knower and the known are contexted to history, politics and society, rather than being entities of a timeless zone of metaphysics. This situating attempt reveals the nature of European necessity for 'understanding' and 'improving' India. The timing of Jones' knowledge enterprise makes it evident that his construction of 'India' happens at a very particular juncture of European history, when discursive practices rather than sole brutalities of conquest are becoming material to forms of ruling. Institutions of knowledge such as the Asiatic Society (1784) straddle at this period the double and integrated realms of reflection and ruling, thereby mediating brute force with 'facts' and 'truths'. English colonization of India becomes both a knowledge enterprise and an administration of socio-political and economic domination.[12] Even though Jones is mainly a humanist—a translator, linguist and a cultural essayist—an examination of his method and content of knowledge regarding India discloses an epistemology for a specific social ontology of power.

Jones' purpose is to re-present India, that is, to create a stock of knowledge about its history, culture and society with an aim to stabilizing these representations so that they can be seen as generally valid. For this Jones establishes a truth claim with regard to his formulations as 'essential' equivalencies for Indian reality contexted to ruling. In this the differences between orientalists such as Jones and utilitarians such as James Mill become subordinated to their overall colonial hegemonic projects.[13] Though Jones' discourse of the sublime, of "Drawing Orient knowledge from its fountains / pure, through caves obstructed long, and paths / too long obscure",[14] may seem an antithesis of the cold Benthamite sneering prose of Mill, yet the claim of 'discovering' an 'authentic India' dominates the colonial texts in general.[15]

The outgrowth of this discovery of 'India', culminating in a sort of mythology, provides the interpretive and interpellative framework for the orientalization of India, or what Inden calls the "symbolic cultural constitution" of the indological construct. The content, or the resulting stereotypes, are either exotic (as with Jones) and/or negative towards India (for both Jones and Mill).[16] Jones' opinions in particular are often ambiguous or contradictory, swinging between respect for and distrust of Indians and India. The sentiments expressed regarding "Asiatick civilizations" in the epigram above, or throughout the first volume of his *Works*, clash remarkably with his opinion of the people of the region expressed as a negatively differentiated cultural category which he calls "the Indian". His dislike for Indians is evident in the following lines, where he requests his friend not to be

> like the deluded, besotted Indians, among whom I live, who would *receive liberty* as a curse instead of a blessing, if it were possible *to give it them*, and would reject, as a vase of poison, that, which, if they could taste and digest it, would be water of life. (Jones 1970: [II]: 847)

An aspiration of "mastery" over a land and its people, as well as their forms of knowledge, inspires and infuses Jones' *Works*. This becomes explicit in Sir John Shore's (Lord Teignmoutt's) "Introduction" to Jones' *Collected Works*. Jones, as Shore puts it, was no mere linguist and translator. Though he "eagerly embrace[d] . . .

the opportunity of making himself master of the *Sanskrit*", he "would have despised the reputation of a mere linguist" (Jones 1799: [I] v). His real motive, according to Shore, was the pursuit of "Knowledge and Truth" regarding Indian culture and society in service to his own country, as he aimed to create a just and benevolent rule over India in keeping with its own nature. Since this was not manifest, according to Jones, it needed to be exposed or represented:

> Such were the motives that induced him to propose to the government of this country [colonial Bengal], what he justly denominated a work of national utility and importance, the compilation of a copious digest of *Hindu* and *Mahomedan* Law, from *Sanskrit* and *Arabick* originals, with an offer of his services to supervise the compilation and with a promise to translate it. He had foreseen, previous to his departure from Europe, that without the aid of such a work, the wise and benevolent intentions of the legislature of *Great Britain*, in leaving, to a certain extent, the natives of these provinces in possession of their own laws, could not completely be fulfilled; and his experience, after a short residence in India, confirmed what his sagacity had anticipated, that without principles to refer to, in a language familiar to the judges of the courts, adjudications amongst natives must too often be subject to an uncertain and erroneous exposition, or wilful misinterpretation of their laws. (Jones 1799: [I] v–vi)

Such statements go to show that the act of territorial possession of India was at the same time an act of construction of authoritative knowledge, particularly 'compiled' and 'selected' as Indian law, by the rulers. This imputation of authority and appeal to a 'real' knowledge hides the interested and immediate (as opposed to 'pure' and transcendental) nature of Jones' version of India, which both encodes and administers domination by an active supercession of 'native knowledge' of their own laws.

Thus Jones' translations or cultural essays, as with any ideological excursion, are structured with and motivated by extraneous knowledge imperatives, their legitimating appeal lying in a metaphysical (universalist/essentialist) mode. This epistemology, which hides the reified and tendentious nature of this knowledge, performs an inversion of subject–object relations. The erasure of history and everyday lives of colonized Indians, the very fact of domination itself, are obscured and written over. The distortion or deformation of content which this results in is part and parcel of the ideological method discussed above. As pointed out above, it functions on a double level: of abstraction or emptying out of historicity and agency, and of filling in these abstractions with empirical illustrations of their 'truth'. Performing metonymic or synechdochal gestures, that is, generalizing a part for the whole or vice versa, this epistemology lays the ground for a power/knowledge exercise which, when articulated to conquest and colonial rule, becomes 'colonial discourse'. A good example of this procedure is Jones' construction of the "submissive Indian" based on personal contempt for the colonized and individual instances of submission or obsequiousness, while ignoring instances of resistance to British rule or his own fear of their subversiveness.[17] The application to Indian society and governments of the notion of 'Oriental/Asiatic despotism', learned during his Persian studies, is another instance of this colonial discourse.[18] The purpose of legitimation is only ambiguously served through the irony that Jones, the Chief Justice of a colonial rule, should berate Indians for a debased and slavish mentality while using this assumption about their nature to justify colonialism. In the "Tenth Annual Discourse to Asiatic Society", for example, Jones felt that he "could not but remark the constant effect of despotism in benumbing and debasing all those faculties which distinguish men from the herd that grazes; and to that cause he would impute the decided inferiority of most Asiatic nations, ancient and modern. . ." (Niranjana 1990: 774).

The ideological method of erasure and categorical construction in Jones' *Works* is connected with his pursuit of metaphysics. Thus, the vindication of his knowledge of India lies in 'purity' and transcendence from history, social relations and other perceived accidentalities. This immutability provides the solid basis or authority for ruling, to be held as valid by both Europeans and Indians, and is central to Jones' project of colonial rule in India. As Niranjana remarks:

> The most significant nodes of William Jones' work are (a) the
> need for translation by the Europeans, since the natives are unre-
> liable interpreters of their own laws and cultures; (b) the desire to
> be a law-giver, to give the Indians their 'own' laws; and (c) the
> desire to 'purify' Indian culture and speak on its behalf. The
> interconnectedness between these obsessions are extremely com-
> plicated. They can be seen, however, as feeding into a larger dis-
> course [of Improvement and Education] that interpellates the
> colonial subject. (Niranjana 1990: 774)

As a representative of the system, Jones felt that India belonged to
England, and in transference, to him. He imagined an India
through his own interpretive schema and symbolic organization,
omitting "unnecessary", that is, unfitting details. Thus the 'purification' or 'sanskritization' which he performed is itself an act of
colonization.[19] Helped by a metaphysical method and artistic/lin-
guistic skills, the special forte of Jones, this self-interested, particularist project of ruling achieves a transcendent and universal glow.
Good examples are to be found in his emulation of vedic hymns, in
which his adoption of the persona of a brahmin truth-seeker keeps
the crudities of the ruling project safely out of sight:

> And if they [the gods] ask, "What mortal
> pours the strain?". . .
> Say: "from the bosom of yon Silver Isle [England],
> "Where skies more softly smile,
> "He came; and, lisping our celestial tongue,
> "Though not from Brahma sprung,
> "Draws Orient knowledge from its fountains pure,
> "Through caves obstructed long, and paths too long obscure."[20]

These Indian conceits and the pastoralism, compounded with the
image of the truth-seeker, add up to a richly textured colonial discourse. They allow the romantic paganism of Jones to coalesce
with that of a universal knower. Yet this knower is also a European
to the west, a Man of Reason, with a mission to reveal the 'real
India'.[21] This ideal knower represents the truly 'human' knower,
as opposed to 'the native' or 'the debased Indian' who can never
aspire to such a status. Thus Jones' quest for knowledge and

"discovery" of India is both an allegory of "Man's discovery of Truth" and a medium for colonization. The mask of the poet and metaphysician (the truth-seeker) hides the brutalities of conquest and the historical particularities and conditionalities of this so-called universal knowledge and representation.

From the point of view of the production of ideology as method, this dual disappearance of the social actualities of both the knower and the known is crucial, as also is their reappearance on a secondary plane of metaphysics as the universal knower and the known object, securely attached to the platform of ruling. Through this transmutation the empirical moments of what is known, that is, what is seen, read or heard in or about India/Indians, are textually refigurated and discursively aligned. Pre-existing discourses of power provide what Marx called "mystical connections"—that is, a coherent 'interpretive schema'—for which the empirical becomes but an embodiment or illustration of an idea previously held. The main interpretive schema or discourse within which Jones writes 'India' is one of 'civilization' and 'tradition', with implicit and explicit binaries of 'improvement', 'native savagery' or 'Oriental barbarism'. The notion of 'tradition' plays a powerful and ambiguous role, switching from one pole of meaning to the other. It must be noted that these discourses are already in place and used in Europe prior to colonization of India. Traditionality and savagery are alternately, or in conjunction, considered the 'essential' character of India, while reason, rationality, improvement and civilization are seen as the attributes of Europe. The metaphysical dimension of this discursivity allows for atemporality, unchangingness and repetition to be built into the concept of knowledge. Thus immovable stereotypes mark the passage of the history of India, and Europe/England and India face each other in an essential ontology of difference. An example can be found in the common practice of equating India with ritual violence and sacrifices.[22] This is then opposed to European civilization or rule of law. Europe therefore is never equated with witch-burning or other frequently held *auto da fé* or brutalities of punishment.[23] These are never considered 'essential' or characteristic to European civilization, while the sporadic occurrence of *satidaha* (burning of a woman on her husband's pyre) in India is seized upon as the 'essence' of Indian civilization and worked into the colonial justice system and the moral regulation of Indian society.

Thus, we can see that an ideological formulation of content is not necessarily 'a lie', or 'wholly arbitrary' in any ordinary sense, but rather an illicit and essential extension of the empirical or the particular into a universal. As noted earlier, this is a matter of fuelling an empirical moment with a metaphysical conceptual dynamic which interpellates the empirical into conceptual frames that are far wider than their immediate scope. The reading of India, therefore, takes place in a European discourse of knowledge belonging to early bourgeois society. Indian colonization as a knowledge project for ruling is thus situated within the European renaissance and enlightenment notions of reason and humanism which are introjected into the construction of India in the shape of metaphors, allegories and images as well as morally regulatory views. Details of Indian life, history and culture are fitted into an overarching elite code of European 'civilization', marked by a deep sense of superiority over 'others'. This epistemological manoeuvre implies interpellative and interpretive processes which render invisible and unnameable actual social relations, values and contradictions in existence in India. In this colonial knowledge universe we are, as D.E. Smith points out, in a blind alley of "phenomena the only practical universe of exploration, or substrate of which is the social organization and relation of sociological [read: colonial/ideological] discourse itself" (Smith 1990: 33). However, we need to explore this formative and knowledge phenomena in greater detail if we want to understand more concretely how the full scope of ideology embraces both form and content.

'India': A Knowledge of Power

By India . . . I mean that whole extent of country, in which the primitive religion and that language of the *Hindus* prevail, at this day with more or less their ancient priority, and in which the *Nagari* letters are still used with more or less deviation from their original forms.

Jones 1799: (I) 23

Anyone familiar with the *Works* of William Jones will

recognize in the above lines some key words in his vocabulary which serve as governing categories for his voluminous opus on India. As stated above, these keywords constellate into a quasi-knowledge paradigm, a discursive organization and interpretation of culture and language. They also ambiguously shade off into value judgement while also speaking of languages. Again the key-words, predictably, are "purity"/"original forms"/"ancientness". They are paired with notions such as "primitiveness" of religion (inclusive of language and culture) and "deviation" from their "original forms". This discursivity is in keeping with Jones' pre-occupation with the ancientness of India and of retrieving or res-cuing it from history and re-presenting it in its essential form. This is how he attempts "to know India better than any other European ever knew it" (Majeed 1992: 24), and to represent it for others, implicitly, Europeans. There is also an assumption here of a trans-parent relationship between reality and its representation as dis-played by all aspects of Jones' construction of India.

Emphasis on this discourse of purity and its perversion (read as corruption produced through socio-historical changes), helps us to read Jones' *Works* in terms of value judgements regard-ing what Jones thought India once was and what it had degene-rated into in his time. This cultural–moral judgement entailed an assessment of what Jones called "the manners", and James Mill, the "Cultures, Morals and Customs" of "the Hindoos". Jones con-trasted these changing "manners" to the immutable "moral" truths enshrined in scriptural–legal texts, such as Manu's *Dharmashastra*. His struggles could be seen as a way to control the chaos of "man-ners" and to keep out history with the fence of edited and anthol-ogized texts. He states as much in his prefaces to the legal digests of muslim and hindu law—*Al Sirajyyah* and *Institutes of Hindu Law*.

Jones' intense awareness of the destabilizing effects of history and changing social/cultural relations and forms is best dis-played in his legal project. A self-conscious decision to textually fix the law is taken in face of the recognition of the power of chan-ging manners and customs. As he puts it in the preface to *Institutes of Hindu Law*:

> It is a maxim in the science of legislation and government, that
> laws are of no avail without manners, or, to explain the sentence
> more fully, that the best intended legislative provisions would
> have no beneficial effect even at first, and none at all in a short
> course of time, unless they were congenial to the disposition and
> habits, to the religious prejudices, and approved immemorial usa-
> ges, of the people, for whom they were enacted. . . . (Jones 1799:
> [III] 53)

And because he is so aware of these customs and prejudices, the
fixation of pieces of texts of hindu ancient law becomes a fetish
object for him. In fact Jones learns Sanskrit only to assure himself
that the *real law* from the texts was being instituted by the Company and crown courts. His fears of corruption and deviation are
enhanced by his perception of deceitfulness in "the natives", showing the chronic insecurity of a ruler who is dependent on local
experts for gaining access to knowledge necessary for ruling. His
vehemence against "the imposition" by pandits and maulavis is
matched by his rhetoric of moral "purity" in the exigencies of ruling. As he puts it: "It is of utmost importance that the stream of
Hindu Law should be pure; for we are entirely at the power of the
native lawyers, through our ignorance of *Sanscrit*" (Jones 1970:
[II] 666). This also made him argue for the learning of Persian by
the servants of the Company—Persian had been the court or official language in northern and eastern India since precolonial times,
and ignorance of it formed a barrier to their trade and advancement activities, as they could not make any local transactions in
writing:

> the servants of the Company received letters which they could
> not read, and were ambitious of gaining titles of which they could
> not comprehend the meaning; it was found highly dangerous to
> employ the natives as interpreters, upon whose fidelity they could
> not depend; and it was at last discovered, that they must apply
> themselves to the study of the Persian language. . . . (Jones 1799:
> [II] 126–27)

If this need for languages was present among the English traders
even in precolonial days, it became more acute, according to

Jones, in the era when the East India Company assumed the task of ruling India and evolving a justice system. Jones' metaphysical and moral drive for "purity" was concretized through a 'fixed text', a core of legal references intended for English judges and administrators, in order to discipline the natives.

Texts and facts, representation and reality, were mediated and constructed through anthologization and inscription of moral codes, of legal and social conduct. This was a totalizing enterprise, as ruling discourse has to be, and it covered all aspects of "native" realities. Even the essays on botany written by Jones exemplify a homology to his ruling project. In "Plants of India", for instance, he emphasized the same inscriptive injunctions which we find in his works of law and culture. Here too he valorized ancient languages on account of their purity and transcendental hold on "truth". His suspicions regarding the vulgar and the vernacular, about fluctuations in popular cultural idioms, organize his essays on plants. An example of this is the following advice to botanists on Indian flora:

> Now the first step, in compiling a treatise on the plants of *India*, should be to write their names in *Roman* letters, according to the most accurate orthography, and in *Sanscrit* preferably to any vulgar dialect; because a learned language is fixed in books, while popular idioms are in constant fluctuation, and will not, perhaps be understood a century hence by the inhabitants of these Indian territories, whom future botanists may consult on the common appellations of trees and flowers. . . . (Jones 1799: [II] 2)

The same ambitions characterize his taxonomy of India's plants as of its scriptural laws, and create a template of ideal reality against which all actuality is to be measured.

Rejection of history and social change marks Jones' political conservatism. The creation of transcendental verities through recovering the 'original' India amount to no more than that. These constructs seemingly militate against his actual experience of living there, but are in fact motivated by what he perceives as the 'debasedness' of Indians in his time. This 'degeneration' of the people is comparable to the vernacular corruption of the original and pure Sanskrit. In this respect Jones shared much with James Mill, both dispensing with experience as a source of 'truth', while constructing their "truth about India" against the backdrop of their unstated experience or view of contemporary Indian society.

Jones was close to the conservative thinker Edmund Burke in recognizing the importance of "prejudices". He supported the establishment of a supreme court in India to protect the British subjects and rule the "natives", with the provision "that the natives of the more important provinces be indulged in their own prejudices, civil and religious, and supported to enjoy their own customs unmolested" (Jones 1799: [III] 5). But this indulgence had its limit, in his canonical version of elite hindu and muslim laws. Through these compilations, colonial rule could claim a legitimacy in local terms even when the actuality was composed of social relations of colonialism and in reality supported prejudices of the Europeans. This legal attempt was meant to remove shadows of usurpation and force from the colonial rule.

Javed Majeed, in *Ungoverned Imaginings: James Mill's The History of British India and Orientalism*, also speaks of Jones' literary and legal works in terms of creating a legitimating indigenous idiom for ruling (Majeed 1992). He shows how Jones' translations and compilations of *Digests* of hindu and muslim laws gradually led to appropriation of power over the local societies and to the supersession of indigenous agencies for self-rule. According to Majeed: "for Jones the apparent monopoly of a form of indigenous knowledge by certain classes could only be broken through translation. This would mean that the *British would be as conversant in their traditions as they were*, and that their idioms would be *desacralized* through the very act of translation" (Majeed 1992: 20 [emphasis mine]). The power/knowledge character of the orientalist construction of India produced a seeming paradoxical relation of repression and dependence between the colonial elite and "the authority of the sacerdotal classes" (Majeed 1992: 20). But actually the project had two stages. Initially indispensable, Indian scholars were slated for elimination once the English translations and compilations were concluded. As Majeed puts it:

> The position of Muslim law officers remained intact until 1817, [when regulation 17] empowered Nizamat Adalat, the central criminal court of Calcutta, to overrule the fatwas of the law officers

in all cases. With this Muslim Law lost its status as the criminal
law of the land, although it was not until 1864, after the Indian
Penal Code was promulgated in 1862, that the institution of law
officers and their fatwas was abolished. (Majeed 1992: 20)

Thus, legitimating colonial rule in an Indian idiom did nothing to
undercut power relations between England and India. If anything,
this peculiar form secured legitimation much more effectively in the
first stages of English rule than an imposition of British law could
have done. The self-assigned creators and keepers of 'truth' about
India were doing the work of ruling effectively. What Majeed has
forgotten to add with regard to English appropriation of Indian
traditions, and Lata Mani and Bernard Cohn remind us, is that
these same "desacralization" procedures which translated Indian
texts also conferred on the colonial authorities the power to decide
and name what these so-called "native traditions" were.[24] They
'invented' traditions as they needed (Cohn 1983).

The results of these inventions were deeply consequential
for the Indian society. Majeed himself refers to this in an undevel-
oped fashion when he remarks on Jones' "mistaken attempts" to
compile *one* uniform code of hindu and muslim law. This one
"true" version of social morality for each community, he feels, "reinforced conservatism", leading to centralization of legal power in
the name of an ideal order, distinct from actual practice (Majeed
1992: 28): "In fact, the insistence on certainty and uniformity, and
the attempt to codify traditions, actually meant that sometimes
Anglo–Hindu law was more orthodox than the Shastras" (Majeed
1992: 27). Majeed's perception is similar to Charles Bayly's, who
in *Indian Society and the Making of the British Empire* speaks of
rigidification of caste through colonial modes of standardization of
knowledge of Indian societies into "rank and grade Indian social
orders" (Majeed 1992: 28). This colonialist knowledge project
increased the social importance of local elite, brahmin pandits and
muslim maulavis on whom the rulers depended, and "[the] scene
was set for the emergence of a more stratified and rigid system of
caste, and a more homogeneous religious practice *within all the
main communities*" (Majeed 1992: 28, emphasis mine). This natural fit between the administrative requirements and standardization

of social knowledge which was produced through the mechanism of an ideological epistemology is hard to ignore.

Jones' own location as a knower within relations of ruling, of Britain over India and Asia, is evident in the following example from "The Second Anniversary Discourse (1785) for the Asiatic Society". Here the relative variations of Europe and Asia in the scale of power and culture are clearly marked out. For Jones,

> Whoever travels in Asia, especially if he be conversant with the literature of the countries through which he passes, must naturally remark the superiority of European talent; the observation indeed is as old as Alexander; and, though, we cannot agree with the sage preceptor of the ambitious prince, that 'the Asiaticks were born to be slaves,' yet the Athenian poet seems to be perfectly in the right, when he represents Europe as a sovereign princess and Asia as her handmaid. (Jones 1799: [I] 10)

This statement provides a visual icon encoding a relationship of dominance and servitude between Europe and Asia (Britannia and India), made seductive by an ambience of grandeur and beauty supplied by Jones' romanticism. It is then qualified and underscored by his position as the representative of the region: "but, if the mistress be transcendentally majestic, it cannot be denied that the attendant has many beauties, and some advantages peculiar to itself [sic]" (Jones 1799: [I]: 10).

These sentiments and images are not, of course, unique to Jones. They are an intrinsic part of a representational apparatus created in the process of European colonization. English patriotic poems or songs such as James Thompson's "Rule, Britannia" and innumerable engravings and etchings of the time show the trinity of Europe or Britannia, a bejewelled white upper-class woman, often a Queen, and her two dark and dusky attendants—Africa and Asia. This colonial iconography is the result of a mediation between written political allegories and a convention in art.[25] This patronizing though romantic attitude is paraphrased by Jones in a more prosaic fashion when he reminds the all-European members of the Asiatic Society not to be too arrogant and dismissive towards Indians or Asians: "although we must be conscious of our superior advancement in kinds of useful knowledge, yet we aught not therefore to contemn the people of Asia. . ." (Jones 1799: [I] 10).

The general style of colonial discourse adopted by William Jones (and other orientalists) deserves a specific discussion. It possesses a peculiarly complex character which expresses domination through classical and orientalist scholarship, Burkeian conservative politics, and a romantic aesthetic. Thus Jones is not to be confused with a "liberal imperialist" (Majeed 1992: 40–43) like Mill and other utilitarians. Though he served the interest of the British empire he did this differently in his style or discourse. Majeed draws our attention to this aspect of Jones' works:

> What has been ignored is the fact that Jones's attempt to define an idiom in which cultures could be compared and contrasted was in part a response to the need for such an idiom that the cultures of the heterogeneous British empire could be compared, the nature of the British rule overseas determined, and the empire unified by the same ethos. For Jeremy Bentham and James Mill, the comparison and contrast of cultures was essential for their formulation of a programme of reform which would be relevant to both Indian and British society, but their approach to this issue was to be very different from Jones's. (Majeed 1992: 16)

If Jones was not interested in 'improving' India and Indians in ways utterly alien, how did he carry out the task of construction of a cultural identity for the country and its peoples? How did he construct the necessary difference between Europe and India? The 'difference' (between Europeans and Indian 'others') was produced through a mixture of arrogance and fascination rooted in an organicist conservative and romantic imagination. He surmised that debased Indians had the possibility of a cultural/moral rejuvenation if, and only if, led by enlightened European guides and rulers like himself.

In order to do this Jones played the insider, and manipulated some of the significational systems from classical Sanskrit literature. He therefore donned the exotic mask of an Indian. As Lawrence of Arabia played an Arab, Jones of India played 'brahmin' and 'pagan' to claim a representational status. Thus his poetic persona embodies cultural essences that were fabricated by Jones himself. His reforms, unlike those of the utilitarians, do not use the discourse of 'rationality' as much as that of purification and retrieval. Many of his poems are hymns to vedic deities, where the benevolent character and intention of the British rule speak an Indian idiom (Majeed 1992: 22) to authentically represent India to the west (at this point Indians were not widely trained in English). The poems accomplish the moral imperatives of British rule in India, and it becomes the ideal condition within which 'the Hindu' or 'India' can return to their pristine glory. This "Hymn to Laxmi", for example, shows such a view:

> Oh! bid the patient Hindu rise and live
> His erring mind, that Wizard lore beguiles
> Clouded by priestly wiles,
> To senseless nature bows for nature's God.
> Now, stretch'd o'er ocean's vast from happier isles
> He sees the wand of empire, not the rod;
> Ah, may those beauties, that western skies illume,
> Disperse the unhappy gloom!
>
> (Jones 1799: [II] 365)

Another poem, the "Hymn to Ganga", is a perfect act of cultural appropriation. It indicates a ruler's right to arrogate the culture of the colonized unto himself. Here Jones represents 'India' as an 'ideal Indian', in accordance to a cultural synthesis that he has put together. The poem is "feigned to have been the work of a BRAH-MEN, in an early age of HINDU antiquity, who, by a prophetical spirit, discerns the equity of BRITISH government, and concludes with a prayer for its peaceful duration under good laws well administered" (Jones 1799: [VI] 383). This naturalized Indian Jones, or the imagined "Brahmen", ends by pronouncing a benediction for British rule in India and prays for its long life:

> Nor frown, dread Goddess, on a peerless race,
> With lib'ral heart of material grace,
> Wafted from colder isles remote:
> As they preserve our laws, and bid our terror cease,
> So be their darling laws preserved in wealth, in joy, in peace!
>
> (Jones 1799: [VI] 392)

This indigenous idiom and the persona adopted by Jones are not to be confused with an act of surrender by the Europeans to Indian culture, but rather understood as a gesture of incorporation. Jones and his colleagues felt the same right to Indian cultural goods as to commercial goods and revenue while simultaneously forging a tool of legitimation. This allowed a control over the colonized in what appeared to be their own moral and cultural terms. This model of ruling, as noticed by many scholars, came from the English perception of the cultural modalities of the Mughal empire. It minimized the fact of the colonial nature of British rule and made it appear organic to the local societies (Majeed: 25; Cohn 1983). And most significantly, the conceptual–imagistic concreteness called 'India' that emerged through these interpretive–constitutive processes of multiple relations of ruling came to be accepted by the west (and in a certain sense, even by Indians themselves) as the 'real India'.[26]

This totalizing aspiration of orientalist knowledge of India is necessarily dependent on flexibility, inasmuch as it has to deal with a non-unified actuality. Thus it resorts to notions of typicality as well as exceptionality and diversity in order to maintain its typologies and essentialist stance. From this point of view, it has been served well by the concept of tradition, which automatically entails the notion of its violation. Through this reading device contemporary indigenous discussions and debates on social conduct and laws of inheritance, property and family could be read and pushed aside as deviation from 'tradition', thereby rendering indigenous discursivities static and un-Indian. Through this process colonial rule became the saviour of India and the orientalists its spokespersons, while representations created by them re-presented Indian reality. This gave a historical agency to the rulers themselves who, like Jones, saw the restoration of the 'original India' as their historic task. Thus the rulers stole from the 'natives' their history, and interposed themselves between a people and their cultural–political past and future, making decisions as to how to rule them, supposedly, in their own idiom.

The enormous power involved in this definitive, antiquarian textualization for contemporary ruling becomes evident in its gigantic proportions if we hypothetically put Europe in India's place. The arrogance and absurdity of ruling a country on the basis of scriptural/legal texts produced hundreds of years ago becomes evident if we propose that Europe be conquered by India or China, and it rules presentday Europe on the basis of an archivally researched, selected and canonized version of Greek laws from the days of Plato and Aristotle. Furthermore, this renders the interim period of development in European thought, between antiquity and now, as accidental and inessential excrescences with regard to Europe's true essence. This is precisely what Jones and others tried to do in India with a considerable degree of success, by constructing mythologies which were also ideologies of 'India', hinduism and islam.

Politically speaking, the orientalist conservatism has to be contexted to the French revolution. It has much of the romantic, organicist conservatism of Edmund Burke. Jones befriended Burke until the impeachment of Bengal's Governor General, Warren Hastings, who was Jones' administrative superior, patron and collaborator in Asiatic research in India. Orientalists were also the heirs of the European renaissance and enlightenment. They were humanist scholars, educated in European classics and classical languages, and admirers of Graeco–Roman antiquities. This expertise and orientation was combined with a mercantalist and physiocratic view of India's economic "improvement" (Guha 1981). All this underpinned their political vision and many, including Jones, advocated 'Enlightened Despotism' for India and contrasted it to 'Asiatic Despotism'. In short, these men inherited and developed personal and political history and an intellectual framework before coming to India. These interpertive devices and frameworks are what they built on both in terms of the form and content of their ideological projects when they sought to 'know' and re-present India. As such, they relied on a common content for constructing 'Asiatic others' prevalent in Europe throughout the postcrusade era, but there were also other stereotypes or perceptions applicable to groups which lent themselves to use in the colonial situation. Constructions or stereotypes of the peasant and rural societies within Europe, the Arab or the Moor, European women and lower classes, for example, have much in common, both in method and content, with those of the later 'Asiatic', 'Oriental' or 'Indian'. Geopolitical mythologies regarding the east used liberally in literature, for example in Christopher Marlowe's *Dr Faustus* or Dr Samuel Johnson's *Rasselas, The Prince of Abyssinia*, in the plays of Dryden or Aphra Behn, travellers' narratives and so on, had existed for a long time before Company rule in India. Upon scrutiny it becomes clear that the orientalist "symbolic, cultural constitution" of India draws on these pre-existing conceptual contents and cultural forms rather than fully inventing brand new ones.

If renaissance humanism, the values of the enlightenment, along with classical antiquarianism, are left unexplored as sources for cultural construction and ideology in the colonial context, the value-laden nature of the term 'civilization' as applied to India would make no sense. The invention of Greece and Rome and the classical past which went with it, along with the invention of 'traditions' which are signifiers of 'European civilization', must all be examined as sources for constructing 'India' and its 'traditions'. The concept of 'civilization', for example, becomes a heavy burden not only because it ceases to signal a process of becoming, an ideal for all societies (see Williams 1983), but instead provides a typological standard already arrived at by Europeans by which 'others' must be measured. This led to India being evaluated through European, especially Graeco–Roman, icons and standards, and occupying an ambiguous position of antiquity on the one hand and being classed as inferior (to Europe) on the other. This ambiguity of 'India' resonates with the shifting horizon of 'European civilization' and its continued bifurcation into Apollonian Greece and Dionysian Asia.

A shifting boundary between Greece and Asia, indicated for example by the status of Egypt, Turkey or Macedonia, contains the elements of orientalism or eurocentrism (see M. Bernal 1993). The humanist fabrication of the 'Apollonian Greece' stands face to face with changing perceptions of Asia Minor and Egypt, characterized alternately as sources of rational, universal thought and of mystery religions or occultism and Dionysian irrationalism. The same ambiguity and shift between admiration and denigration is also to be found in the orientalist perception of India. The same historiography as found in Europe, with its notions of ages and stages, is applied to it. A history of decline is also perceived here, evolving to decay, from the golden age to the contemporary era.

In Europe itself this historiography had invented time and traditions which went into the construction of the European 'middle ages' (the middle of what?) or the 'dark ages' (contrasted to 'enlightened'), of 'renaissance' and 'enlightenment'. The same perspective, with its curious mixture of romanticism and rationalism, of neoclassical aesthetic and the sublime, was brought to bear on India and produced representational images and knowledge. European paintings, etchings or verbal descriptions of the time produce 'India' through these same modalities.

Conclusion

This paper considers the issue of representation specifically in the colonial context with regard to a fuller understanding of the concept of ideology, encompassing both the content and the form or method of production of knowledge. The elaborated theorization is then sought to be made apprehensible through a discussion of William Jones' *Works* in terms of production of ideology. No doubt more could be said of them, as his opus is voluminous, but the paper concentrates instead on uncovering how historical and social relations of his ruling enterprise informed the (ac)claimed metaphysical disinterestedness of his work. This essay should also go a little way towards understanding how ideological knowledges arise which are not only current in their own time, but persist through time into further stages and modes of power. The method of metaphysics constructively applied to historical moments, as Jones does to his encounter with India in the last years of the eighteenth century, flies the produced "knowledge" way beyond the confines of its locale and its time, and settles into the status of truth and fact. So it is that Jones' 'India' becomes the lens through which not only his contemporary colonizing Europeans but many future nationalist Indians saw their country and themselves.

Notes and References

[1] For different approaches to history writing and historiography, see E.H. Carr (1964); E.P. Thompson (1966); Philip Abrams (1982); J.W. Scott (1988); and the introduction to Ranajit Guha and Gayatri Chakravarty Spivak (eds) (1988).

[2] There are numerous examples of this. To name a few we can cite Said (1979), Henry Louis Gates Jr (ed.) (1985) and Mary Louis Pratt (1992).

[3] See Smith 1990: chapter 2, "The Ideological Practice of Sociology", in its entirety for the reading of ideology I have evolved for this paper.

[4] For Smith's notion of ideology, especially as a discursive/epistemological form of "relations of ruling", see chapters 2 and 3 in Smith (1990).

[5] This is borrowed from the title of D.E. Smith's book, *The Conceptual Practices of Power* (1990). It is a code name for the *doing* of ideology as social relations of ruling.

[6] This is D.E. Smith's (1990: 43) version of Marx's formulation.

[7] See Derrida (1978), especially the essay "Violence and Metaphysics: An Essay on the Thought of Emmanuele Levinas".

[8] See also Smith's notion of the circularity of ideology in 1990: 93–100.

[9] See also Abdul Jan Mohamed, "The Economy of Manichean Allegory: The Function of Racial Difference in Colonialist Literature", in H.L. Gates Jr (ed.) (1985).

[10] For Spivak on "epistemic violence," see "Can the Subaltern Speak?" in Nelson and Grossberg (eds) (1988).

[11] On knowing as a relation and ideology as ruling, see the "Introduction" in Smith (1987).

[12] These knowledge activities brought about by the occasion of colonization involve putting together a stable mode of textualization, of inscription and transcription, which encode and organize administrative forms and relations of ruling in concretely ideological terms. See R. Guha (1982); E. Stokes (1969); G. Visvanathan (1989).

[13] For similarities and differences among orientalists and utilitarians, see J. Majeed (1992).

[14] William Jones, "A Hymn to Surya", as quoted by Niranjana (1990: 775).

[15] This language of exploration and discovery is pervasive in the European colonial enterprise. From Columbus to William Jones to Henry Morton Stanley and beyond, this discourse helps to obscure the dimension of force, brutalities and denigrations integral to colonization. Within this overarching discursivity, the notion of authenticity and exposure of the real, the true, the original, etc., find their place. The metaphor or trope of "caves" or hidden and lost knowledge is present equally ubiquitously. A modern example of this is the complex use of the cave in E.M. Forster's novel *A Passage to India*, charting the journey of the colonial English psyche into the cave of 'India' and beyond. The aesthetic of the sublime that is found in these metaphoric discursivities, present in overabundance in William Jones' poetry, is a major genre of visual depiction of India to Europe. For an excellent example, see M. Archer and T. Falk (1989).

[16] See the chapter on "Manners, Morals and Customs" of hindus in Mill (1968 [I]) for examples of negative stereotypes, also partly shared by Jones (for example, in Jones 1970: [II] 712).

[17] On this projected evil, and fear of the colonized other in their various forms, see the classic text by Joseph Conrad, *The Heart of Darkness*, and its critique in F. Fanon (1963). It is brought out eloquently by M. Taussig: "Hated and feared, objects to be despised, yet also objects of awe, the reified essence of evil in the very being of their bodies, these figures of the Jew, the Black, the Indian, and woman herself, are clearly objects of cultural construction, the leaden keel of evil and mystery sta-

bilizing the ship and course that is Western History". (1992: 139)

[18] The discursive legacy of this has been discussed by Edward Said (1981). The notion of Oriental/Asiatic despotism and assumptions about Asiatic society embedded in it developed through James Mill (1968), A.C. Lyall's *Asiatic Society*, Marx's and Weber's essays on colonialism in India and Indian society, among others, enters into the later sociological and his-torico-political assumptions of Barrington Moore, Perry Anderson and many others. 'Despotism' becomes synonymous with the 'east', providing in both early and later periods of history a legitimation for colonial rule and other dominations.

[19] 'Sanskritization' literally means purification, and 'Sanskrit', the language, literally means that which has been purified. Sanskrit, interestingly, has never been a spoken language, i.e. a vernacular, for any particular social group.

[20] "A Hymn to Surya" [the Sun], quoted in T. Niranjana (1990: 775).

[21] See in this context a short but useful discussion in Majeed (1992: 31–40) regarding Jones' reading of Indian history and its expression in his poetry. Majeed and others, for example V. de Sola Pinto, have situated Jones within the tradition of English romantic poetry.

[22] This view of India as a land of ritual violence is as old as Herodotus. Rich examples can be drawn from British writings on *satidaha*. See L. Mani (1992) or S. Bannerjee (1989).

[23] As, for example, outlined by Michel Foucault (1979), numerous studies on the evolution of European criminal laws, or studies on the European counter-reformation and the Inquisition, especially historical works on the treatment of witches and heretics.

[24] See E. Hobsbawm and T. Ranger (1983), especially the Introduction.

[25] Much, for example, has been written on Manet's Olympia attended by a black maid, onto whom the European male gaze has shifted the white woman's burden of an unregulated sexuality.

[26] Making India 'traditional', while reifying or inventing traditions, put in place an interpretive framework which has lasted from orientalism to the current phase of international development. It should be obvious by now that Jones considered the colonial project as one of ruling India for her own good, as a gesture of rescuing and restoring. Thus, he considered the task of the East India Company's servants to be twofold: intellectual–moral, and legal/administrative. He was not alone in this understanding, but his predecessors and colleagues, such as Warren Hastings, Halhed, C.T. Colebrook, and H.H. Wilson, all conformed to this vision and task. Learning languages, translating, selecting, compiling and canonizing texts, fixing and constructing characteristic traditions—in short, project-ing the real "genius" of the country—were their fulltime occupation. The purpose was to create a representational apparatus of India which would provide a controlled and predictable (for the colonizers) ground for ruling.

Beyond the Ruling Category to What Actually Happens

Notes on James Mill's Historiography in
The History of British India

> Knowing is always *a relation* between knower and known. The knower cannot be collapsed into the known, cannot be eliminated; the knower's presence is always presupposed. To know is to always know on some terms, and the paradox of knowing is that we discover in its object the lineaments of what we know already.
>
> D.E. Smith, *The Conceptual Practices of Power* (1990)

Introduction

The concept of tradition is always with us even though, perhaps because, we live in North America or Europe, coded as the west. Associated with certain parts of the world, their peoples and cultures, characterizing them as 'others' not 'us', tradition and its conceptual satellites appear in an automatic gesture of compreending and creating difference. Tradition serves as an interpretive and constructive device, providing a discursive staple for newspapers and television shows, scholarly texts, feminism and fashion magazines, development policies and UN-sanctioned bombing of Iraq. Sections of the world, variously called 'the east', 'the south', or 'the third world', contrasted to 'the west', 'the north' or 'the first/developed world', have been designated as domains of tradition.

Edward Said, very early in a long line of critics of colonial discourse, noted a historical knowledge–power relation encoded in

This essay was first published in *Knowledge, Experience and Ruling Relations*, eds. M. Campbell and A. Manicom, Toronto: University of Toronto Press, 1995.

the category 'the east' or 'the orient'.[1] He drew our attention to an essentialist, homogenizing representational apparatus which levelled, with its imperial gaze, diverse non-European regions into imaginary geographies and vast historic–cultural blocs. One of the interpretive devices that helped to accomplish this task was 'tradition'. The adjective 'traditional' (relatedly underdeveloped, backward, as opposed to 'modern', progressive, advanced or developed) seems to synthesize disparate cultural characteristics to the satisfaction of the west.[2] Associated with stereotypes of mysticism and spirituality, dowry, wife-burning, female infanticide, over-population, primitive technology, peasants and villages, India in particular has been projected as a 'traditional' society. It has long held a binary relationship to the west's self-representation, ramified through its package of science and rationality, technological–economic development, 'open society' and political freedom.[3]

Deconstructing this traditional 'India' as an ideologically representational category by unpacking the constituent social relations and epistemological method of its production implies an examination of the notion of tradition as a mode of reification. Furthermore, to return this 'imagined India' to the realm of history necessitates its disarticulation from the notion of tradition which dehistoricizes the cultures of Indian peoples.[4] This chapter attempts a part of that task by examining the epistemological mechanism, the social relations embedded within that notion, and the resulting representational character of 'India' as produced by James Mill in *The History of British India* (first published 1817). The importance of this book in terms of representing India in the west, and also to India itself, is difficult to exaggerate.

Text, Rule and Ideology

We could, I imagine, be easily asked, why ascribe a single text such importance, and what power can conceptual practices have in the creation of hegemony? What, in short, is a written text or epistemology to ruling?

The answer to these questions lies in a Gramscian understanding of the concept of hegemony. According to this, even though force is the fundamental content of hegemony, it does not reside only in physical brutality or a machinery for direct coercion.

The initial moment of conquest has to be translated or mediated into an administration of power. The work of intellectuals who interpret the reality to be ruled and inscribe this into suitable categories provides the administrative basis for a sustained, reproducible ruling (Said 1979).[5] In the case of India, orientalist scholar–administrators of the East India Company, along with those of the colonial state, provide this conceptual or categorical framework.

On this basis an 'India' is constructed from the standpoint of European colonial rule. It consists of a set of "virtual realities vested in texts and accomplished in the distinctive practices of reading and writing" (Smith 1990: 62). The ruling nature of this construction is evident from the fact that it tells us less about that country than about the social imperatives of the producers of that knowledge (Said 1979: 4–9). The importance of texts which transmit knowledge, especially about "distant amorphous" places (Said 1979: 9), to the west from whence also colonialism and imperialism spring, must always be kept in mind. They provide the building blocks for cultural and ideological representation of these areas. Socio-cultural relationships between these spaces are conducted mainly through what Smith calls "the textual mode" (Smith 1990: 61–65; 83–88). Furthermore, these constructed "objects of knowledge" claim authority for neutral or unbiased representation. No allowance is made for the possibility that the knower's, for example Mill's, intention or location in relations of ruling are implicated in the types of discourse deployed and developed (Smith 1990: 14–18).[6]

This epistemological erasure of the social, through the adoption of a metaphysical mode entailing occlusiveness, displacement and objectification, is named as ideology by Marx in *The German Ideology*. Here ideology is not solely the *content* or a collection of particular ideas and stereotypes, but also, and mainly, *an epistemological method*. A close reading of *The German Ideology* shows that not only are the "ruling ideas of any age . . . the ideas of the ruling class", but also how these ideas are implicated forms and products of social relations necessary for ruling (Marx and Engels 1973: 5). We begin to see constructive and reflexive relations between the apparatuses of ruling and knowledge.

This ideological method which degrounds and obscures the historical/material dimension of ideas naturally postulates a superordinate and separate realm for them. In "Ideological Practices of Sociology", Smith transposes Marx's critique of philosophy to the standard knowledge procedures of conventional (bourgeois) sociology and insists that they are neither "objective" (except reificatory) nor "pure" (see Smith 1990: 14–16; 66–70). The productive tools and impacts of these procedures, when queried on the ground of everyday life, amount to a categorical and segregated organization of relations of ruling, involving specific semiotic systems. They are, for her, "isomorphic with relations of ruling" and necessarily invert the actual lived subject/object relations. They write over subjectivities, experiences and agencies of peoples in history (Smith 1990: 83–88).

Smith's Marxist critique of sociology as ideology can be extended to historiography of colonial history. I have chosen James Mill's *The History of British India* for an exploration of its epistemological processes with the intention of uncovering how Mill's 'India' is an ideological constellation, what Ronald Inden calls an "imagined India" (Inden 1990).

Making India British: James Mill and Colonial Historiography

It is certain that the few features of which we have any description from the Greeks, bear no inaccurate resemblance to those which are found to distinguish this people at the present day. From this resemblance, from the state of improvement in which the Indians remain, and the stationary condition in which their institutions first, and then their manners and character, have a tendency to fix them, it is no unreasonable supposition, that they have presented a very uniform appearance during the long interval from the visit of the Greeks to that of the English. Their annals, however, from that era till the period of Mahomedan conquests, are a blank.

James Mill, *The History of British India*

Mill's *The History of British India* has stood in for "Indian history", even though Mill encapsulates his real project in the very title of his study. The title holds, as does the book, an actuality and an ambition within one cover. India at the time of his writing (1805–17) was not fully under British control, either in terms of occupation of territories or in terms of knowledge. A comprehensive task of creating knowledge for ruling had been already undertaken by the orientalists in the eighteenth century, but an 'India' equal to the task of colonial rule had not yet been fully formulated. Besides, both in England and India there were many turns and reversals in political philosophy of governing and practical politics. The notion of 'British India', therefore, projects both a partial actuality and a desire of full domination, as well as their conceptual bases (Mill 1968: 118–19). Mill's India is thus an ingested and aspired to social space for colonial rule. The book's towering status as a colonial text is evinced in securing Mill the job of the Chief Examiner of India House, the highest post in England of the most lucrative instrument of colonial rule. Administrators, legislators, missionaries and businessmen engaged with India, among others, read this book as a compulsory text. An important footnote is John Kenneth Galbraith's preface to the 1968 edition (Mill 1968). Galbraith read Mill before venturing out as American Ambassador to India. His preface abounds in admiration of Mill for giving the modern reader a fundamental grasp on Indian reality.

This preface supports Mill's claim that *The History of British India* would stand as an enduring representation of India for the west. An assessment, thus, of this crucial text as ideology should be conducted along the following lines:

1. The epistemological method and historical context, including the social positionality of the author;

2. The particular content with regard to ascriptive stereotypes of concepts and images;

3. The overall political implications of these textual and conceptual practices with regard to the type of social subjectivity or historical agency ascribed to the Indian people.

Speaking of context, James Mill is primarily known as the apostle of Bentham's utilitarian philosophy and its application to matters of government. It is less known that in earlier life Mill was an evangelical preacher, and he remained close to Wilberforce and the Clapham sect. He was admired by William Bentnick, the Governor General of Bengal, and by important parliamentarians such as Thomas Babington Macaulay. For his formulation of 'British India' he relied on the archival compilations of the East India Company and translated resources of the orientalists. But his particular interest, unlike theirs, did not lie in the antiquities and their revival, and he successfully ejected parts of the earlier approach which combined a negative cultural–moral judgement of the contemporary Indian society with a respect for India's ancient civilization.

Mill's history project, and thus his historiography, obviously stems from the standpoint of a colonial empire. It is not in 'discovering' India as an historical entity but in vindicating the moment of colonial rule that he found his intellectual motive force. His purpose was to unfold the implications of events which marked the "commencement of the British Intercourse with India; and the Circumstances of its Progress, till the Establishment of the Company on a durable basis of Act of Sixth of Queen Anne" (Mill 1968: 1). The scope of the three-volume project consists of:

> recording the train of events, unfolding the Constitution of the Body, half political, half commercial, through which the business has been ostensibly performed; describing the nature, the progress and effects of its commercial operations, exhibiting the legislative proceedings, the discussions and speculations, to which the connexion of Great Britain with India has given birth, analysing the schemes of government which she has adopted for her Indian dominions, and attempting to discover the character and species of relation to one another in which the mother country and her eastern dependencies are placed. (Mill 1968: 2)

The attempt consisted of situating and legitimizing British colonial rule in a pattern of ruling successions in India. Emphasizing force and repeated invasions by foreigners, characterizing the Mughal empire in particular as foreign rule, and portraying the Mughals as despotic and a degenerative influence on the hindus, Mill argued for the necessity of an English empire in India. It was as a rule of reason and a civilizing mission that he justified this rule. Throughout his first chapter, on the English mercantile companies and the foundation of the colonial empire in Bengal, Mill presents an innocent commercial history. All European atrocities of conquest and commerce, including slave trade, are erased while presenting

English achievements and superiority in "the spirit of commerce".
The only moral judgement is levelled at the Dutch for executing
nine Englishmen in the "massacre at Amboyna". The Mahome-
dans, however, attract heavy condemnation on the ground of savagery and ruthlessness, while "that brilliant empire, established by
the English" was entirely legitimated in India (1968: 33). It was
even portrayed as sanctioned succession, as in the following statement: "A firman and decree of the Emperor, conferring [these] privileges was received on the 11th of January, 1643; and authorized
the first establishment of the English on the continent of India, at
that time the seat of most extensive and splendid monarchies on the
surface of the globe" (1968: 21). The "recording of train of events"
was thus no neutral narrative venture for Mill. *The History of
British India* had but one main objective, to project and promote
British rule in India.

This objective required a representational characterization
of the object of rule—namely, Indian peoples. The remainder of the
three volumes is dedicated to this enterprise, the construction of a
definitive socio-moral version of India, beginning with the most
extensive chapter on "manners, morals and customs of the hindoos". This is followed by a temporal history, also laced with
moral and cultural judgements. Together they contained both justification and direction for the development of the colonial state.

Mill's history consciously eschews any archival or empirical research, including the knowlege of local classical or vernacular
languages and texts. Thus it is not impeded by or accountable to
information that may not fit in the introjected ideological schema.
This colonial historiography is distinct from that of writing European history, where the historian attempts a direct familiarity with
the sources and records events in time. In colonial historiography,
however, the historian, according to Mill, plays the role of a judge
who is faced with a crime and a set of circumstances and testimonies of witnesses. These he must construe as "evidences" of a
typical event, as well as decide on the credibility of the witnesses.[7]
He must then read or hear the testimonies, etc., with the legal provisions pertaining to this crime. Whether something is an "evidence" at all will depend on what it is an "evidence" of, that is, on

the pre-existing legal construction of that crime. Mill's legal discourse contains explicit epistemological principles and statements.
Beginning with the premise that he 'knows' 'India' (the crime) even
before he undertakes his task, he employs a principle of relevance
and logic in selecting and sorting evidences for this preconceived
knowledge which originates outside his research. Thus the text is a
fully fleshed version of his presuppositions, details of which are to
be read as illustrations of his preconceptions of Indian history and
society. The attempt results in a seamless 'imagining' or construction of 'India', unaccommodating of complexities which might
have problematized this construction.

   Mill's proudly stated historiography, which adopts a metaphysical mode as a tool of social research, could be termed an
idealist rationalism. This method was critiqued by Marx as the
epistemological method of ideology. Discrediting the need for a
material basis or actual research, etc., for writing history, Mill
starts with an essentialist version of a 'real India' as opposed to the
phenomenal one, which is qualitatively different from and un-
accountable to the empirical and social. Logical deductions and
interpretations rely, thus, on this prehistorical and empirical essentialist notion of the 'real'. Merging the formality of logic with the
universal claims of metaphysics, Mill purports to provide his readers with the 'real truth' about India. He never questions his pre-
sumptions about India, their sources, or the existing social relations
between a colonial investigator and a colonized reality. Totally
unselfconscious, he characterizes his method as that of "positive
science", resting on notions of "true" and "false" causes, "witnesses" and "evidences" in order to come to the right socio-moral
judgments about India (Mill 1968: 6–7). However, in this process
Mill not only creates moral judgments; they also became 'facts'
about India which function as metaphysical and foundational categories for classifying, judging and administering Indian peoples
and societies. Thus, the writing of history becomes a production of
ideology, content and epistemology matching each other, occluding
constructive relationships between consciousness and society.
Unlike the sciences, Mill's method dispenses with verification, with
the obligation to test preconceptions and so forth against the

archival, empirical sources, both vernacular and European. He discourages new research, since he considers that a "sufficient stock of knowledge was already there" (Mill 1968: 5).

The standpoint of domination is also implicit in the fact that Mill never considers the ability or the right of Indians to define and represent themselves. His text as a whole is both a device and a justification for that silencing. The only voice and image permitted to 'the native' would be those she/he would acquire in the course of the colonial narrative.

The ideological character of Mill's enterprise, which fears any threat to his ideal type, emerges in his complex intertextual relationship with the English orientalists.[8] Since no narrative even remotely resembling a history could have been written without previous records and translations, Mill was highly dependant on the orientalist archive. Though he did not in all points share their view of India, the "lineaments of what they already knew" provided the pedestal for his project. But he resorted to a strategy of abstraction to decontextualize and incorporate previous research and interpretations, and manipulated stereotypes and attitudes as he needed them.

Mill's major debt to the orientalists for an ideological version of India lay in the polyvalent concept of 'tradition'. It is this grab-bag category of cultural interpretation and representation which provided Mill's staple or modality for constructing 'difference'. It created a ground for essentialism and thus generalization, since everything found in or about India could be read in light of this pre-established concept. The peculiar relationship held by this concept to time and social agency, bespeaking an arrested time, fixity and repetition, allowed any reading of India through the lens of tradition as both chaotically mobile and rigidly fixed. This imputed changeless, passive lack of agency was then put forward as an intrinsic characteristic of Indian peoples and their histories. Caught in the conceptual grip of 'tradition', events and changes of a few thousand years could then be seen as "blank annals" (Mill 1968: 118–121) or an eternal repetition.

The deployment of the concept of 'tradition', which did not originate in the colonial encounter or in Mill but pre-existed in Europe for other and similar sense-making purposes, became a major device for constructing both the "crime" and the evidence for Mill the historian–judge. Orientalist scholar–administrators such as William Jones had already established traditionality as an essence of Indian society, and of the "Hindoos" in particular. In fact, from the era of Warren Hastings in the 1770s to the time when Mill was writing his book, colonial civil legislation in India continually assumed and constructed 'tradition' through translation of hindu and muslim scriptures and a selective compilation of their personal laws.[9]

The concept of 'tradition', when deployed in the otherization of India, entailed the related notions of 'civilization' and 'antiquity'. While concepts such as 'tradition', 'antiquity' and 'civilization' were invested with positive connotations for the colonial conservatives of the eighteenth century, they also served as conduits for varying moral judgments about colonized societies at each stage. What was meant by 'civilization' or its importance at each stage decided whether a country with an old history and complex socio-cultural organizations could be called civilized. Thus, the attitude toward civilization and traditionality, as well as the ascribed types of traditions, decided whether a country was 'civilized' or 'barbaric' or 'savage'. And those who had power and the need to define the "truth about India", claiming self-transcendence, had decided that it was a traditional country. Thus, it was at once in and out of time and history, replete with peculiar "barbaric" traditions. Mill also went by categorical formulations of 'India' as accomplished by the India Office, but unlike the orientalists, denied either the value or the existence of an ancient civilization in India. As a utilitarian and Malthusian economic liberal he not only had little interest in traditional societies or ancient civilizations, but even less in eastern ones.

Mill's book therefore begins by disputing the orientalist ascriptions of antiquity and civilization to India. His version of this country is projected in no uncertain terms at the very outset: "Rude nations seem to derive a peculiar gratification from pretensions to a remote antiquity. As a boastful and turgid vanity distinguishes remarkably the oriental nations, they have in most instances carried their claims extravagantly high" (Mill 1968: 107). He goes on to criticize orientalist accounts of hindu creation stories and the

hindu methods of record-keeping and chronicle writing. Dubbing
the orientalist acknowledgement of hindu claims to antiquity as
duped submission to the "national pride of barbarians", he dis-
misses indigenous records, literature and other archival sources as
worthless for writing "history" (Mill 1968: 118–19). "Judging"
the sources and "witnesses" in this peremptory way, Mill simultaneously displays his power location as a reader of Indian reality
and manipulates, controls and constructs socio-cultural 'facts'
about India according to his own discursive organization.

This disregard for matters indigenous to India, echoed
later by Macaulay in his influential "Minute on Education for
India" (Curtin 1971) as "monstrous fables" of barbarians, often
pits Mill against the orientalists. He is particularly dismissive of
their impartiality and accuracy, since they knew Indian languages,
lived there and enjoyed the literature that they found. Thus, they
lacked the necessary detachment which Mill considered essential
for a judge–historian, and he found himself eminently suitable for
this task on the very grounds of his lack of knowledge of languages,
direct connections with or experiences of India.

H.H. Wilson, on the other hand, an orientalist scholar–
administrator who went on to become Boden Professor of Sanskrit
at Oxford, subsequently edited *The History of British India* and
provided extensive footnotes correcting Mill's "errors" in representing Indian culture or history. Asserting that Europeans cannot
"know" India without learning its ancient and modern languages
and reading extensively to develop a cultural literacy to be com-
plemented by life experiences and discussions with Indians, Wilson
offered in his "corrections" a text parallel to Mill's.

Wilson's footnotes and commentaries highlight Mill's
enormous ignorance of India and his even greater arrogance that
his very ignorance was a prerequisite for knowledge. Mill was one
of the earliest propagators of the notion that India did not have a
'history', a notion that was to be found from William Jones to
Marx though to modern times. For Mill, India lacked 'history'
both in terms of an intellectual discipline and in terms of a social
progression or evolution in time, expressive of agency and origi-
nality. Presenting hindus both as infantile liars as well as the real
"natives" of India, caught in fantasy and blind to the difference

between fact and fiction, and Indian muslims as foreign invaders who only kept minimal records, Mill regarded European historians such as himself as the real historians of India.

Mill's view of himself as the definitive historian of India, while denying India any history, creates crude inconsistencies in his text. On the one hand, his own lack of willingness and ability to do primary research on India makes him reliant on early Greek and later European sources. He is thus constrained to say that orientalists "had studied the Indian languages" and "acquired the means of full and accurate information" (Mill 1968: 118). On the other hand, they were seduced by that very knowledge into a positive view of India, especially of the hindus. Mill draws instead upon the Greeks for denigrating social features which "bear no inaccurate resemblance to those which are found to distinguish this people at the present day". Consequently, he states in the same breath that "we have no reason to suppose that their knowledge of the Hindus was valuable" (1968: 118). Mill's double project is to degrade and deny Indians any worthwhile historical and cultural agency and thus any history of its expression. His ultimate aim seems to have been the establishment of an empty historico–cultural slate for India inscribed with barbaric traditions. He shares with the evangelical missionaries the conviction that Indians (mainly hindus) are essentially degenerate and full of "insincerity, mendacity, venality and perfidy" (Niranjana 1990: 776–77).[10]

Mill's pathological dislike of Indians, and the colonial context and the content of his book, are secured by his manipulation of categories such as 'tradition', 'civilization', 'barbarism' and 'savagery'. He constructs simultaneously a social space that is rigidly ordered and enclosed and yet formless and primeval. A telling example of this is to be found in his reading of the caste system, which he sees both as atavistic or irrational and forged with "iron laws" (Mill 1968: 153). Wilson's extensive footnote on this topic, however, not only shows up Mill's scanty reading and reliance on rumour, but also illustrates the complexity of caste as a form of fast-mutating social practices and organization rather than a mere discourse of tradition (Mill 1868: 125 n1). Mill's ascriptive confidence actually rests on the *a priori* notion of European social superiority over conquered 'others'.

What also becomes evident from the struggle between the text and the footnotes is that the modalities of colonial rule vary in historically specific moments. The goals and practices of a mercantile monopoly (East India Company) differ substantially from the ideological aspirations of a rising colonial state. Thus, Mill's dismissal of the need to research Indian history can be contrasted to Wilson's view that research on India was in "the veriest of infancy", or that Mill's opinions of Indian society, "to say the least of them", were "premature".[11] Wilson's view of India as 'traditional' was coherent with a positive ascription of 'civilization', qualifying its decline. But for Mill a steep decline follows the Aryans, whom he erroneously sees as "aboriginal" to India. After the Aryan "golden age" India becomes a static yet chaotic society. Further degenerating under muslim invasions and rule, it remains stagnant and decadent until the arrival of the British (Mill 1968: 113). Thus, Mill creates his own "Robinsonade" (Marx 1977: 83–85) through this teleology of European and Indian history moving towards capital and colonization, using enlightenment notions of civilization and humanism together with the moral lens of evangelicalism. That is to say, he creates a history of India as a part of an overall current political and ideological project.

As such, Mill denies or distorts all political developments within India, particularly that of a state formation and the development of social government and legislation. He invents a nomadic stage of Aryan pastoralism which he inlays with an English nuclear family form (Mill 1968: 122). This happy pastoral stage, according to Mill, is followed by a tortuous route of decline. But orientalist and other European insistences force him to impute to India a highly qualified form of barbaric 'civilization'. "The first rude form of a national polity" is to be found in "fully as early a period as any portion of the race" (1968: 122). But he also adds that the "cautious inquirer will not probably be inclined to carry this era very far back" (1968: 122 n1). The legislative texts of earlier periods, such as Manu's *Dharmashastra* as translated by the orientalists, are seen by Mill as exceptional achievements of "superior spirits" rather than as the result of a general development of political and social government (1968: 124). According to him:

> The first legislator of the Hindus, whose name it is impossible to trace, appears to have represented himself as the republisher of the will of God. He informed his countrymen that, at the beginning of the world, the creator revealed his duties to man in four sacred books, entitled Vedas; that during the first age, of immense duration, mankind obeyed them, and were happy; that during the second and third they only partially obeyed, and their happiness was proportionately diminished; that since the commencement of the fourth age disobedience and misery had totally prevailed, till the Vedas were forgotten and lost; that now, however, he was commissioned to reveal them anew to his countrymen, and to claim their obedience. (Mill 1968: 125)

Wilson's comment on this is telling: "The whole of this is imaginary; there is no such legislation, there are no such assertions in Hindu tradition" (1968: 125 n1). Flying in the face of all available evidence encoded in *Dayabhaga* property laws, Mill also claimed that there was no private property, revenue or justice system in India, nor a system of public finance and public works, nor a knowledge of the art of war. For this lack he resorted to explanations based on the "laziness of the hindus" (1968: 133 n1). Wilson's comments, therefore, establishing his difference from Mill, allow for variant readings of a colonized society from within the very precincts of colonial rule. These debates from within also expose at their clearest the articulation between knowledge and social relations of power, and their historical specificities.

All disagreements notwithstanding, the overall colonial project comes out loud and clear when we see that Mill develops as a key in his history one orientalist theme to its fullest—that of Asiatic Despotism, which should be distinguished from European Enlightened Despotism. In this formulation converged negative perceptions of the 'two peoples' of India. The sources of this despotism were traced to both caste-bound, "traditional" hindus (with their self-enclosed village societies) and muslims, already renowned in post-crusade Europe as absolute despots, with racial and religious propensities in this direction (Said 1981). Unlike Europe, 'Asiatic' political institutions and economies are claimed to be sustained by brute force, superstition, authoritarianism and tradition

(Mill 1968: 141). Mill projected this stance through the conflation of the typology or the iconography of the monarch and the actual or practical system of government in different historical stages. Taking statements from Manu literally, oblivious to similar European iconography of the monarch (for example in Hobbes' *Leviathan*), Mill posited a monstrously totalitarian system of government for India as an intrinsic expression and requirement of the peoples (1968: 141).

The eurocentrism or racism inherent in the concept of Asiatic Despotism is a manipulation of the concept of 'traditional society'. This is exposed through Mill's and Wilson's contradictions with each other, as well as through the contradictions within Mill's text. For example, the rigidity of this notion and Mill's ascribed chaos and formlessness of Indian cultures and polity are both accommodated by 'tradition', and as a whole play condemnatory roles. Wilson's copious footnotes also signal to the complexity of actual political practices, in sharp contrast to Mill's construction of symbolic fixities. Wilson questions both Mill's claims that the government which "almost universally prevailed in the monarchies of Asia . . . was contrivance extremely simple and rude" (Mill 1968: 142), and that the hindu king/sovereign combined all functions of the state in himself (Mill 1968: 143). Instead he draws attention to the similarities between European and Indian governing systems, remarking that: "In the more skillful governments of Europe, officers were appointed for the discharge of particular duties in the different provinces of the empire . . . [and] . . . all together act as connected and subordinate wheels in one complicated artful machine" (Mill 1968: 145). The notion of Asiatic Despotism in India should therefore be seen as less descriptive than ascriptive, as a conceptual artefact for colonial legitimation. It allowed Mill and others to justify and advocate despotic rule for India by marshalling the concept of tradition and locating it as India's cultural essence. It is through this device that India was judged as fundamentally unsuited to democracy and positively responsive to authoritarianism. The same sentiment was expressed by James Mill in his *Essay on Government*, while his son John Stuart Mill (1972) in *On Liberty* justified a despotic, though enlightening rule of India on the same grounds.[12] Later Indian demands for a constitutional rule could be thus dismissed on this very ground. Marx's essays on colonialism and India, along with the thesis of lack of history, contains the same credo of Asiatic Despotism.

Developing further the colonial project of ethnicization, Mill constructed hindus and muslims into separate and self-enclosed cultural categories and organized Indian history into three periods of rule, namely hindu, muslim and British, with a particular social ethos ascribed to the rulers. This process of fragmentation and categorization, commencing in the eighteenth century, became a developed historiography in *The History of British India*. It lent itself to a periodization pattern of European cultural and social history. The "golden age of the Aryans" thus declined into the "dark middle ages" of muslim conquests and rule, followed by the enlightened rule of Britain. Contrary to all evidence, muslims were projected as foreigners or outsiders, and the composite or hybrid culture of north and east India were ignored. All this provided a distortion of Indian history while providing the bases for a colonialist strategy of divide and rule. While the British presence was legitimated by trade permissions and land grants given by the muslim emperors and lesser muslim rulers, the muslims themselves were portrayed as usurpers. Indeed the fear that they were seen by Indians as invaders and usurpers was never allayed for the British even by their massive military might. The equation, therefore, of themselves with the Mughals as equally and a better type of outsider, as well as the negative depiction of the muslims, gave the English a moral prerogative to rule. It is therefore not surprising that Mill's claim for Europeans as better rulers rests upon negative stereotypes of muslims as warlike and full of "saracenic" fanaticism with an inbuilt tendency towards sensuality, cruelty and luxury. The fact that the muslims made a self-conscious historical effort by writing biographies and descriptions or keeping state records, or produced great art, architecture, mathematics and philosophy, did not redeem them in Mill's eyes. Nor was he able to see Indian islam as a specifically Indian and syncretic formation, or muslims as Indians in diverse groups in their regional cultural varieties.

By reinforcing the orientalist notion of the hindus as the (ab)original sons of the soil, Mill 'hinduized' India in a highly effective way, while taking away from "Hindu India" the attributes of a progressive or significant civilization. Thus the "Hindus" were greatly in need of being civilized, which the muslim rulers, who were themselves barbaric and, unlike the English, had succumbed to the "Hindu" culture, could not provide. Distancing himself from the seduced orientalists, Mill had no project for restoring India to its pristine ancient glory. The ancient venerable India of the orientalists is for Mill mainly a moment of civilizational immaturity, "the dawn of childhood of human kind". As a patriarchal and patrician stern ruler and judge, rather than an indological scholar, Mill advocates discipline and punishment for the good of this "wild, barbaric, savage and rude" people (Mill 1968: 123 n1). As far as he was concerned, Indians were "a people over whom the love of repose exerts the greatest sway, and in whose character aversion to danger forms a principal ingredient" (Mill 1968: 153).

It is interesting to note how Mill slides between binary notions, such as age and childhood, order and chaos, nature and culture, barbarism and tradition, in his ideological construction of 'India'. He resolves the contradiction between tradition and savagery or barbarism by positing that their traditionality is itself an indication of savagery. It is this elision between tradition and savagery, or culture and nature, or better still, culture as nature (see Dirks 1992: 1–3), which allows Mill the maximum leverage to accommodate diverse cultural features without himself suffering from any sense of contradiction (Niranjana 1990: 776). It also allows him to systematically introject inferiority into the difference between Europeans and their Indian colonized subjects. This silences the Indian prerogative of self-representation and justifies colonial rule as an expression of progress or improvement.

Mill completed his project in 1817, but his historiographical method, which produces ideology, separating forms of knowing from ways of being both in history and in presentday social organization, continues. The project of inventing cultural categories to accomplish the task of ruling continues unabated. The attribution of 'tradition' to any society is still a legitimation for domination, and an excuse to modernize, that is, to recolonize.

Notes and References

1 See Edward Said (1979) regarding cultural–colonial construction of 'the orient' or 'the east' as a knowledge/power category, and the implication of 'the west's' cultural–political identity and politics.

2 See Raymond Williams (1983: 318–320) for an evolution and application of this concept.

3 See the discussion of modernization theorists of the MIT school in the context of 'development', such as S. Kuznets (1966) and W.W. Rostow (1985), for an overall grasp of this position.

4 See Ronald Inden (1990) for an extended discussion of this colonial cultural–political construction of India, which attempts a project partially similar to Said's *Orientalism* (1979).

5 See also Smith (1987: 181–85) on the notion of 'standpoint' of knowledge, and Smith (1990: 31–57) on the ideological (i.e. ruling) role of intellectuals (sociologists and others) in the construction and maintenance of the ruling apparatus.

6 See also Smith (1987: 49–69) on the implications of knower's location in the production of knowledge.

7 See Mill's "Preface" to Volume I for the full exposition of his method of history writing and his conception of what properly constitutes 'history'.

8 Throughout Volume I, Book II, Mill disputes with the orientalist historians and translators, just as much as he disputes the fact of India having a history.

9 For Hastings and personal law, see the introduction, Sangari and Vaid (1990).

10 See also R. Hyam (1992) for a reworked version of masculinity and personality of colonized males.

11 See Wilson's footnotes (Mill 1968) on issues of caste and other social practices in Chapter II, and on government laws in Chapter III, especially pages 126–40.

12 "Despotism is a legitimate mode of government in dealings with barbarians, provided the end be their improvement, and the means justified by actually effecting that end". (J.S. Mill 1972: 73)

Age of Consent and Hegemonic Social Reform

Until recently colonialism in general and British colonial hegemony in India in particular has been largely considered in terms of economic exploitation, military repression and direct political administration. This view of hegemony as unequivocally coercive omits to consider its legitimation-producing aspects. This subtle and complex dimension of hegemony amounts to a reorganization of the civil society of the colonized which is accomplished through a diffusion of cultural–ideological constructions and moral regulations.[1] Though this legitimation aspect of hegemony is present in most colonial enterprises in varying degrees, depending on the nature of the enterprise, it is the case with India that British colonialism sought to legitimize itself through self-characterization as rule of law and social reform.[2]

Significant legislation pertaining to social reform which sought to penetrate deep into the everyday life and culture of Indians (in particular of Bengal) marked the passage of British rule in India. This legislation involved such intimate and private aspects of life as marriage, motherhood, women's relationship to their bodies, sex and sexuality and, less intimately, property laws and education. The processes leading up to the enactment of reform legislation entailed the elaboration of colonial cultural constructions and modes of moral regulation. They accomplished the process of colonial state formation in India by ascribing cultural–

This essay was first published in *Gender and Imperialism*, ed. C. Midgley, Manchester and New York: Manchester University Press, 1998.

moral identities to the indigenous population which served in the capacity of ideology for ruling.[3]

In this enterprise patriarchy and the reorganization of gender relations provided the most crucial elements. Patriarchal colonial–moral imperatives came into nineteenth-century Bengal deeply inflected with British/European ideas of "race" and difference. The laws therefore actually far exceeded their stated legal purpose and in effect provided a set of norms and forms for the society to adhere to.[4] This was particularly effective with the rising Bengali middle classes, who were formed in the terrain of colonial rule. One such law, perhaps the most hegemonically charged, is the Age of Consent Act of 1891. This paper explores this Act's ideologically hegemonic dimensions with respect to the production of identities for Bengali hindu middle-class women. Since these female identities are conceived with reference to their male counterparts, a discussion about them is necessary. These hegemonic identities were not restrained within the boundaries of the Act and they continue to texture all manner of social legislation and discussion which surrounded them.

On 9 January 1891, the Viceroy of India, Lord Lansdowne, introduced before the Supreme Legislative Council a Bill to amend Section 376 of the Indian Penal Code, which would effect an amendment of Schedule II to the Code of Criminal Procedure of 1882. Drafted and presented at length before the Council by the Honourable Andrew Scobble, circulated for opinion to a large number of colonial administrators, both Indian and British, medical and legal practitioners, including notables among the muslim and hindu communities, the Bill was passed with unprecedented speed on 19 March 1891. Entitled "The Age of Consent", raising the age of legally permissible sex for girls from ten years (the limit set in 1860) to twelve years, this Act became the most controversial of reforms legislated by the colonial state.

The objective of this Bill, soon to become an Act, was a final definition and settlement of the age at which any female of the Indian communities could become the object of male sexual penetration. The violation of this age limit would constitute a criminal offence irrespective of the marital status of the female or the relationship between the female and the male offender in question.

This Act was crucial in the state's attempt to regulate sex and forms of sexuality among the Indian subjects. It defined legal sex as being heterosexual and penetrative, while equating sexual transactions both within and outside of marriage, including prostitution. The same legal provisions would thus hold for rape, statutory rape and illegal solicitation, and implicitly impact on the population growth of the country.[5] This state regulation of the private lives of the colonial subjects also had a profound moral dimension, on the basis of which the reform was proposed and justified. That entailed a negative cultural–moral construction of the local population which was perceived by the colonial authorities to be in dire need of reform.

The Bill created an overwhelming reaction among the indigenous male population at its consultation stage. Huge rallies were organized in protest, especially in Calcutta and Bombay, as well as petitions and signature campaigns. Though some support for the Act was also forthcoming, in the main the state faced the accusation of a high-handed imposition (see Kosambi 1991: 1857–68). Anticipating this, the colonial state performed various exercises of legitimation. It not only went through the motions of public consultation but also created a Viceroy's Council which minimally took care of the issue of representation. Of the fifteen members, four were Indians, two each from the hindu and muslim communities. In addition a Select Committee was appointed to review the objections raised about the Bill, and a few minor changes suggested by it were incorporated into the Act. Of the two hindu Council members, one voted negatively, despite being a loyal legal practitioner. The Act in its final state made compromises. A husband's offence, considered non-cognizable, removed for him the penalty of transportation for life,[6] as well as made provision for the case to be tried by the District Magistrate (a post reserved for the British), rather than being arrested and investigated by the police.

This large controversy surrounding the age of consent in its Bill stage was not a struggle between two homogeneous groups, namely the colonizers and the colonized, embodying the principles of modernity and tradition, respectively.[7] As research has shown, preoccupation with social reform and modernity, or social order and tradition, is in no consistent way the project of the British or Indians ranged in oppositional relation. During different phases of colonialism British attention shifted from 'tradition' to 'modernity' or vice versa. The British sought to create a colonial ideological apparatus for ruling just as much on one basis as on the other. Lata Mani, for example, has shown this effectively in terms of the invention of tradition in her work on *sati* and colonial representation of Indian women.[8] Colonial rule in nineteenth-century India meandered along a tortuous path between the traditionalism of the orientalists and the modernizing drive of the utilitarians, all in search of developing a technology for legitimation and social control which would elaborate a hegemonic reorganization of the indigenous civil society.

The same hegemonic aspirations marked the indigenous male elite, who were also preoccupied with the same issues of social reform and social control.[9] They took opposing stances to the proposed colonial legislation, and in some cases constructed reasons other than those of the states for proposing or demanding laws. Being pro- or anti-reform cannot therefore be read as simple signs of being pro- or anti-colonial, that is, of being a colonial loyalist or a nationalist. There were many instances when loyal British subjects disagreed with the proposed Age of Consent Act or the legislation against *sati*.[10] Boundaries to intervention seemed to be drawn by loyalists and nationalists alike, mainly in the matter of domestic life consisting of legislations regarding women, the control of their bodies and sexuality, marriage and family.[11]

Since neither the issues involved nor the project of social reform as such were unknown and unacceptable to the local male elite, we are left with having to answer why this particular Act called for such reaction rather than the Act of 1860, which fixed the age of marriage and sex for girls at ten years. Not even the banning of *satidaha* (1829) nor the introduction of widow remarriage created such an organized protest. Though more research needs to be done in this area, some speculation might be in order. One could begin from the shadow cast over the 1891 Act by the death of a ten-year-old girl, Phulmoni Dasi, in 1889. Many, even colonial officials, blamed not only her husband but also the British government for allowing the act of sex with a ten-year-old girl. Reformers of all types found this reprehensible and the state responded to their criticism by raising the age of consent to twelve. This change was considered insufficient by some, while others thought the decision should be left to family members and other guardians. All of these responses were catalyzed at the consultation stage of the 1891 Bill, probably because it was the second such act of social legislation[12] to regulate the social morality of the 'natives' related to the issue of control of marriage and sexuality. The state was again posing as the guardian of 'native' morality, claiming to be the protector of Bengali/Indian women, and making charges of immaturity, brutality and incompetence against local males.

This attempt at social and moral interference in the private sphere of Bengali homes and sex lives seems to have unsettled the unofficial trade-off between the local male elite and the state. The 'home and the world split', which has been identified as the base of the national(ist) identity (P. Chatterjee 1989: 233–52),[13] was certainly severely challenged by such a reform proposal, precipitating moral contestation and political turmoil. Interpreted as a virtual assault on indigenous rights to self-definition, objections came not only from *shastric*[14] individuals but also from others asserting the principle of non-interference. If the Act of 1860 marked the threshold of local tolerance, then that of 1891, following thirty years of deepening anti-colonial politics, created a massive upsurge. To this was added a sense of betrayal since this Act reneged on Queen Victoria's 1858 proclamation of non-interference in indigenous social or private life, which she made after the onset of the Great Rebellion in 1857.[15]

It is obvious that the debate over the 1891 Act involved an extensive dramatis personae, as the project of hegemony involved colonial rulers and their champions and diverse opponents. This paper, however, does not attempt to cover the full spread. Instead, it focusses on one selected group of protagonists and examines their representational discursivities with respect to hegemonic colonial social reform. It is the ideological and cultural premises of the state's proposals and their creation of a body of representation or a "symbolic cultural constitution" (Inden 1990) of indigenous women, and relatedly of men, which are under scrutiny here. This focus can be justified on two important grounds. I concentrate on the dominant or the governing group which sets in place a political–cultural agenda which provides the terms for hegemonic contestation. In this agenda patriarchy, organized through a colonial racist perception, projects a site of contestation, a specific and concrete object of rule—namely women, their bodies, and familial and sexual conduct (K. Sangari and S. Vaid 1989: 1–26). This war of moral and cultural attribution, identity and self-definition is centred on or carried through reform projects that seek to define and organize the lives of local women. This means the regulation of the conduct of families where the control of the conduct of women was to take place. The moot issues are therefore the moral construction and regulation of a 'Hindu' culture and a 'Hindu' woman, which are equally at stake for the colonial and the local male elite.[16] This is an indelibly patriarchal project for both. But what is central for us is that the cultural–normative terms and regulatory boundaries are initiated by the colonial state: others respond to these even when they create overlapping or oppositional ideological spaces. This chapter concentrates on the discursive–ideological forms arising from the state's proposals and considers them as moments of evolution in the 'ruling discourse' of colonial India. The representations of Bengali/Indian hindu women, their male counterparts and society need to be read in the wider context of British colonial rule as a global project for social/cultural hegemony. My purpose is to focus on these identities and their role as forms of moral regulation and mediation within the textual apparatus for ruling.

Whose Consent? At What Age?
Discursive Constructions, Ideological Interpellations
and the Colonial State

The reforming impulse of the British colonial state in India had little to do with the protection of women and girls, though initiated in their names. This becomes evident from the fact that the issue of the woman's or the girl's own consent is hardly discussed in the official documents. Nowhere is there a provision in the Bill for a direct role to be played by the very people whose bodies are to be the discursive battleground between indigenous men and a patriarchal colonial state. Texts of submissions by and to the state make it apparent that the notion of 'consent' is only a nominal gesture towards women and girls as objects of a legal and social transaction.[17] In actuality they provide the legal guardian (father or custodian) with permission to alienate his (or her) daughter's or ward's body to a male user as husband, client or sexual keeper, and also to initiate her pregnancy. Legal penetration and impregnation thus crucially depend on the determination or definition of 'the age', which would provide the state with a fixed and justifiable criterion for 'consenting' to the guardian's 'consent'. It is this definition which was to confer 'womanhood' upon a 'child' or a 'girl', with or without individual onset of puberty, and thus prevent charges of rape and violent assault against the sexual (ab)user, sparing him, the parents, guardians and pimps the danger of legal prosecution.

The determination of the criterion for 'the age', however, lay with legal, scientific and religious experts as well as community leaders mobilized by the state, and aimed beyond questions of violence against women or children, to an overall definition of an acceptable moral and social order. As this moral order was to be the core of the reform attempted by the state, it needed contrasting points of reference to both an ideal and a degraded type of morality. Thus, through a complexly woven set of legal, scientific/medical and moral discourses, marked with inflexions of christianity and humanism, the state created legislative proposals which served as a social terrain for ruling through the imperatives and models of reform. These legislative practices and their discursive–ideological presentations are simultaneously forms of state regulation and cultural moralization. At once instruments of legitimation and a penal apparatus, they projected an 'enlightened' self-identity of the colonial power which then sought to rule and reform the colonized 'other' for its own good.

Ascribed identities, put forward as 'difference' produced in a colonial context, have little substantiveness to them, but are rather ideological projections articulated from within the relations of ruling. This type of difference, therefore, is not initially articulated by the population under rule, and as such are not socio-historically 'intrinsic' to their society. Thus, the characterization of India as an essentially religious/traditional society has less to do with India itself than with being a marker which is invented to differentiate it from England/Europe as rational and secular spaces. This difference is a reforming design which contains a perceived

degradation of the 'other' and the 'enlightened' benevolence of the
colonial reformer.

The reforming desire of the self-proclaimed moral and
rational colonial ruler, the ascribed degraded nature of the object
of reform, and the tropes of Indian women's abuse at the hands of
Indian men and white men rescuing brown women, in short the
entire baggage of the colonial project, stand out in the following
quotation from the Honorary Secretary, Public Health Society of
Calcutta, summarizing reports and submissions from medical practitioners. He reports on the opinion of Dr K. McLeod, Brigade-
Surgeon and Professor of Medicine at Calcutta Medical College.
This helps us get a sense of the power-driven and complex meaning of reform as encoded in the Age of Consent Act.

> The desired reform is one which will serve to remove a blot from
> our Indian codes, which will *ameliorate and elevate in a wide and
> deep reaching manner the condition of the women of India*. It
> seems to the Council that *it is to the improvement of that condi-
> tion that the attention of all who seek for well-founded and per-
> manent reform in India should mainly be directed*. . . . [The] evi-
> dence of history goes to show the high status [of women] attained
> in European countries has proceeded slowly, it may be, but nece-
> ssarily and surely, ever since the period when the status of women
> was first elevated, and when she first began to be regarded not as
> the mere toy and slave of her husband, but as his equal and fel-
> low worker. *Here again the legislature can give a right direction
> to popular opinion in this country, and can serve an educational
> purpose, the value of which is almost impossible to overestimate.
> The evils dealt with in this letter sap national vigour and moral-
> ity*; and the reform which the Council of the Health Society seek
> to press on the attention of the Supreme Council of the Health
> Society, to press on the attention of Supreme Government, seems
> to be the natural and necessary corollary of all those beneficent
> schemes for raising the physical, moral and mental status of the
> native, and of which the noble institution founded by the Count-
> ess of Dufferin is one phase. (Government of India 1882: 419–
> 20, pt 15, my emphasis)

This submission from one of the most important members

of the colonial medical administration in India attests to a white man's burden attitude, endemic to reform projects of this kind. This responsibility for reform encodes the colonial/European self-identity and the 'difference' between them and the constructed 'native other'. Through this reforming gesture the colonizing country posed as the universal standard of perfection, as a prescribed social model, upon which to base the moral improvement of the colony. The condition of women is evidently used as an index of both societies, of the perfection of one and the baseness of the other.[18] The superior agent for change, the colonial state, claims to deserve and reserves the right of interpretation and implementation at all times. In keeping with this exalted role, Dr McLeod invests the colonial legislature with the legitimate task of providing the "right direction to popular opinion in [India]" and thereby serving "an educational purpose" for uplifting the "native's" morals. This moral legislator and educator was to eradicate "evil" practices, particularly so when associated with sexuality, among an uncivilized subject population which is yet to reach a proper adulthood or maturity. The "native" (always male) was allegedly indulging in sexual activities which "sap national vigour, and national morality", in particular by cohabiting with "underage" girls, which spelt "the degeneration of the Indian race" (Government of India 1882: 424, pt 2).[19]

'Native' sexual practices are categorically considered by McLeod as the most important issue before the government which "has a wide bearing in a social point of view as regards the native community, and also with reference to the importance of the race" (Government of India 1882: 424, pt 2). These references to "the race", "the nation", and "the native community" signal to a perception of the collective perverse and infantile sexual identity of the other, "Bengalis in particular", who are "enervated by this unnatural custom". The unnatural practice is seen as pervasive enough to wear away "the stamina to withstand the baneful effects of malaria and cholera germ" (Government of India 1882: 426, pt 5).

In striking contrast to this degenerated 'native' is the morally superior, sexually contained, thus more physically robust European. A submission provided by a Bengali doctor, himself using colonial discourse and working for the medical administration, states: "After years of observation of the worst epidemic diseases of Bengal the conclusion is reached that placed in an equally unhealthy environment, the European may be said to enjoy an immunity to which the Indian is an utter stranger" (Government of India 1882: 426, pt 5). This same European model of socio–sexual morality, consisting of restraint as health, is used by the British administrator who seeks to interpose himself between the "native" man and "his" woman, as her rescuer from the "native's" unnatural sexual appetite. For this he has to legislate against the 'native', but by doing so he accomplishes "beneficent schemes for raising the physical, moral and mental state" for the whole of the 'native' society. The Age of Consent Act is thus considered the most "important step towards improvement of the race". The lofty character of the colonial reform/civilizing mission thus expands out into ever-widening circles of responsibility and achievement. Thus "reform is demanded in the interests of the state, of native society, of the Indian peoples, and of humanity. . ." (Government of India 1882: 420, pt 16).[20] And in this grand scheme of civilization the European/British man is an embodiment of civilization, posing as both a teacher and a judge.

The construction of the 'native' as a microcosm of a degraded society is a general colonial practice with a common epistemology, but it is also culturally specific to each colonial situation. In the case of India, the social space itself was declared to be "traditional" (read 'backward', 'superstitious', 'pagan' and so on), while its inhabitants were religiously identified as "Hindu" or "Musulman". "The Hindu" and its counterpart were then ascribed certain moral and cultural characteristics which were also differentiated in terms of gender. Within the colonial semiotic range 'the Hindu' had a special feature—it was an ideological category that allowed an articulation between the colonial project and the local population. Its ideological status is evinced by its homogenizing and essentialist character, and its morally regulative function was best displayed by its sexual and reproductive ascriptions to the subject population.[21]

Reform, it was felt by the state, can only come to 'the Hindu' from the outside, from the civilized Europeans.[22] In the first instance, "it is not supposed that a reform of a deep-seated custom in the domestic life can be carried out without a persistent opposition". The state, therefore, must legislate this and "should not leave it to the growth of improved public opinion" (Government of India 1882: 416). After all, was not India, as translated and represented by Jones, Colebrook, Wilson and others, a land of traditions? Even if reform, introduced by the British, "for at least a generation engaged the thoughts of the best men of all of the native communities" (1882: 417), 'the Hindu' could not be trusted to come through on his own. The state could not, therefore, "pursue a gentle course of non-interference, especially with regard to something so fundamental yet sensitive, the matter of sexual consummation" (1882: 417). As stated in one submission: "It [the age of consent] is a question extremely difficult to deal with, because there gather about it the silent but coercive force of traditions, the sanctions of immemorial customs, and the misunderstood [by the hindus, not the British] injunctions of religion. . ." (1882: 417). In fact some of the administrators regretted that there was a certain softness shown by the erstwhile colonial state to the "Indian tradition" as regards the social life.[23] Nonetheless, the civilizing responsibility had to be discharged by any means necessary: "Reforms introduced from the outside require force as a factor in their acceptance by the people or communities they may concern, and it may be doubted if they are ever thoroughly assimilated" (Government of India 1882: 417).

However, the rulers had to be circumspect about this use of force and seek hegemonic consent from local sources. The Age of Consent Act should not only "commend itself solely to the Anglo–Indian community", though it would provide the model. The sympathy of the people in England, "and especially of [English] women", was crucial, but the colonial state would need to draw on all of that surreptitiously. It would be "an evil if the impressions were to get abroad that the Government of India in a matter of this sort found the springs of its actions in the sentiments and wishes of the people of England" (Government of India 1892: 417). One would have to make a show of seeking local assistance and the loyal part of the hindu subjects, the westernized 'reformers', could perhaps be of some assistance. There was, after all, "a stir, attention in public press in India" brought on by the case of "the unhappy child Phulmoni Dossee" (Government of India 1882:

417). The death of a ten-year-old girl, produced legally through marital rape, became an occasion for legitimation, that is, expansion of hegemony, of the colonial state.

Discursive Construction of 'Hindu' Sexuality and Reproduction

The colonial discourse of racial identity and inferiority which characterized the 'Hindu' as a construct was intrinsically patriarchal, with regard to both the men and women of Bengal. To begin with, subjectivity and agency were accorded only to the male, as the 'native' was a masculine construct, and the 'native society' under reform was 'his' and seen as suffused with his cultural characteristics. The British (also referred to by a masculine singular noun) could only conduct businesses with the males of 'other' societies. The 'native females' were rendered invisible through a double move of possession and objectification. As 'Hindu women' they were seen as the subject of male governance in their own community and claimed as objects of reform by the British state. At least that much was tacitly agreed upon by both male parties in this hegemonic contestation. But social reform purporting to 'improve' or reorganize the colonial society threatened this equilibrium of power relations. With the Age of Consent Act matters reached a head. As far as the hindus were concerned the colonial state sought now to usurp the authority of the 'native' or 'Hindu' male, since he was claimed to be an unfit, brutal governor of women of his community.

The British state argued that 'Hindu' women and girls were also to be treated with some consideration as Her Majesty's subjects, since they lived under men full of "moral abominations" (Government of India 1882: 416). Their situation was an index of the fundamentally degenerate state of the society and the hindu men they lived with were to be seen as no more than child rapists. The official documents claimed that they were "subjected to more or less frequent acts of connexion with their husbands" (1882: 416), even when below the legal age. Unique to the 'Hindu' character was the fact that "legalized love of child-wives in marriage" was "represented by lust for female children outside of marriage" (1882: 423). This perversity, if tolerable with prostitutes, when manifested within marriage was to be considered criminal rape, and punishable by life imprisonment and transportation.

This condemnation of the 'Hindu' male would have been more than a mere ideological stance had any regard been manifested for actual variations in social practices, and had any consideration been displayed by the state for Indian/Bengali women and girls as legal and social persons by providing them with a real role in debates around the Age of Consent Act. Instead, we find in these colonial legal constructions a deep contempt towards the women themselves. The colonial administrator saw the 'Hindu' woman as a partner in the degeneration of 'Hindu' society, and she was even more of a degraded object for him than the 'Hindu' male. Preoccupation with 'the age' rather than consent made the girl/woman little more than a body and a reproductive system to be regulated and investigated. In fact the moralistic stance towards the 'Hindu' male and his society hid the instrumental use of the theme of violence against women for the purpose of condemnation of local societies, and provided the legitimation of colonial domination. It created for the state a space for conducting research in the areas of sex and reproduction in the name of science and civilization. The practices and objectives of the colonial medical establishment leading to this Act converts the body of the 'native/Hindu' woman or girl into an object of scientific penetration and vivisection (see Whitehead 1995: 187–209; Forbes 1979: 407–19). The construction and publicization of the private life of 'Hindu society' tore to pieces both the 'Hindu' male and the female. The white man condemned the 'Hindu' as both weak or effeminate and predatory or brutal, and posed as the ultimate guardian–patriarch who could legally and medically control the 'Hindu' woman's sexual and reproductive life.

To appropriate legal control and the moral definition of a whole society's sexual and reproductive life, and particularly to create a valid atmosphere of objectification, it had to be proved that the terrible lot of the 'Hindu' woman and girl was due to a moral failure of her own society which sprung from its own intrinsic nature.[24] This essential quality, which distinguished 'Hindus' from Europeans, was that of 'tradition' and an identification between being a 'Hindu' and being 'traditional'. Everything about 'Hindus', according to this view, signalled iron laws of orthodoxy, as opposed to the European rationality and progressivism as well as the morality of christianity. An example offered of this 'tradition-ality', presumably peculiar to 'Hindus', was their attitude towards marriage. The writer of *Hindu Law*, and an 'expert' on hindu society, Sir Thomas Strange, is quoted by the administrators in order to characterize the 'Hindus' and to justify the need to reform. According to Strange:

> Marriage, from a Hindu point of view, is a religious duty in the nature of a sacrament invested with sanctions of the highest character, which retain their hold upon the sympathies and customs of the people, because they can be traced back with exceptional freedom from modifications to very early times. Wherever there are Hindus there marriage holds a place it is difficult for other nations to comprehend. (Government of India 1882: 421)

This definition obliterates the christian or any other religion's approach to marriage as a sacrament and a commitment for life, and provides a directive of difference through the concept of 'tradition'. This relegates 'Hindu' society outside of history and time, and confers on it an opacity or density which puts it outside of European comprehension. In being beyond European comprehension this 'traditional' 'Hindu' society becomes the ultimate other of Europe/Britain and beyond the pale of reason or change. The unchanging quality of this society is further reinforced by drawing upon statements of indigenous colonial administrators:

> Girls in our climate could not be left unmarried up to fourteen years, nor would a girl of that age submit to the present system of marriage. . . . Unlike *sultanism* [concubinage], marriage is interwoven with the whole texture of our society, especially the Hindu society. You cannot seriously alter the marriage system without altering the whole fabric. (1882: 421)

The Age of Consent Bill was a peculiar concession to traditionality in so far as the colonial authorities consulted local scriptural experts and claimed to continue non-interference with the age of marriage if not of consummation. Since wives were supposedly "indispensable" to hindus for religious observances, they would be allowed to marry any time they wanted, and to a girl of any age. Colonial administrators spoke on this matter with the authority and tone of brahmins when they commented on the "four orders" [caste] which in "the Hindu view of life . . . distinguish the different periods of human life" (1882: 417). They were willing to concede to the 'Hindu' belief that marriage "completes the expiatory ceremonies of sinful taint contracted in the parent's womb", and for women and *sudras* (low caste) this was the only expiatory rite allowed (1882: 417). British men argued, with scriptural quotations, that marriage provided the only important "obligations to women" and they were equal to "the ordinances of the vedas". There were cautionary remarks on "the difficulty and delicacy of tasks before the government", and how reform must thus "be moderate in extent and must be as far as possible a return from a deteriorated custom and compliance. . ." (1882: 417). A "return" to what, one might ask, and the answer, curiously, refers to an earlier state of civilization of the 'Hindus' themselves, of being "Aryans". For Bengalis in particular, reform would consist of becoming equal to more "manly races" in India at the present time (1882: 417). Aryans, it seemed, waited to consummate their marriages, or even married at a later age than was the present practice in Bengal. It is noted that marriage "takes place earlier in Bengal than in the Hindustan provinces, where it may be supported that among a more purely Aryan population the custom approaches more nearly to the ancient practices. . ." (1882: 417).

This concession to "traditions of Hinduism", both as constructed by the British and especially those regarding marriage, meant little more than a contemptuous tolerance of "degenerate" practices in keeping with the perceived negative moral characterization of this Bengali/Indian society. In fact it is this very concession, with its ascriptions of depravity, which gave the state the reason or excuse to extend its jurisdiction over the sex life of its subjects as a whole, and over women's lives in particular. While marriage must be allowed, it was felt that "the consummatory home-bringing of the wife stands upon no such special and peculiar ground; and may be considered in the interest of the people and in these interests be regulated and defined" (Government of India 1882: 417). This consummatory homebringing, referring to "the age" at which a girl could be sexually used, brought the British authorities directly into contact with the bodies of Indian/Bengali girls and women. They were perceived as a biological organization of a certain type of human species rather than as substantive human beings, or even as objects with any sexual connotation for the white male. Throughout these submissions, the female of the hindu species, unlike the male, was credited with no personality, subjectivity or agency, no matter of what distorted variety. She could only be perceived as a vehicle for 'Hindu' (male) sexual perversity and as a breeder for that society. This status as 'the native female' or 'tropical girl/female' determined the ideological discursivities revolving around her.

It is important to note that this pathologization, in addition to presenting Bengali/Indian women as passive bodies, also has a degraded sexual connotation which is informed by the prevailing racism of European medicine and social anthropology.[25] These disciplines experimented or speculated upon black or dark-skinned people, the inhabitants of the tropics. They were invested with dangerous disease-carrying potential and degraded sexual stereotypes.[26] Whether deployed by a local or a British doctor, the discursive composite of "the native female" or "tropical woman/girl" contained a passive yet oversexualized connotation. The geographical and sexological homologies between females of the tropics and its warm climate and lush vegetation fantasize an early puberty for the tropical woman (as fruits/vegetation mature quickly in the heat) and an eager sexual readiness.[27] This conflation gave the European enlightenment's generally patriarchal equation between women and nature a profoundly racist twist. This discourse explains the curious fact in the Age of Consent documents that the doctors, who do not subscribe to the hindu *shastras*, at the end of their medical–rationalist arguments against them, accept the age of twelve as 'the age of consent'. Though they often state the "medical fact" that puberty does not arrive properly before the ages of fourteen to sixteen either in India or in England, they end by concluding that "in this country" twelve could be acceptable as "the age". This racist patriarchal discursive apparatus of difference modifies in the last instance the scientific, charitable or humanitarian concern of the medical man and the scientist.[28]

The central point of these discussions or representations was the girl's or woman's body.[29] There is almost no mention of any personality, volition or moral agency of the girl or the woman. Physicality, paralleled with passivity, is the core of this discursive construction of "the tropical woman/girl", especially where 'good' women or girls, deserving of protection and charity, are mentioned. A hint of female sexual agency, always conceived as perverse, comes through when older female relatives or older prostitutes are mentioned as engaging in unnatural activities of manipulation of the girl's genitalia in order to facilitate premature coitus. Often this "evil practice" of child marriage and premature consummation is blamed on older female relatives in the context of the family.[30] A positive female sexuality is utterly inconceivable within this discursive framework. The 'Hindu' woman is invariably seen as a sexual object of 'Hindu' males, an instrument for his use and a vessel for biological reproduction. It is through this view, either as a wife or a child prostitute, that she constitutes a site for the extension of the state apparatus of criminal and medical jurisprudence, and also provides an avenue for the expansion of European/British scientific/medical knowledge.[31]

This degraded identity of the 'Hindu' girl or woman is essential to an overarching moral condemnation of the subject. If the colonized male is portrayed as brutal and infantile, with a perverse will and a tradition-enclosed mentality, then the female is the physical substrate of this society. As such, the search for "the age" operationalizes that degrading construction and ascription. It begins with an imperative and assumption of the following kind:

> it is necessary to ascertain the minimum age at which a girl acquires her capacity for sexual intercourse, and the minimum age at which she attains to full maturity for maternity. Such minimum age is, as a rule, lower in a warm country like the plains of India, compared to countries in cold latitudes. (Government of India 1882: 424)

Though some medical practitioners sometimes doubt the geographical dictation of female puberty, more or less the same sentiment extends through the dossier of C.C. Stevens. Scientific experts who are concerned about the effects of climate on "race" determine in the main the way in which the 'native female' is perceived.

The language of medical submission is an active discursive process of objectification—through physicalization and pathologization—of women and girls. The texts are a curious and even macabre mixture of scientific interest and a kind of pity which is generally shown towards an animal. Women and girls are constantly described in terms of their sex and reproductive organs and events of rape, childbirth, mortality and autopsy. Though a protective attitude is put forward regarding them, this is done in terms of moralistic, victim-creating pronouncements, never attributing any active, intelligent, feeling humanity to them. Not only do these women/girls not speak in the texts, they very rarely even appear with a face or a personality, except as anatomical–biological organs or pathology and a doctor's probe on a dissection table. Except for one or two memos in a large body of submissions, women/girls remain non-humanized, without an outward body or appearance, and even those texts display features of objectification. The following is an example:

> Premature sexual intercourse tells also by its remote effects on Indian wives. Mechanical dilation of the hymen, conical dilation of the vagina, displacements of the uterus, and peculiar hyper-tropical condition of the labiae are its local effects. With an undeveloped pelvis pregnancy entails very often serious consequences, viz. difficult labour, puerperal complications and heavy infantile mortality. Among its constitutional effects I may note down the arrested development of body and mind. A victim of this atrocious practice is known by her girl-like face, hands and feet, with the body and figure of an old woman, a description that applies to most Indian women. A mechanical submission to domestic drudgery and tyranny is a sufficient test of her intelligence. (Government of India 1882: 426)

Written by a Bengali doctor, this description, with also its brief reference to the fears and tears of a young girl visiting her husband's home, is the only vaguely humanizing reference to women and girls as sentient beings. This may be joined with that of a British doctor who compares the fate of a young girl unfavourably with that of an animal, stating that a female animal has more freedom from sexual and reproductive tyranny than a child wife/mother in Bengal (1882: 425).

The submissions supporting the Act, and many against a merely legislative or the present legislative solution, testify to horrible cruelty against women and girls. Allusions to injuries, rape, pain and blood fill the pages. However, only a few of the submissions partly call into question the mythology of the early sexual maturity of girls in the tropics. Some experts are ready to say that the age of twelve is not satisfactory: "It is absolutely no test whatever that maturity for the purpose of maternity [for that matter, for the act of sex] has been attained" (1882: 418). Some make a distinction between "puberty" and "nubility", and deplore the 1860/61 penal code (1882: 418). One states that the law "instead, almost seems to sanction the infliction of injuries which in many instances prove fatal, and in still more numerous cases seriously affect the future health and well-being of native women" (Government of India 1882: 418–19). One doctor speaks of "the terrible strain of premature maternity" and points out that "at least in 20 per cent of marriages children were born to child wives" between twelve and thirteen years. The injuries are repeatedly detailed: "difficult and delayed labour, laceration and sloughing of the passage, death of the child, exhaustion, fever, abscesses, contractions, and fistula" (1882: 419). "Minority", "maternity" and "mortality" are inseparably joined in the reader's mind as s/he progresses through the dossier.

This fleeting awareness of cruelty does not mitigate, but in fact deepens, the pathologization marked by the typicalities of "race". This "raced" female has no possibility of going beyond matter and nature; she is even more of a physical entity than the European woman.[32] Her pathology then has the anthropology of "inferior races", and is mainly considered in terms of breeding or reproduction. The life-cycle of this 'Hindu/tropical female' falls into two periods: the earlier, briefest period called childhood, which is presexual and prereproductive; and most of her life, in which she serves as a male's sex object and reproduces. These two aspects are uniformly collapsed into one. The dividing line between two parts of life—of childhood and womanhood—is the blood line of menstruation, and the only question worth asking about her is "the aptitude of [her] sexual organs for intercourse with an adult man" (Government of India 1882: 425). This simultaneously translates out in concerns for her ability to conceive and have a healthy pregnancy, and these are the features which supply the legal formula for 'the age'.

Bodies of women and girls, therefore, were studied in great detail. The entire working apparatus of an extensive colonial medical establishment, also featuring 'native' doctors, launched forth into an in-depth exploration. "Unanimous in their abhorrence of the present custom" (Government of India 1882: 422), they debated with each other, speculated upon and penetrated these bodies with scalpels in hand, bodies which would show them the secrets of human reproduction in general but also that of a "tropical species". Social statistics, medical and scientific literature from Europe, general studies in anatomy and physiology, all converged on this project. Brigade-Surgeon McLeod and others refer to long-standing research on Indian girls/women and reproduction. He cites thirty to thirty-five years of research contained in Dr Allen Webb's *Pathologica Indica* (1850s), Dr Harvey's work which analyses 127 cases, journals such as *Indian Medical Gazette* and others, and extensively cites his own work, "Child-wives", in the *Gazette* (1882: 423). As a responsible medical scientist and doctor he discharged his duties solemnly: "I have brought the whole subject before the Calcutta medical society with a view to eliciting additional facts and ascertaining the opinions of native medical men" (1882: 423). Piece by piece, from autopsy reports, surgical dissections, hospital and private cases, police reports and records, a sizeable body of information emerges. Bengal in particular, the seat of the empire, but also other parts of India, become a vast laboratory of research on reproduction, on the mechanism of copulation, on population, and maternal and infant mortality. But along with this incremental increase in scientific knowledge there is an equally incremental solidification of an ideological moral stance towards both this population under rule and 'tropical' others in general. This creates an extension of the medical notion of pathology into moral spheres and a social anthropology, a *Pathologica Indica*, which becomes the colonial perception of India. The old

orientalist discursivities constellated around 'tradition and civilization' are fed into medical science and jurisprudence, and further
amplify otherization and negative difference by connecting with
pathology. The 'native' is not only "traditional" and "savage", as
Jones and Mill would claim respectively, but by the same token
pathological and perverted. These traits constitute the essence of
'his' society. The 'Hindu female' is not very much more than a cow
or any other animal, to be probed into, to be construed as an index
of the degradation of the society of which she forms a part, to be
an open book on sex and reproduction in the tropics.

Indeed there is an overweening curiosity among various
types of experts, bordering on indecency, regarding the gynaecological and obstetrics life of the 'native female'. Documents which
otherwise exude the coldness of morgues and the precision of
autopsies resonate with a righteous scientific wrath at being pre-
vented access into the deepest recesses of their objects' homes, functions and bodies. 'Native' customs of midwifery, as well as gynae-
cology, are deeply resented and discredited by these experts, as are
the practices of 'Hindu medicine' or *ayurveda*. At this point,
diverse interpretations of the *shastras* (scriptures) become useful as
a tool for discrediting any Indian claim to science and medicine.
Not only are 'Hindu' medical practices, either of popular or elite
variety, condemned, but so also the 'Hindu' household which prevents the outsider, especially male (white and indigenous) doctors,
from entering into it. *Purdah*, the *zenana* or the *andarmahal* are
railed against as obstructions in the way of saving lives and, worse
still, for obstructing science.[33] An atmosphere of rumours is created
around these homes and what happens within them, including
sexual and gynaecological knowledges of older women and midwives that the medical establishment is not privy to. It is also stated
that rapes and deaths of women frequently occur there, particularly connected with premature sex and motherhood. As one writer
put it: "The death of Phulmoni has only brought before the public
an evil the existence of which is no new development of recent
years, and which is far from being coextensive with the limits of the
experience of medical officers, coroners and juries sitting in Presi-
dency towns" (Government of India 1882: 425). The concept of
'race', which is ubiquitously present in this otherizing–identifying

discourse, dovetails neatly with European scientific and moral concern with motherhood and breeding which is present both in and
out of colonial discourse. In the case of Bengali/Indian (read as
'native/tropical' women), notions of motherhood and breeding are
collapsed into the broader discourse of physicality and animality.
Fertility, fecundity and population growth, rather than lofty and
sentimental notions and images, dominate any consideration of
motherhood. If there is any genuine concern for the health of
women and girls in the Indian context, it is mainly in terms of
eugenics.

The central question here is of regulating copulation and
reproduction, and in the proper propagation of the "race". In fact
"race" and motherhood became functions of each other in this discourse as they constitute each other as signifiers in this situation.
Women and girls are to be seen primarily as a race of mothers and
as mothers of races. The official concern with the weak masculinity of Bengali males finds its cause in the weakness of the "race",
that is, in premature, overactive sex life and unregulated breeding.
Motherhood within this discursive framework is not connected to
the socially active verb of 'mothering', but rather to that of breeding. The importance of this discourse lies in the fact that this
approach is shared equally by the 'native' and the European/British
doctors, and provides the basic theme which echoes in different
ways in different aspects of the controversy surrounding the Age of
Consent Act.

Conclusion

This exercise in decoding what the colonial authorities
meant by 'Hindu' women, men or society makes it evident that the
discursive specificity of British colonial cultural politics in India has
a global context. 'Colonial discourse' holds a generic sort of quality to it, showing up in other European countries' textual/inscrip-
tional forms of colonial ruling. Though our task here has been to
explore a single strand in that repertory, we find similar ascriptions
containing comparable forms of moral regulations elaborating
from a ground plan of domination.[34] The 'Hindu' woman/girl of
these documents marks a moment in the overall 'symbolic cultural constitution', not only of a colonial 'India' but of a global

European identity politics, where we see projected binary identities of inferior 'others' *and* of the 'enlightened self' of Europe.

These cultural and moral identities, the 'Hindu' woman/ girl for example, were both static and pejorative. As a contrast to European idealized identities this is a form of difference, but of an exclusive and negative nature. The real subject, the European/ British male ruler, is however hidden or spread ubiquitously through the pages of the documents without any necessity for self-naming (Bannerji 1995: 17–40). The entire discussion emanates from the 'I/eye' of the colonial administrator, his values and relevances produced in the cause and course of rule.

No matter what its content, colonial discourse is reifying and concretized by social relations and cultural forms of power, coded as gender, "race" and class. In spite of a wide and complex range of constructions, it is ultimately a 'master/slave', 'black/ white', 'patriarch/woman' binary discourse. The importance of studying this undiluted form of colonial discourse, baring its raw edges, is essential for understanding how totalizing power of any kind develops and operates beyond a simple functional project. If there is a colonialism it must have a discourse which is coherent with it and characteristic of it. One cannot help but notice the autonomy and strength of colonial discourse. A worldview, a cultural grammar and a political ideology having a tenacious and un-varying direction have come into being. This does not make it a rigid or monolithic template of concepts and images. It develops at different levels and stages, opposing images and notions constitute its body; but at any given moment, in any shape or form, it remains reificatory—an instance of power/knowledge. It is strong enough to enter not only into middle-class nationalist discourse, but also into discursivities of both European and third-world socialist/com-munist revolutionary and feminist politics.

We should also insist here that all of the European/British political–ideological world is not to be seen as monolithic in dis-course and intention. Just as in the colony, the metropole was also divided by ideological and factional disagreements. By the late nineteenth century some British feminists, doctors and missionaries had their disagreements with or evinced some criticism of colonial India. But the purpose of this paper is not to explore these 'other' discourses of England, and perhaps it is worth stressing that these 'other' discourses cannot be wholly disarticulated from colonial discourse and are often underwritten by colonial christianity—a discourse of charity and civilization, or a discourse of horror. These critics did not necessarily contradict the state's language and attitude of hegemonic reform and rescue. We cannot therefore either decentre or minimize attempts at negative otherization such as the one examined here. While similar otherizations were at work at 'home', that is, in England, objectifications there took other turns, consequences and contestations. In the case of India, it is still imperative to see what became of these ruling forms of consciousness and modes of reification as they played out their identity games in the heart of the empire, mobilizing "race" to the purpose of patriarchal class rule.

Notes and References

[1] See P. Corrigan and D. Sayer (1985) and also P. Corrigan (1981).

[2] See B. Cohn (1983: 165–210); also Cohn (1985: 276–329).

[3] See H. Bannerji, "Beyond the Ruling Category to What Actually Happens: Notes on James Mill's Historiography in *The History of British India*", this volume; also Bannerji, "Writing 'India', Doing 'Ideology': William Jones' Construction of India as an Ideological Category", this volume.

[4] On the role played by the creation of difference and "race" in the course of ruling, see M. Sinha (1995: 33–68).

[5] A Malthusian way of viewing both 'home' and colonial society in terms of 'population growth' was in place by the time the Age of Consent Act is passed. It forms an active part of governance in both spaces, and is also connected with this interest in reproductive biology, eugenics, women and motherhood. See J. Whitehead, "Modernizing the Motherhood Archetype: Public Health Models and the Child Remarriage Restraint Act of 1929", *Contributions to Indian Sociology*, 29: 1 and 2 (1995), 187–209; see also D. Arnold (1993).

[6] A "non-cognizable" offence was bailable; "transportation" for life meant a life sentence.

[7] See Sinha (1995: 1–32) for an extended discussion of this position. See also A. Stoler (1989: 134–201).

[8] See L. Mani (1989: 88–126) for a discussion of *sati* and the deployment of the categories 'tradition' and 'modernity' in the service of patriarchal 'race'-inscribed colonial hegemony. Also see G. Chakravorty Spivak (1988: 271–313).

[9] See H. Bannerji, "Fashioning a Self", this volume; see also H. Bannerji, "Textile Prison" (1994: 145–68).

[10] See S. Sarkar (1985: 1–17). Sarkar speaks of loyal British subjects, such as Radhakanto Deb, who did not support the anti-*satidaha* stance.

[11] See T. Sarkar (1987: 2011–15); (1992a: 213–35); (1992b: 213–35).

[12] The first regulation of marriage and consummation was the Act of 1860.

[13] See also P. Chatterjee (1994).

[14] *Shastric* refers to individuals who subscribe to the *shastras* or religious/scriptural injunctions of the hindus.

[15] The Great Rebellion, or *Mahabidroh*, refers to the armed resistance against British colonialism in 1857. It is also known as the Sepoy Mutiny.

[16] See U. Chakravarti (1989: 27–87); L. Carroll (1989: 1–26); A. Burton (1994); and T. Sarkar (1992a: 213–35).

[17] See Government of India, Legislative Department, *Papers (Nos. 4, 11, 12) Relative to the Bill to Amend the Indian Penal Code and the Code of Criminal Procedure, 1882* (India Office Library and Records [IOLR]), London, for a full file of the submissions.

[18] The colonial reformers here write within the discursive tradition of using the social status or the 'condition' of women as an index for 'civilization'. This European enlightenment measure of self-identity and difference from 'others' is to be found in Mary Wollstonecraft, John Stuart Mill, and Frederich Engels, among others.

[19] This construction of the 'native' is complex. It ranges through depictions of an infantile, immature, weak, hypersexed, undersexed, animalistic, decadent and brutal sexuality—leaving no consistent stereotype in view. The element that is consistently present is objectification and denigration, expressing a relation of dominance and its terms rather than an unvarying body of content. This is clearly brought out in M. L. Pratt (1992). R. Hyam (1992) describes this phenomenon, though uncritically. Sinha's text (1995) is another critical and rich exposition on this construction of the 'native' (male) as a sexual colonial subject.

[20] Dr McLeod and his medical colleagues' sentiments are entirely shared by C.C. Stevens, Chief Secretary to Sir Stewart Bayley, Lieutenant Governor of Bengal, as well as all the other administrators whose opinions he compiles in his file of submissions to the highest colonial authorities. These documents are copy-book exercises of the integrity of discourses on social reform and colonial rule. Their foremost accomplishment is the degraded characterization of the colonized society in totality, particularly as microcosmically reflected in the character of the 'native'.

[21] See H. Bannerji, "Writing 'India', Doing 'Ideology'", this volume. This 'seamlessness', a result of an essentializing epistemology, has been noted by many critics as a characteristic feature of power/knowledge. For the most influential critique of this, see E. Said (1979). For India, see H. Bannerji, "Writing 'India', Doing 'Ideology'", and T. Niranjana (1990: 773–79). The emergence of this category 'Hindu', and its identification with 'India', with its own peculiar ideological and cultural baggage, extended over a long period. It was in the making beginning in the era of the orientalists, of the East India Company's accession to the status of government of Bengal and of the post-mutiny (1857) inclusion of India into the empire (1865). Every stage of legislated social reform, from *satidaha* (burning of widows on their husbands' pyre) to widow remarriage and to the Age of Consent, added to the formulation of the notion of 'the Hindu' and to the typification of its content. The last in particular was

the widest in its scope of debates and discussions and the culminating step in this process of construction and ascription of a national identity to the ruled, thus finalizing the most comprehensive 'difference' between Europeans and Indians. The ideological nature of the category 'Hindu', its essentialist, dehistoricized and homogenized character, becomes obvious from the way in which the texts produced by colonial administrators and medical and legal experts exorcise from that category all of its cultural and historical particularities.

[22] Thus, in the interests of colonial hegemony at different levels, colonial administrators and experts, both foreign and local, either suppress facts or contradictions among them, or leave them unaddressed in the text. They adopt a strategy of refusal to draw any logical conclusion from them. Interpreted in this fashion, indigenous reformers are referred to as Europeanized supporters of the state, but ignored as a substantive body of social agents and critical thinkers. At best there is an ambivalence towards them. But even this ambivalent relationship to 'educated men' and to 'a strong and a very intelligent body of public opinion' does not destabilize the ascribed typicality of the notion of 'the Hindu'. In fact, these local 'reformers' are depicted as exceptions which prove the rule of orthodoxy and tradition in 'the Hindu way of life'. What remains underlined is Stevens' assertion that this "practice [*garvadhan*] is favoured and enforced by the educated men of the community" (Government of India 1882: 416).

[23] There was, for example, that proclamation made by Queen Victoria in 1858 which promised non-interference in religious and daily life, made in fear in the period of the Sepoy Mutiny. As an anti-traditional member of the Council of the Health Society of Calcutta put it, "the history of British rule and the working of the British courts in India manifest a distinct leaning towards, and non-interference with, the customs and religious observances of the Indian people" (Government of India 1892: 417). The rulers largely agreed that such a stance was obviously no longer needed with the final eradication of armed resistance to British rule and the solidification of the empire. Besides, as science and civilization were considered to have progressed apace in Britain and Europe in the meanwhile, the contrast between these enlightened societies and those of the traditional, benighted 'natives' was deemed much sharper than earlier in the century. The earlier orientalist perception of an ancient Indian civilization was to be replaced by that of James Mill and his intellectual successors, in tandem with that of the christian missionaries. Assertions of Indian "savagery", "rudeness" and "the perfidy, venality and mendacity" of "the Hindus" abounded in official textual spaces. Now science, medical expertise and medical jurisprudence could be summoned to impose a civilizing order upon a barbaric traditional society. Since much of India had been thoroughly colonized economically and militarily by the 1870s, the annexation of the civil society had to be stepped up. The hazards of doing this were also recognized, particularly as 'the Hindu' might not be able to morally assimilate this enlightenment, even if he did intellectually comprehend it.

[24] See P. Levin (1994: 579–602), which draws on connections with other

critiques of moral and social purity stances, on social histories of ruling as implying moral regulation.

25 Other than sources already cited in this context, see S. Gilman (1985: 223–61); also S. Harding (ed.) (1993) for a comprehensive context to the colonial scientific/medical construction of the colonial subject in India.

26 See P. Levine (1994) on disease-carrying potentials as well as on a basically 'abnormal', diseased view of the subject population.

27 For an introjection of climate and geography in creating negative and reifying views of 'others', and in creating racialized forms of difference as an area of critique of colonial and neocolonial discourse, see C. Lutz and J. Collins (1993).

28 For a complex view of the medical/scientific experts' approach to the questions of "the age" (a question which consumes them with a need for facts), a generally committed relationship to the colonial project, and their Hippocratic and humanitarian concerns, the entire set of submissions by Drs Harvey, McLeod, Webb (author of *Pathologica India*), Chandra, Gupta, Chevers, etc., in the India Office Library and Records file has to be read and carefully scrutinized (Government of India 1882: 420–26). Their stance becomes clearer when we keep an eye on how they speak of girl brides/wives and prostitutes.

29 The archetypal medical description of "the girl's" body necessary for ascertaining "the age" comes from a Bengali doctor, Major B. Gupta, whose expertise is developed on the same grounds as that of the British doctors. An M.B. officiating as a civil surgeon in Hooghly, he gives us the clear clinical view. See Government of India 1882: 426.

30 Allusions to female relatives as evil influences and sadistic participants in "the girl's" life are made frequently by different functionaries of the state, both British and Bengali. These allusions to older women, who "prepared" "the girls" for their use by husbands and male clients, need further research.

31 The formative conjunction of science and the legal apparatus of the colonial state emerges and evolves as medical jurisprudence. Much of the scientific endeavour is at the service of the development of a legal apparatus. This extends on the one hand into comparative statistics (Government of India 1882: 426), close physiological and anatomical studies of "the girl" (1882: 422; 425), and on the other hand into acrimonious, resentful reports of "secrets" of native childbirths, closely guarded by midwives and female relatives.

32 G. Lloyd (1984) and M. L. Shanley and C. Pateman, in their Introduction (1991), show how establishing a transposable relation between European women and nature contra-indicates women's assumption of citizenship. This connection becomes an absolute equation when used towards women of the colonized spaces. See Gilman (1985) and M. Alloula (1986).

33 See note 30 on the resentment against midwives and female relatives and native family relations and daily social life.

34 For an interesting reading of colonial identities as sites of domination and resistance, where stereotypically ascribed colonial women subjects take up the project of shaping themselves through lived forms and fantasies, see L.J. Sears (ed.) (1996).

Attired in Virtue

Discourse on Shame (*lajja*) and Clothing of the Gentlewoman (*bhadramahila*) in Colonial Bengal

In those days there was a particular rule for women. Whoever became a *bou* (bride/daughter-in-law) was to veil herself for an arm's length or so, and not speak to anybody. That's what made a good *bou*. Clothes then, unlike now, were not made of such fine fabric, but were rather coarse and heavy. I used to wear that piece of heavy cloth, and veil myself down to my chest, and do all those chores. And I never talked to anyone. My eyes never looked out from within that cloth enclosure, as though [I was] blindfolded like the bullocks of the oil presser. Sight did not travel further than [my] feet.

Rashasundari Dasi, Amar Jiban (My Life), 1860

The starting point of these reflections was usually a feeling of impatience at the sight of the naturalness with which newspapers, art and commonsense constantly dresses up a reality which even though it is the one we live in, is undoubtedly determined by history. I resented seeing Nature and History confused at every turn, and I wanted to track down, in the decorative display of what-goes-without-saying, the ideological abuse which, in my view, is hidden there.

Roland Barthes, Mythologies (1973)

Introduction

Judging by the moral and legal preoccupations of the colonial state and the indigenous intellectual elite (wholly male), the

---

This essay was first published in *From the Seams of History*, ed. Bharati Ray, New Delhi: Oxford University Press, 1994.

nineteenth century of Bengal could be called the Age of Social Reform.[1] The rapid process of colonization, the type of colonialism brought into India by the English and new class formations in Bengal gave rise to a radical sense of disjunction and changes in existing social relations and values, precipitating a sense of social and moral crisis.[2] Questions ranging from religious to everyday life, inclusive of sexuality, gender relations and the family, erupted in endless public discussions, debates and disclosures. Persistent and vigorous attempts at social legislation and institutionalization, for example of education, accompanied these intellectual efforts at reorganizing and reconceptualizing the new social relations, values and their practical demands. These moral utterances and social projects of the Bengali middle-class intelligentsia did not form a monolithic whole but rather consisted of ideological–discursive strands which converged, competed with and contradicted each other.[3]

Interestingly enough, the largest bulk of these reforms and discussions were aimed at women and gender relations prevailing in the family, thereby seeking to reorganize much of the existing social forms and functions. The heart of the social project was 'the degradation and the decadence' of society, typified by the state in which Bengali women and families of the propertied classes existed.[4] Tanika Sarkar, for example, has commented that the Bengali male intelligentsia's interest in women's 'improvement' bordered on the obsessive.[5] But to ameliorate the living conditions of Bengali (middle-class) women, to improve their minds and morality, to regulate their conjugal and household roles, signified a concern for the upliftment of Bengali society as a whole. The 'natural' constitution of the female mind, it was felt, along with women's social condition, needed a serious 'recasting'.[6]

Constructed through the colonial discourse of 'civilization' (later 'improvement' or 'progress'), used both by the 'enlightened' or westernized middle-class hindus and their reformed, non-idolatrous counterparts, the Brahmos, 'the woman question' emerged as a highly controversial one. The idea was to bring the women members of the propertied classes within the purview of 'civilization', 'progress' and utility. Tracts, plays, farces, novels and even poetry on domesticity, conjugality, and moral and practical education for women, swamped the printing presses. This process, however, was not a unilinear move of submission to colonization or 'westernization'. Attempts at understanding what 'civilization' is and how to achieve it contained thorough searches of and reflections on both indigenous and European practices and values. Ambiguity and criticism regarding both marked most of the attempts at synthesizing and imitating.[7]

In any case, a strand of the Bengali male intelligentsia, whose consciousness had a formative and positive relationship with European thought, took on the role of Pygmalion and sought to fashion for themselves a Galatea. This was to be a moral or discursive portrait of the ideal feminine, otherwise known as *bhadramahila* (the gentlewoman). The moral–cultural configuration of this discursive image or sign was embedded in, and endowed with, duties, pleasures and graces appropriate to the cultural commonsense of the 'westernized' sections of the middle classes. No aspect of this construct was beyond (male) utterance, both in formulation of character (moral–domestic) and in appearance (moral–erotic/aesthetic). Men sought to become experts in all matters pertaining to women, flouting existing social proprieties deeply grounded in a sexual/cultural division of labour.[8]

A signal example of this ideological–aesthetic meddlesomeness was the attempt by 'enlightened' hindu and Brahmo men to 're-dress' the women of their own classes. The image was to simultaneously express and construct their overall class culture, that is, also their morality. Sartorial experiments on captive household females provided a concretization of reform aspirations, as we see in Swarnakumari Debi's "Sekele Katha" (Story of Old Times) (1916), the scope of which entailed a basic change within the everyday life of the household. The need for a sartorial change was initially contexted to the entry of non-kin males within the 'inner quarters' of the household. The move came in several steps, building the sartorial project into the social–moral life of women and the household:

> At the time of this new improvement of our household/home, Keshab babu became a disciple of my esteemed father. Into the inner quarters, impenetrable to the rays of the sun [a hyberbolic

metaphor to signify its aristocratic honour], he was the first un-
related man, who was greeted like a close relative and welcomed
to enter. Many people marvelled at this great act of courage. But
that my venerable, sage-like father, who forsook friends and relatives for the sake of the right religious conduct [*dharma*], who did
not hesitate to give up all earthly comforts, would receive Keshab
babu (who was an outcaste of his home for converting to the true
religion, seeking refuge with his wife, as a disciple) into his own
home with a father's affection, was not a matter of surprise.
(Swarnakumari Debi 1916: 3. All translations from Bengali in
this chapter are mine.)

Next came another male, both a teacher for the girls and women
and a disciple of her father, Debendranath Tagore, the founder of
Brahmo Samaj, a form of ecumenical reformed hinduism: "My
esteemed father was disappointed in the education supplied [to the
women of the household] by 'mems' [white governesses]. The new
preacher of the Adi Brahmo Samaj Strijukta Ayodhyanath Pakrashi
was employed to teach in the inner quarters" (Debi 1916: 5). Several women and girls were to study with him. Both events occasioned an 'improvement' in clothing appropriate to the notion of
feminine civility:

> On this occasion clothes of the denizens of the women's quarters
> were reformed, [due to the fact] that it was impossible to appear
> in front of men [non-kin] in the Bengali women's usual garb of
> only a *sari*. My older sister, maternal aunt and sisters-in-law used
> to come to the study in a kind of civil and refined outfit of a
> *peshawaj* [outfit of aristocratic muslim women] and a shawl. My
> esteemed father always had a distaste for the clothing of Bengali
> women, and deeply desired to reform it. He did not stint in
> efforts to realize this wish, at times on my *Didis* [older sisters],
> but tirelessly on the infant daughters. In those days, the youngest
> children in our household wore clothes similar to the girls and
> boys of Muslim aristocratic families. After we grew up a little, we
> wore a new type of clothing every day. My father looked through
> a large number of paintings and ordered new designs. The tailor
> attended him every day and so did we. (Debi 1916: 30–31)

Even though the vagaries of style and the moral dimensions of these 'reforming' experiments elicited ridicule from the anti-reformist middle-class hindu male faction, the situation as a whole revealed the general male preoccupation with the question of an appropriate social subjectivity for women.[9] They all postulated a relationship between the inner and outer selves of women, and saw her clothing as a moral signifier of her social role and thus of what they saw as the culture of their *samaj* (society) or class. The covering and uncovering of her body, the particular parts which were to be hidden or disclosed, and the style/manner in which this was done, were contested grounds for moral and aesthetic visions among males.[10]

This male monopoly on the aesthetic form and moral content of ideal femininity came to an end in the last decades of the century. Even though the social context remained the same and patriarchy provided the basic philosophy for the appropriate investiture of the female body, educated middle-class women of 'enlightened' homes themselves had much to do and say regarding both the discursive–ideological and actualization processes. Summoned into education and cultural activities by the hegemonic agenda of their classes, informed by the moral and intellectual atmosphere generated by male reformers, middle-class women stepped into the world of public utterance approximately from the 1870s and added to the existing discourse of 'reform'. Through various journals and magazines, this rudimentary female intelligentsia participated actively in fashioning their own subjectivities as expressed in the sign called *bhadramahila* or the gentlewoman. One has to remember that Debendranath Tagore's moral–sartorial dream was finally fulfilled by a woman, his daughter-in-law, Gyananda Nandini Debi. As his daughter Swarnakumari Debi puts it:

> But he could not settle on a costume/attire after so much experimentation. His dissatisfaction came to an end when [my] middle sister-in-law returned from Bombay, dressed in a civil and elegant attire in imitation of Gujrati women. This attire, an integral combination of indigenousness, decorum and modesty, was just what he had wanted. It suited what he desired and removed a fundamental deprivation of the daughters of Bengal. (Debi 1916:31–32)

Malavika Karlekar, in her book *Voices from Within* (1991), remarks on this negotiated self-making, showing how women both compromised with and pushed the boundaries of the class patriarchy of the Bengali middle class.

A long discussion ensued among educated middle-class women through magazines such as *Bamabodhini, Bharati, Sahitya, Pradip, Mukul,* and *Sakha*.[11] The discussion was a serious attempt to think through what an 'appropriate reformed female' subjectivity, coded as *bhadramahila*, should be, and how that should be projected as a visual–moral sign. The notion of 'appropriateness' was conceived with reference to gender and family relations in the new context of the colonially-inflected, respectable middle classes. Appearance, in the sense of body–self presentation through clothing, was a particularly important theme. The morality of the *bhadramahila* was to be translucent in the self-composition through clothes, and this theme of self-composition, along with that of the body, provided the discursive organization for the women's texts. In spite of the fact that the women reformers came into a pre-organized moral–discursive space, their own discourse on women, femininity and clothing was tempered by a recognition of the power of gender roles. Even though they did not fashion it in its entirety, they substantially inflected the sign of *bhadramahila* —the moral/aesthetic/erotic configuration of women of propertied classes in Bengal.

This paper examines the discursive organization of sartorial morality as put forward by some of the women writers of major Bengali magazines, especially with respect to the forms of class subjectivities they propose for Bengali women. The concentration here is minimally on fashions or styles but rather on the emergence of a social morality which seeks to serve, and to some extent does serve, as an unofficial form of moral regulation created by civil society. This demarcates, at the level of proposals or ideology, social spaces, personal interactions between men and women, and the kind of moral personality a *bhadramahila* should have. Attitudes towards the female body and sexuality are a part of this insignia of virtue and vice. The clothes are meant to propose a definitive relationship between the women and their class/social status.

Significations of the moral and the immoral, the sexual

and the social (posed as asexual and therefore virtuous) are never kept out of sight. In fact, the position that the sexual and the social are in some ways antithetical captures a process and a project of profound privatization of sexuality which, in reality, is publicly and discursively constructed. Here we need to remember Michel Foucault' response to S. Marcus' *The Other Victorians*, where he challenges Marcus's "Repressive Hypothesis" and points out the public, discursive nature of the very project of privatization of sexuality in nineteenth-century western Europe. Hearing the bubble/babble of voices on morality and the notion of the appropriately 'feminine' (a euphemism for female sexual conduct), we cannot but ask Foucault's questions with regard to the projects of social reform in nineteenth-century Bengal:

> Why has sexuality been so widely discussed, and what has been said about it? What were the effects of power generated by what was said? What are the links between these discourses, these effects of power, and the pleasures that were invested by them? What knowledge was formed as a result of this linkage? The object in short is to define the regime of power–knowledge–pleasure that sustains the discourse on human sexuality [in our parts of the world]. (Foucault 1980: [I] 11)

The negative revelation of the female body as an absent signifier through explicit forms of prohibition, and thus the covert allusion to its sexual potentialities, is publicized and made central to the sartorial project for the gentlewoman. These essays by women writers, full of rich descriptions, critical comments and exhortations, allow us to provide a semiology and ideology of culture and class in a concretely embodied and engendered fashion. And we can begin, as Foucault suggests, to question and situate our sources and voices,

> to account for the fact that [sexuality in various names] is spoken about, to discover who does the speaking, the positions and viewpoints from which they speak, the institutions which prompt people to speak about it and which store and distribute the things that are said. What is at issue, briefly, is the 'overall discursive fact', the way in which sex is 'put into discourse'. (1980: [I] 11)

Clothing as Embodiment or Sign

Are there objects which are *inevitably* a source of suggestiveness as Baudelaire suggested about Woman? Certainly not . . . . *for it is human history which converts reality into speech*, and it alone rules the life and the death of mythical language. Ancient or not, *mythology can only have an historical foundation, for mythology is a type of speech chosen by history: it can not possibly evolve from the 'nature' of things.*

> Speech of this kind is a message. It is therefore by no means confined to oral speech. It can consist of modes of writing or of representations.

Roland Barthes, *Mythologies* [author's emphasis]

In order to treat proposals and images for women's clothing as historical and ideological constructs or signs, we should explore the particular relationship displayed in them between bodies of women (of the middle classes) and their clothes, thus aiming towards the spatio–social meaning of the location of these bodies. Thus clothes are to be seen as forms of moral investiture. As the editor of the magazine *Antahpur*, Hemantakumari Choudhury, remarks, clothes are to be seen as a sign of progress, marking moments in moral/cultural advancement from primitivity to civilization:

> What are clothes and why are they necessary? Only those are clothes, wearing which the body may be fully covered, and which cover/prevent shame. It is known from reading the history of the most primitive stage of humanity that human kind then had no clothes to wear. Tree barks, leaves, animal fur or leather covered the bodies of different groups/peoples. The proof of this is to be found today among savage deep-forest or mountain dwellers. The ancient aryans, when they first arrived in India, dwelt in the forests near the Himalaya mountains. Initially they felt the need of clothes in order to prevent themselves from feeling the cold. . . . But as humans became more civilized they used their intelligence to fashion material fit for covering their bodies . . . and God has always given to women a love of beauty and a sense of modesty. (Hemantakumari Choudhury 1901: 137)

This version of the evolution of clothes claims that the human body itself has to be always understood as a vehicle which is capable of signifying a moral and historical stage (of civilization), and the case of women as special within that.

The essays on clothing in the magazines and other supporting texts[12] support a similar evaluative perspective on human and female bodies. This perspective, however, makes little sense unless contexted to the notion of class, understood in its broadest and originary sense of social relations between mental and manual division of labour, inclusive of the sexual division and thus extending 'class' into areas of both social production and reproduction. These magazines and tracts make it clear that the female body of the propertied classes is not to be seen directly in terms of its potentialities for reproduction or social labour (as befitting for non-labouring classes as a whole). The kind of social reproductive activity or labour which involves middle-class women is primarily viewed through the lens of morality, of the ideologically class-gendered notions of appropriate behaviour or decorum such as *sabhyata* (civility), *shobhanata* (decorum/propriety/decency) and *lajja* (shame/modesty). Of the three, the first two, understood as civilized behaviour or refinement, are applicable for both males and females of the middle classes, though inflected in an appropriately patriarchal way, implying an overall moral unity of the civilizing project with gendered differentiation. But the concept of *lajja*, which is also a morally judgmental term and should translate more as 'shame' than 'shyness' or modesty, governs or underlies all references to civilized 'proper' behaviour when applied to girls and women. This is so central a notion that Kumari Soudamini, among others, writes in *Bamabodhini Patrika* a small treatise on *lajja*. In tackling this topic she instantly applies it to women in a manner that straddles the realms of both manners and morals:

> Shame is of two types. Of these one prevents human beings from sinful deeds, the other is peculiar to women. This essay is about the kind pertinent to women. There is no race/peoples on earth that deny that 'women should have a sense of shame'. Shame resides in the hearts of women in every country. There is only one difference, that some have more of it in their hearts than others.

> According to social customs, it is expressed differently in differ-
> ent countries. Whatever is regarded as a sign of shame in one
> country, in another may be considered a sign of shamelessness.
> . . . Another name for real sense of shame is modesty, and those
> women who are really possessed of a sense of shame, are also
> 'modest'. . . . [O]ne cannot be truly modest (possess a sense of
> shame) simply by veiling one's face and not speaking to anyone.
> In fact not speaking to people might express pride. Those who
> are truly modest cannot have hearts which contain pride or inso-
> lence, they are adorned by gentleness, politeness, good manners,
> tranquility, etc. (Kumari Soudamini 1872: 99–100)

It is to be noted that Kumari Soudamini repeatedly speaks of shame
as an internal quality, links it with innocence along with refinement, unlinks it from hypocrisy and distinguishes it from 'savage',
that is, uncivil or impolite behaviour:

> Those who are truly possessed of modesty/sense of shame can
> never be hypocritical. Their hearts are adorned with the virtue of
> innocence, and their behaviour/manners express this sense of true
> modesty/sense of shame. . . . One should not behave like an
> uncivilized person to show modesty/sense of shame. That gives it
> a grotesque look. Many women of Bengal are in the thrall of this
> grotesque type of shame/modesty. (1872: 99–100)

She firmly establishes this sense of shame as a behaviour particularly appropriate to male–female relations and as a way of under-
cutting female provocation of male sexuality and of initiation of
sexual response on her own part. The following passage shows the
link she establishes between shame, exposure and covering of the
female body and passionate enactments and utterances, and further
clarifies the sexual theme, though the writer's own sense of
shame/modesty prevents her from blatantly stating any of that:

> They [upper-class women] wear very fine [transparent] clothing
> and appear at ease in front of their male and female servants.
> Some women veil themselves but scream ugly things and carry on
> a fight with someone. That person who has never seen her face
> can [however] hear the crude words which emit from her mouth.
> (1872: 99–100)

Her concern about the sexual implication of the exposed female body and uncensored behaviour becomes explicit when she offers a 'civilizing' suggestion to counteract women's current bathing practices. "Bathing, rubbing down of bodies [of women], etc., are done in places which can be seen. Therefore there should be a rule that male or female servants won't enter anywhere without permission, and bathing etc. will take place in privacy or secrecy" (1872: 99–100). Sexuality permeates every corner of the social atmosphere she creates where possibilities of 'indecencies' are always present. From clothes to conversation, all must be ruled by 'shame': "However one should converse in such a way that it does not give rise to any untoward [bad/sexual] thoughts in the minds of [the male] interlocutors" (1872: 99–100). Thus the colonial notion of civilization, with propriety, gentility and refinement as corollaries, to which only the new propertied classes aspired, can always be extended to sexuality, with which can also be associated the custom of enclosure for feudal, pre-British aristocracy. To be civilized is to have a sense of shame, and it is the antithesis of sexual provocation brought on by explicit sexual display or seduction which is indicated in terms of clothing by the degree of exposure of the female body. Revealing and hiding it selectively thus works both as a lure and a deterrent to male lust, and confers on it the status of a significant and fetish object in the context of the social morality of the new propertied classes.

The overall discourse on/of shame or *lajja* is a curious blend of indigenous and colonial values regarding women, nature and the body. Here misogyny blends with a rejection of the natural or physical in any form. The female body and sexuality are read through the notions of the primitive and the savage. In essays such as "Sindur" (Vermillion), all ornaments and colour decorations on the body are despised as savage and sexual, and women are portrayed as savages within 'civilization':

> With the improvement in education and growth of civilization bad popular customs slowly disappear. Savages do not pay attention to the beauty of [their] mind, but rather adopt ways to enhance their physical beauty. They draw designs on their bodies, use vermillion in their hair, and pierce their ears and noses to

wear ornaments. Since these bad popular customs of this country
are associated with religion, their persistence is more severe.
Piercing ears, nose and wearing vermillion by women of Bengal
are the foremost among these. The Hindu scriptures enjoin: 'only
those may be considered as good wives who colour their bodies
with tumeric powder, use antimony or mascara and vermillion'.
But among our women readers, whose minds have been minimally enlightened by knowledge, there has developed a profound
disgust for female customs and superstitions. (Anon. 1869:
121–23)

Certain behaviours, therefore, are classified as 'lower types' of
body-behaviour, and contrasted to higher, intellectual–moral, or
civilized ones of Europe. 'Exposure' and physicality also provide
the hinge on which turn the themes of 'civilization' and 'savagery'
or 'barbarism.' Hiranmayee Debi's essay "Sutikagrihey Banaratwa" (Apishness in the Nursery) (1892a) further builds into it the
relevant element of social Darwinism.[13]

Hemantakumari Choudhury, in her essay on women's
clothing, "Striloker Paricchad" (Women's Attire), states: "The
more civilized humans became, the more clothes they made",
marking the stages of civilization from body to mind, paralleled by
going from nakedness to wearing clothes, valorizing the mental
over the manual and the physically reproductive (H. Choudhury
1901: 137–40). The civilized man or woman is well covered and
plain, unadorned by ornaments, which she considers, as do the
christian missionaries, clearly as fetishes. The plainly clothed English gentlewoman or the low church preacher, for example, as ideal
female and male images, are contrasted to the well-adorned florid
Bengali *babu* who is 'effeminate', and his female sexually provocative counterpart, the *bibi*, who is pagan hedonism/decadence
incarnate.[14]

The project of essays on shame or decency, as characteristic traits of the *bhadramahila*, is to render upper-class/caste
women's body and physical life invisible, attempting to rarefy and
ideologize as far as possible the actual everyday life of women and
all their bodily functions. The *bhadramahila*, which is no more or
no less than the sign of genteel womanhood, is thus the inter-

pellating device for middle-class women whose lives must illustrate particular gender–class relations of their time. Thus shame is 'an adornment of women', an especially commendable feminine virtue which both displaces the upper-class/caste woman from her body as well as identifies her with it. Going beyond the sense of common social decency, *lajja*, as applied to women, also incorporates within it a keen awareness of sexual possibilities, infusing elements of denial, forbiddenness and guilt within female sexuality. As a concept it subsumes all kinds of physical and social needs and functions within a sexual discourse, enclosed in a general imperative of self-censorship. Essays such as Krishnabhabini Das' "Strilok o Purush" (Women and Men), or articles in *Bamabodhini*, situate shame as a central concept in 'femininity' and explicitly connect it with 'civilization', which implies both a de-sexualization and a de-physicalization. Opinions vary as to whether as an emotion it is learned or innate, but all the writers agree on creating a social ethics of denial and repression.

A transparent homology is established between the body, sexuality, and savagery or primitivity. Discounting both the long existence of public and common bathing as a daily practice in villages or of ritual occasions, the writers emphasize the sexual possibilities inherent in it. The women bathers are seen as 'whores', though this word is carefully avoided as a 'bad' or 'indecent' expression. The adjective *jaghanya* (repulsive/abhorrent) is endlessly repeated through the text, particularly with regard to visibility of the female body. Accepting that civilization means the denial of the body, and the female body in particular, the theme of shame becomes a way of defining and institutionalizing virtue and vice. Virtue is unphysical and thus unfemale, and also not the prerogative of those who engage in physical production. It is not connected with anything biological or manual in nature. It is non-reproductive and intellectual,[15] and proposes a new type of segregation which is maintained by self-surveillance.

The female body is invested in different ways in private and public spaces and in terms of the onlooker. Her clothes and presence thus possess a set of architectural and social correlates coded as *andarmahal* (inner quarters) and *griha* (home/hearth), and as 'home' and 'the world'. This spatial organization is imbued with moral–cultural imperatives which are embedded in a specific social reproduction entailing its own sexual division of labour. With the proposal for change (only partially actualized) in the organization of social reproduction, where the 'inner quarters' give space to the notion of 'home/hearth', in which the household is a joint enterprise of men and women with 'free mixing', there arises the idea of women's 'emergence' from the inner quarters to the presence of non-kin males. The necessity and origin of the sartorial innovations and renovations are always referred back to this notion of 'emergence' and the presence of male company, connected in turn to 'civilization':

> The kind of clothing women wear here [in Bengal] is not considered reprehensible because it is customary. But upon even a slight consideration it will become apparent that it is slightly better than remaining naked by throwing a piece of cloth [over the body].
>
> How perfunctory clothing may be, can be seen among women of this place. This may indicate a lack of show/pride, but it cannot protect one from the winter's wind or allow one to maintain civility, both major criteria of clothing. In no civilized country is there a custom of this kind of clothing, many laugh upon seeing it. . . .
>
> Any civilized nation is against the kind of clothing in use in the present time among women [literally, "weak ones"] of our country. Indeed it is a sign of shamelessness. Educated men [literally, "those who have mastered knowledge"] have been greatly agitated about it, almost everyone wishes for another kind of civilized clothing.
>
> There is a custom here of [women] wearing fine and transparent clothing, which reveals the whole body. Such shameless attire in no way allows one to frequent civilized company. If it happens that there is wise counsel being offered about religion/proper conduct, it may so happen that we cannot attend to those wise words because of the clothes around. This shows how such clothes can stand in the way of our [moral] improvement. (Khastagiri 1872: 148–52)

The phenomenon of 'emergence' is noted by Swarnakumari Debi in the context of her own sister-in-law's experience:

> My middle older brother returned from England in 1864, and his service began in 1865. In those days the enclosure [of women] in the inner quarters was fully alive. Then women had to go in a covered palanquin, with a guard running beside it, even to go from one house to the next within the same compound. If mother got permission to bathe in the Ganges after much pleading, they plunged her in the river along with the palanquin. When middle older brother was taking his wife to Bombay, even then he could not make her walk through the front yard. It was such a shameful deed for the daughter-in-law [of a good family] that everyone expressed particular disapproval. Therefore she had to get into the ship in a palanquin. (Swarnakumari Debi 1916: 37)

But times moved inexorably:

> Two years later when middle older brother came home with his wife, then no one could ask the daughter-in-law/bride to come into the house in a palanquin. But the tragedy that was enacted by witnessing the bride of the family descend from the carriage in front of the house [in public] like a white woman, is indescribable. (1916: 37)

Hemantakumari Choudhury expands on the theme of Bengali women's clothes by speaking of a need for change in the attitudes of women towards their own bodies:

> Indian women, imitating the Begams [wives] of the Nawabs, started using very fine or transparent clothes. As a result of this, wives of Bengali homes felt no shame in going to bathe in the Ganges, or attending invitations. But finally many have begun to realize the bad taste involved in the custom of wearing one transparent/fine piece of cloth. (Hemantakumari Choudhury 1901: 139)

These statements imply a basic change both in reality to some extent and, certainly ideologically, in the social context of female presence in Bengal. Reproductive labour carried on primarily by women within the household, outside of male participation, in large joint family structures, gives place to a reorganized emotional–moral space approximating the model of a nuclear family, at least conceptually and morally. Women writers such as Nagendrabala Mustafi decried the old arrangement, calling it an "enclosure" and speaking of the horrible degeneracy among women as a result: "We are trapped like birds in a cage of enclosure, our mental capacities are gradually becoming sluggish, our hearts are not able to blossom in the light of knowledge." (Nagendrabala Mustafi 1896: 30–31) The 'emergence', then, contrasted to 'enclosure' or 'seclusion', came to be seen as *stri swadhinata* (women's freedom), a goal of social reform and an indicator of social 'progress'. But depending on the ideological stance of social critics, this could also mean an inversion of the desirable social/ moral order (noted as *ghor kali*, or a fallen age).

The discursive organization of physical exposure, including veiling or leaving bare the face, is created by the usual mixture of colonial and precolonial moral categories for social reform applicable to all aspects of social life. They are posed as moral binary terms:

> civilization/barbarism
> modern/traditional
> spiritual/physical
> rational/irrational
> decent/indecent
> virtuous/sexual or sensual.[16]

These form a moral and interpretive cluster and pose a constitutive relation between sexuality and society. They inscribe the (female) body with distinct sexual–social meanings. Accordingly, this body and its sexuality enter the realm of morality, both at the level of action and of desire. This creates a basis for both an everyday and institutional administration of sexuality in general and female sexuality in particular. The formal/sartorial presentation of the female body in particular becomes a powerful signifier of the success and failure of a moral regulation, and offers a scope of controlled sexual expression as much as of suppression. It maps out the moral boundaries of the propertied classes, and subsumes within them the question of the practicalization of desire.

This regulatory construction of sexuality, with a manipulation, fear and negation of the body, expresses the upper classes' notion of sexuality. It reveals at the same moment the social relations between, and ideological positions on, mental and manual labour. The relationship of the body or 'nakedness' to 'civilization', expressed as sexuality versus rationality and visualized as clothing, encodes the evaluation of, and power relations between, mental and manual labour. It typically valorizes the mind (and its functions) over the body or nakedness (and its functions). *Lajja* or physical shame (this does and does not approximate the christian notion of guilt) becomes a pro-rationalist moral measuring concept which establishes the criteria for 'civilization'. It calls for privileging the domination of nature, body and passion or 'irrationality' by various 'higher' mental capacities. The control of the female body through the moral mechanism of *lajja* or 'shame' becomes an expression of contempt, control and fear of female sexuality and the body as being quintessentially physical or 'natural'.

This misogynistic and controlling attitude is most blatantly expressed in an anonymous piece on women's public bathing. 'Civilization' provides the focal point of judgment from which the bathers are viewed. The unsigned piece deserves to be quoted at length:

> Education helps to change many disgusting/revolting habits. As people become more civilized, they engage in civilized customs and practices, as befitting of the times. But habit has such an overwhelming power that people continue to nurture many disgusting practices because of it. Women's bathing customs in this country are one of these highly disgusting matters. . . . How it is that civilized and educated people engage to this day in this disgusting/revolting custom I cannot tell! No doubt habit is the cause. But if they are not vigilant about such disgusting/revolting things they will become obstacles for women's improvement.
>
> Genteel/civilized, as well as uncivilized women of villages bathe without any reservation together with men. This is not a matter of little disgust! And bathing [here] does not simply mean returning home after a dip. If only that were the case, even that would be no small matter of disgust. But [instead] women,

eschewing all shame, stand next to men and clean their body parts in a most revolting manner. . . . On top of that, the kind of fine [clothing] material they wear is not fit to go out in society, and when that material becomes wet and clings to the body, then there is no difference between being naked and dressed. Many a time a decent man hesitates to get out of the pond in such clothes, but women, displaying remarkable ease, get out of the pond and walk home in their wet clothes.

Finally, it is respectfully submitted to women that they do not engage in such a disgusting activity. It is far better to go for a week without a bath, or even to go to the pond at dawn. Yet it is never reasonable to wash the body or clothes that are on, in front of men. I don't know when you will learn the real use of shame!! (Anon. 1871: 71–73)

It is evident that this discourse and the actual principle at work in the designing of the attire are both obsessively centred on control through the segregation, obscuration and obstruction of movement of the female body.

Woman's Body: Enclosure and Exposure

The sense of crisis that we have mentioned before came to be crystallized in the theme of women's 'emergence' into the public/male domain and also the entrance of men into the household. Ideological consideration on the social crisis pivoted on the theme of women's transgression and the permissiveness of progressive men. The conservative literature of the time echoed with fear and anger about women's public presence. But scrutiny reveals that it is not the presence of women in the public space as such which created this fear and anger, but rather the type and context of the space and presence.[17] The earlier public activities by women did not challenge the established sexual division of labour and the relatively stable and segregated domains of social reproduction. Therefore, it is not just the spatial transgression that upset the anti-reformists.[18] It is rather the 'unnaturalness' of their social presence in the capacity of intellectual interlocutors of men, as students, and as actual and potential professionals, such as teachers or doctors, which produced an ideological/moral response of managing the crisis.[19]

If this was the 'conservative' concern, the male reformers' concerns were no less anxious and acute. The female body and its moral–social–functional implications in the context of changing social reproduction overwhelmed them just as much. While advocating an education for women, and their 'emergence' from the 'inner' domain, they sought just as anxiously to curb any possibility of gender destabilization or any real autonomy for women. Thus the attempts to re-dress them in 'civilized attire' may have had less to do with the fact that they wore a single piece of unstitched cloth in the women's quarters than with the fact that they were feared to be found where they should not have been, doing 'what men do'. This is not to say that there was no resistance to a regular form of exposure, or an advancement of the inner quarters or the *andarmahal* as a woman's 'natural' place. Even a writer like Krishnabhabini Das, who felt that economic independence was a positive gain or at times a necessity for women, in her essay "Striloker Kaj ar Purusher Kaj" (Woman's Work and Man's Work) put forward this division of labour normatively. This 'natural' labour was as much about appropriate activities as about the placement of the female body or where such activities should take place. She should 'naturally' be found at 'home', keeping out of men's way, not competing with them and leaving the public space at their disposal. The sartorial recasting, therefore, meant much more than an introduction of women's fashion or style in clothing, but rather a proposal to recast both at an ideological/ moral and a social/practical level a prevalent social organization. Anxiety, signified by new experiments at dressing, reflected an anxiety over the loss of patriarchal power in a new form of social organization. Articulating in diverse ideological propositions the actual and possible shift in social relations created by colonialism, the male reformers also sought to shape or direct these changes. Thus women 'emerged' in a new moral and social regalia which sought to counteract any threat to patriarchy. The clothing project meant the investiture of the female body in a new enclosure—a sartorial enclosure.[20]

This problem posed by the female body and its relative exposure was curious since Bengali men lived with both in life and art until well into the British rule.[21] Suddenly we are reminded of the 'uncivilized' appearance of women in their 'traditional' garment of an 'unstitched' piece of cloth, lacking undergarments to conceal their breasts and lower bodies. This new awareness could only have been due to the recognition that the prevailing patriarchal social organization would undergo a shock in the new context. The possibilities of male–female relations, no longer regulated through appropriate kinship conduct and established modes of biological–social reproduction, occasioned much speculation and articulation of moral strategies. Tanika Sarkar addresses this very issue when she says: "When we look at the nineteenth century household manuals and contrast them with the ancient, . . . we find that the real point of departure in our material relates not so much to the strategies of control but to unprecedented possibilities in the conditions of the women's existence." (1989: 3) But Tanika Sarkar makes a mistake in not seeing the reform project as building in control in the very texture of how possibilities are conceived. The situation contained a special problem of signification in continuing and reorganizing patriarchy. A discourse on shame and attempts to practicalize it through clothes and other moral imperatives restrained and incorporated "possibilities" of women's fuller subjectivities within a patriarchal class project.

The attempted reconstruction was therefore a reconstruction through both older and newer ideological and social norms and forms. The 'emergence' was also a continuation of the 'enclosure', a continuation of control of women's bodies, labour and sexuality into the new phase of colonial middle-class formation. As such, in the matter of appearance, which provides us, as do all visual signs, with a more flexible and spacious signifier, the enclosure/emergence opposition undergoes a formal and moral elision. Even though the icon/sign signals to what may be called *new* possibilities, it also signals *new* restraints. The new image incorporates much of the old enclosure through a formal and an ideological reshaping. The attempt is represented as 'virtue', as a consciously designed textile–moral contraption. The woman of the 'enlightened' middle-class Bengali home was to present herself as the sign called *bhadramahila*, attired in virtue.

Lajja, National Culture and Women's Clothing

The social meaning of the body goes beyond what is functionally understood by sexual reproduction. It relates to the social organization as a whole, and involves a general morality and politics not exclusive of sexuality. The importance of physical appearance with appropriate signifiers for cultural representations is obvious in the context of Bengal's nationalism. This national culture implies and aspires to a certain kind of morality and constructs the Bengali women's ideal sexuality, and projects this as the sign of the *bhadramahila*. *Lajja*, or a sense of shame, is integral to this construct of femininity in nationalist terms, and the sartorial project consists of designing a 'national' visual form. As cultural nationalism gained momentum from the 1860s onward, European women's clothes were not seen as just 'alien' or 'foreign' but actually 'shameful' in the national context . The question of direct imitation always gave place to attempts of construction. A minuscule section among the elite wore gowns while saris were being experimented with. But it is interesting to note that saris won the day. The reason for this outcome is the elision between feminine shame/modesty and *deshiata*, or 'nationalist' cultural authenticity, which includes a restrained female sexuality. Writer after writer in the women's magazines creates a transparency between a proper female sexual morality and a national apparel. As Soudamini Khastagiri puts it:

> Relatively speaking [relative to wearing one piece cloth] clothes of nations such as those of the English may be better. But in some aspects they are a thousand times worse than ours. Therefore, if we seek to imitate them, we get rid of some faults only to embrace their deficiencies. (S. Khastagiri 1872)

She states that such clothes are a betrayal of national identity and what is culturally appropriate femininity for 'us'. It is hypocritical and artificial for Indians to wear western clothes, and by so doing they become marginalized in both societies. An anonymous writer quotes approvingly from another woman, Rajlaxmi Sen: "Therefore whatever preserves national culture, and enables all to identify [one] as a woman of Bengali homes and covers the body thoroughly, and is appropriate for both the rich and the poor, allowing at the same a free movement of the body, should be worn." (Anon.

1872: 2) An essay by Jyotirmayee Gangopadhyay written many years later echoes exactly the same sentiment: "There was a time when the new promoters of women's emancipation, both male and female, adorned themselves in western clothes. . . . They adopted these clothes as an expression or symbol of their views." (1922: 1055) But she also stated: "We have many proofs of the fact that educated men and women did not wish to wear western clothes, since they conveyed an anti-nationalist mentality. Most educated women, and it is not an exaggeration to claim about 99 per cent, do not consider gowns as tasteful as saris." (1922: 1056) The same sentiment is echoed by Soudamini Khastagiri:

> It is never as enjoyable to imitate clothes of other nations, as to create one from one's imagination, and which is suited to both *national characteristics* and is also *civilized*. And besides, there is a sense of artificiality if Bengalis wear the clothing of English or any other nation. They are considered of that culture and are treated as such. If a Bengali person dresses like the English and frequents their society, they engage in reviling the Bengalis in front of him, which he has to listen to with patience. Such clothes also deprive one of full acceptance among one's own people. (1872)

Or further:

> It is a duty to keep characteristics/signs of one's nation/culture in people's clothing or manners. Therefore it is not fit to imitate other nations wholly, this expresses lowness in status. We will accept the good things about religion and conduct [moral character] of other countries, but there is no need to imitate them in matters of appearance. Even when the [female] attires of the English, or Northern or Western Indians, or Muslims or the Chinese may be beautiful, Bengali women should not wear them. The duty consists of wearing clothing which shows one's national culture, covers one's body fully and which indicates instantly that one is a woman of Bengal. (1872)

As we saw in Swarnakumari Debi's description of her reformer father Debendranath's sartorial experiments, a combination of 'shame/modesty' and a patriarchal nationalist aesthetic have always provided the bases of new designs. Sarala Debi's essay, "Swadeshi Poshak" (Nationalist Clothing), is also a good example of what is meant by a national cultural identity. Concepts such as *shobhanata* (appropriateness/decorum), *shabinata* (decency) or *shilata* (courtesy) are shown to be the moral underpinnings of the fashion design of nationalism. This 'national' and sexually moral apparel also marks out the good from the bad woman, and advocates a complete sexual repression and sartorial segregation for widows. This is also the opinion of Soudamini Khastagiri, who states:

> Nowadays some women wear *kamij* [a type of long shirt with long sleeves], jacket, sari and shoes. That is fine, but even some bad/loose women of this country wear them. For this reason one should use a shawl covering from head to toe, which especially hides the upper body. This will indicate a daughter of a respectable family. . . . And one should also adopt a way of distinguishing married women from widows. (1872)

She and others suggest a recipe for dressing in ways signifying respectability (class, national culture and shame/modesty). For wearing at home, an *ijar* (bloomers or drawers), *piran* (a short-sleeved shirt) and a sari, or a long *piran* and a sari. For going out an *ijar*, a *piran*, a sari, pyjamas, shoes and socks, though the latter are optional, female 'shame' not residing in the feet. The experiment is obviously never complete and always on the verge of a collapse under scrutiny, and even this figure of modesty, national culture and 'good' class is not considered 'authentically national' or modest by a large section of hindu conservative society. It is still considered 'anglicized' and 'masculine' both in morality and form, and ridiculed in the caricatures of the street painters of Kalighat.

Lajja, put forward as a major female ethic, projecting a high social status and an indication of national authenticity, serves as a subjective regulator of female physicality or sexuality. As an internalized censor, uplifted to virtue, it becomes the most personal, therefore moral, way of controlling women. A good example is the portrait of Krishnabhabini Das in a hindu widow's garb after her rejection of western clothes. It is an act and an image through which she redeems herself in the eyes of her previous critics through her acceptance of a garb of purity signifying sexual self-effacement and self-sacrifice.

> Almost every day at the mall I saw a woman well-dressed in European clothes. It surprised me a little, because even though she was dressed in European clothes, the expression on her face was sweet and gentle. . . .
>
> Where was that woman dressed in English costume now? This was a widow of Hindu homes in front of me! She was worth being worshipped. She knew of no good qualities to boast of in herself, nor had she any temptation in that direction. She never wanted to be famous. Becoming one with the very earth in humility, she carried on her tasks. Her white and pure attire of a widow created such a sense of respect and awe [towards her]. (Sarojkumari Debi 1923: 742)

In keeping with her image of white purity is her personal morality: "After becoming a widow she gave up all kinds of comfort. She never slept in a bedstead anymore, but rather made a bed on the floor. Never ate anything good, such as fruits or sweets. She gave up everything." (1923: 742) By discarding the European garb of her former married state and the definition of herself as an individual, with limited self-interests, she enters simultaneously into the orbit of shame and cultural national authenticity. Her portrait serves as a radiant icon of female purity which reaches its climax with widowhood. Sexuality can now be erased completely both in the name of virtue and national culture.

An obsessive concern for well-coveredness of the female body and the visual projection of purity are the negative signifiers for female sexuality—a perpetual reminder of what lies within and what a woman must not disclose except at the risk of being outcast both personally and politically. A passive sexuality is thus established for the middle- or upper-class woman where, lacking the volition of exposure or disclosure, she becomes a contained but persistent zone for activating male sexuality. The cover of clothing is presented as the future promise of uncovering by an outside agent. Unveiling her, or 'freeing' her from a fabricated encasement, becomes a male prerogative and pleasure. The passivity of the construct called *bhadramahila* is ensured by the fact that her *bhadra*ness (gentility or modesty or class status) is dependent upon her desexualization. She must be constantly aware of male gaze and avoid being or doing anything sexually provocative. From this point of view 'shame' becomes the ideological construct on which pornography (not the same as erotic literature) is hinged. Nineteenth-century male reforming literature is full of indirect allusions or moralizing on what is forbidden or hidden. Thus shame, or decency, while considering female clothing, supersedes discussions on beauty or is equated with it.

The sartorial moral philosophy of Bengal, whether produced by women or men, implies an invisible and constant male gaze at women. The purpose of this gaze, or rather its origin/ occasion, is domination, to create an ideological object, a sexually circumscribed 'other'. Women themselves, through their own subscription to the discourse of 'shame and civilization', participated in the same enterprise. Their construct of femininity is thus not only opposed to the masculine, through sharing the premise of gentility, but also self-divided and self-censoring. It consists of the moral notion of appropriately gendered 'goodness', 'otherizing' the woman's own sexuality from herself through patriarchal prescriptions. The antithesis of this female goodness is the bad woman, epitomized in the notion of the prostitute.[22] This self-division is reflected in the divide among women themselves, towards other women, and regarding the attitude towards their own body and eroticism. And it should be noted that the ideology of 'proper clothes' designed for women of the urban propertied classes is held out as a typology to all others, and is part of a general hegemonic design. Its 'naturalization' as appropriate aspiration for gentility creates a mythology, a system of signs, which encodes a reconstructed morality of a nationalist but anglicized section of the urban propertied classes.

The nature of this new morality as indicated by *lajja* for women cannot be understood outside of Bengal's colonial context. The sense of crisis that filled the air manifested itself as much in idealizing/ideologizing the collapse of the older organization of social spaces, as in attempts of reprivatization and in directing the course of change, particularly as regards women and the family. It contains a colonial response, both in an anger towards and a submission to European judgment on the decadence/savagery of Indians both male and female.[23] The prescription for female sexuality, constructed within a colonial context, shifts from being direct to that of a repressed Victorian christian ladyhood. This becomes clear if a contrast is established between the icon of the desexualized gentlewoman and the pre-anglicized version of female sexuality in eighteenth-century Bengal, when a woman's sexual initiative is portrayed with respect and frankness by male poets such as Bharatchandra. In this epic poetry from the eighteenth century, the woman is not an 'object' of male desire, as is to happen later, when this very male desire is circumscribed by a general ideology of desexualization of the human body through a narrative of vice.[24] The much advocated serene, unsexual moral female image, which is only nuanced by indirect and repressed physicality, is a sign of 'femininity' rather than of womanhood or femaleness. It also desexualizes or contains male sexuality, or rather is an expression of its containment, since it is at its most 'feminine' in a passive form, and does not solicit a directly sexual male attention.

The colonially inflected patriarchal world view of the middle classes of Bengal, however, should be understood as being both local and foreign. The sign of the *bhadramahila* is a great example of this reconstruction of consciousness. It is in a sense a reworked or anglicized version of the older Bengali *sati* (the chaste woman-wife). In its current phase of a gentlewoman the direct physical control and violence of patriarchy has been domesticized and substituted by an ideological encirclement of clothing and other forms or morality which mix chastity and sacrifice with the moral code of a utilitarian christian lady.

After the first half of the nineteenth century, 'the feminine' emerges as a notion among the western educated population in Bengal. It is found everywhere—from education to clothes. It is not surprising therefore that many women, in search of a direct agency and strength, turned to the colonial–nationalist myth of the Aryan Woman or notions of the mother goddess. If we compare women's and men's use of the construct of the Aryan Woman we find that women are attracted to the myth in search of notions such as dynamism and clothing designed for public and open spaces, while

men to the Aryan Woman's moral qualities which are passive, such
as constancy, chastity and sacrifice:

> The clothes worn by Aryan women in ancient times bear no
> resemblance with the present time. In those days women had
> freedom. Women frequented war zones and courts freely. In
> many cases wives or sisters had to ride on horses with their hus-
> bands or brothers. This is why it was not suitable for them to
> wear just beautiful clothes. There was a great similarity between
> male and female clothing. (H. Choudhury 1901: 138)

The same may be said of the typology of English and American
women used by Krishnabhabani Das, Hiranmayee Debi and others
who represent freedom, agency and self-sufficiency, without fully
displacing women from the private or domestic sphere.

Conclusion

These essays by women on civilization, shame, the body
and clothing both organize and express the consciousness of a significant strand of the developing 'westernized', reforming middle
classes of Bengal. They display the commonsense of classes created
on a colonial terrain which also contain competitive 'national' aspirations. In the case of the garb of the *bhadramahila*, however, much
more so than in the area of education, for example, the colonial
context and content overdetermine the hegemonic forms of these
classes. This sartorial–moral enterprise is profoundly English nineteenth century in its ethos. Fundamentally distinct from precolonial, feudal notions of grandeur or status, this attire is an
intrinsic response to and an absorption within a colonial influence.
The ideology of Victorian femininity provides the lens through
which is perceived and configured the indigenous dominant ideology about womanhood.

The *bhadramahila*, both in form and content, is the Bengali males' response to European accusations of their barbarism.
The configuration here depends on a particular set of social relations which express the gender organization of the propertied
classes. Here we have multiple but coherent discourses of patriarchy in so far as local and colonial elements of gender and class

ideologies converge into an overall misogyny and a general rejection of the physical. As we noted before, class, in the sense of division and valorization of mental over manual labour, extends into a positive hatred of the body and sexuality as embodied by women as 'nature' and 'the primitive'. Racism itself is concretized with patriarchy and classism in the European stereotypes of animality and sensuality of Bengali/pagan women in particular, but also men.[25]

If this seems like an exaggerated way of stating the colonial ideological design, we need to only look at Kenneth Ballhatchet's book on racism and sex in the Raj, which gave the 'Hindoos' and their women in particular a savage, evil and corrupting role with regard to Europeans. Accusations of barbaric sensuality and primitivity fill the pages of Mill's *History of British India*, the missionary tracts, letters, travelogues and drawings of Europeans in India/Bengal.[26] Rationality, or access to reason, is seen as a faraway dream for Indians, so close are they supposed to be in religion and everyday life to sensuality and nature. Their spirituality or literary creation itself is seen at best as a product of a sensual, distorted imagination rather than of spiritual transcendence.[27] And if the Indian/Bengali society as a whole, characterized in terms of its males, is such a natural excrescence, then how much more so the Bengali women, whose identity with nature has not been ruptured by any rational interruption. The European enlightenment's moral–social schema, which rests on 'civilization vs. barbarism/moral decay' of Indian males, or an ambivalence towards 'tradition', expresses itself in a man-to-man condemnation of Indian males (as sensualists and females manque) as oppressors of 'their women', and confers on the colonial (male) rulers the role of protectors or reformers of Indian women. For Indian males, vying for the same status of reformer–protector, this means a combination of self-hatred (for being 'female/effete') acquired in the colonial context, and a hatred of women (for being natural, uncivilized, etc.) which is both colonial and precolonial.

The project of social reform for women therefore allows for externalizing or displacing their views of the self and self-hatred onto society at large and women in particular. It also calls for curbing 'naturality' (femaleness) in themselves. In the same sexually

repressive configurated design aimed at women, morally–
sartorially, the project of self-improvement is collapsed with self-
repression for men. Thus domination of nature as embodied by
women could be projected as social reform, offering examples of
rationality (therefore true masculinity à la old brahmanism and
European enlightenment/utilitarianism) on the part of the Bengali
male intelligentsia. Indians such as Rajnarayan Bose (and many
others) expressed just this conjuncture when their reforming zeal
was expressed in terms of "she must be refined, reorganized, recast
and regenerated". This introjected colonial judgment, along with a
reorganized older patriarchy, provided much of the middle classes'
hegemonic self-definition. It could therefore be said that the clothes
designed for the *bhadramahila* inscribed on women's body the
moral–political agenda of the same classes. Krishnabhabini Das
and Swarnakumari Debi, describing changes in the social organization of a household, speak of growing male control over all
aspects of women's lives. Much of their own writing aims to establish a relative autonomy for women while maintaining a somewhat differentiated social domain.

The virtuous attire designed for the gentlewoman of Bengal is a reworking of existing and incoming social and cultural
forms. This convergence, negotiation and fusion on grounds of cultural commonsense and ideology between colonial and indigenous
patriarchal class values can only happen because the European
forms and norms are not dissimilar to those prevailing in Bengal.
The intelligibility of colonial, foreign notions actually rests on prior
social organization in Bengal or India. A highly evolved division
of labour as expressed in the caste system and forms of class,
valorization of mental production by placing brahmins (priest-
scholars) at the head of the society, the deprivation of women (even
of the brahmin caste) and low-caste physical-manual producers of
intellectual prerogatives, all contain a basic similarity to European
social organization in terms of gender and class organization. The
pre-existing social organization thus provides enough ground for
weaving in or reworking colonial misogyny, elitism and racism.
Fundamentally patriarchal, brahminical rationalism and asceticism
is also characterized by a basic hatred and contempt towards
women (as natural, physical entities) and the lower castes/classes as

unreconstructed body or nature, and thus collapses the woman and the *sudra* (low caste).[28]

This predisposition could not have been inimical to colonial–capitalist class distinctions, protestant christianity, utilitarianism and Cartesian rationalism, all of which were fundamentally anti-woman, anti-physical/manual producer and racist. Frantz Fanon has written about colonial discourse as a discourse of Cartesian masculinity in which the colonizer/ conqueror is the sole male or intellectual subject and the colonized is an object, a body, an animality and, by extension, a femaleness (Fanon 1963: 35–43).[29] The equation of women with nature, with the reproduction of physical life, womb and instinct and, expandedly, with feelings and primitivity, was equally well known to both India and Britain. This is why the woman of India and the savage, and the Indian/Bengali woman as the quintessentially savage, must be reformed and clothed or reclothed. This is not to say that the European attitude towards European women was any different or better. European contempt (and hatred) for females of the conquered species was disguised as paternalistic charity. This charity, mediated through notions of civilization and progress, offered both an indictment of Indian society and a legitimacy for colonial rule.

The women writers of the magazines share to a great extent, in spite of their nationalism, the colonial view of themselves and their society. They adopt the same trajectory of historiography originating from James Mill, starting with the golden age of the Aryans, moving through the dark ages of muslim rule to the present moral and intellectual decay, to the English era of enlightenment which calls for social reform.[30] These sartorial innovations therefore represent a recovering of a higher, intellectual–moral self, a disguising and a muting of the 'natural', through consciously eliminating sensuality/sexuality signalled by hiding of the female body. If nothing else, through the reform attempts the basically reproductive natural femaleness is tempered with virtue, taming sexuality and animality into sweet sentimentality and mothering. The colonially proferred image of the Victorian, christian middle-class woman which overshadows this sartorial project, less the grand lady than the helpmate of missionaries and social reformers, represents the icon of a civilized society, while holding forth the possibility of moral improvement to a section of Bengali women.

Much more so than in education, where the feminist thrust of the women's self-improvement project is strident in spite of subscription to norms of a class-patriarchy, it is in the area of clothing and the body that a guilt-ridden, shameful, indigenous-cum-colonial patriarchy holds women in thrall. While the same women are unashamedly demanding in acquisition of intellect and reason, they are held in place by 'shame' in the matter of their body, sensuality and sexuality. It is with 'shame' that middle-class women are most inexorably riveted to patriarchy. The life of Krishna-bhabini Das is a prime example of this situation. It shows what suspicions she had to allay for going to England, being educated and independent, what she traded off in order to gain a morally correct image. That white-robed icon of the hindu widow which hides her femaleness in a heavy garb of coarse cloth, which mutes all expressions and potentiality of sexuality, which tempts no male, is her uniform of legitimacy for being a 'modern' woman and advocating women's emancipation and education. Only attired in virtue can she fully expiate her past of transgressions. So even she, critical and strident as she is, a tireless promoter of reason and knowledge, subscribes to the same discourse of shame, to the triumph of male brahminical–colonial rationality over the female mind and body.

If we are to consider the issues of subjectivity and agency of women in nineteenth-century Bengal, it becomes apparent through this sartorial–moral project that middle-class women are held hostage between colonialism and nationalism, patriarchal class subjectivity and their resistance to it.[31] In helping to create an icon/sign for the emerging aspirations of a Bengali culture and Bengali nationalism, women capitulated far more to a patriarchal fashioning of themselves than in any other area of social change and development. The values they represent sartorially are in no way contrary to those of men, and in fact the more 'enlightened' they are, the more they compensate by sacrificing their social–sexual agency for their encroachment in the male domain of reason and public service.

In the end, we might say that though middle-class women 'come out' or 'emerge' by overstepping the boundaries of an earlier 'inner quarters' in terms of location in space and an earlier division of labour, their sartorial morality indicates an object–subject ideological status which they themselves are active in bringing forth. As relegated agents of an objectified subjectivity, they enter a textile prison, fashioned by male tailors and fathers of Bengal's social reform. This prison is constructed from lace, linen, cotton and silk, and from the sober and sombre tints of shame and guilt adding up to virtue.

Notes and References

[1] Themes of social reform and social change in various ways dominate studies on nineteenth-century social and cultural history of Bengal. Books as diverse as M. Borthwick's *The Changing Role of Women in Bengal 1849–1905* (Princeton: Princeton University Press, 1984), V.C. Joshi's edited volume *Rammohun Roy and the Process of Modernization in India* (New Delhi: Vikas, 1975), T. Raychaudhury's *Europe Reconsidered* (New Delhi: Oxford University Press, 1988), Susobhan Sarkar's *On the Bengal Renaissance* (Calcutta: Papyrus, 1979) and *A Critique of Colonial India* (Calcutta: Papyrus, 1985a), A. Sen's *Ishwar Chandra Vidyasagar and the Elusive Milestones* (Calcutta: Riddhi-India, 1977), among numerous others, speak of these topics with different social analyses and interpretations.

[2] See the preface to T. Raychaudhuri (1988: ix–xvi) and note: "But whether the change was introduced by self-conscious effort or impersonal influences, one notes an all-pervasive concern, almost obsessive, in their social and intellectual life—an anxiety to assess European culture in the widest sense of the term as something to be emulated or rejected" (xi). The terms and forms of this assessment are considered in their complexities and contradictions by S. Sarkar (1985a); see also Jasodhara Bagchi (1985) and G. Forbes (1975).

[3] H. Bannerji, "Fashioning a Self: Educational Proposals for and by Women in Popular Magazines in Colonial Bengal" (this volume): "The social location of the significational aspect of ideology supplies the multiplicity of meanings, fissures, the openings and closures (always semiotically signalling out), which even the most thought-out ideological formulation cannot escape" (142). It should also be noted that "writers on ideological formations in nineteenth-century Bengal are, not surprisingly, preoccupied therefore in dealing with 'shifts and slides', 'liminality' and so on—pointing to a multidimensionality within one ideological position or its class articulation (143)."

[4] The assessment of the state of Bengali society and 'civilization' by judging the condition of women from a European/christian standpoint is pervasive in missionary literature, for example. Also Mrinalini Sinha, in her essay "The Age of Consent Act: The Ideal of Masculinity and Colonial Ideology in Nineteenth Century Bengal" speaks of the overall English colonial disposition to "Victorian sexual ideology" and "specific gender identities" and their imposition on an "alien culture inextricably linked to the pursuit of colonial economic and political power. . ." (1995: 2–3).

This ruling and condemnatory design is also spoken of by K. Ballhatchet (1980).

5 T. Sarkar writes: "subjection for most sections of the [male] intelligentsia meant loss, albeit with some potential for progress. Against this fundamental and all-encompassing loss of self-hood, the only sphere of autonomy, of free will, was located within the Hindu family: to be more precise, with the Hindu woman, her position within an authentic Hindu marriage system and the ritual surrounding the deployment of her body. . . . [T]here was a thorough examination of every aspect of the problem." (1989: 1)

6 The criteria for social reform, though not strictly an expression of or an agenda for colonizing the Bengali mind, are evolved in the colonial context and in relation to colonial content as well. The *Autobiography* of Shibnath Shastri, for example, provides an excellent sense of what is entailed in such social reform, while a book such as *Re-casting Women: Essays in Colonial History* (edited by K. Sangari and S. Vaid [1989]) offers a feminist reading for such attempts at 're-forming' or 're-casting'. See the Introduction to that anthology, which takes its name from Koilashchandra Bose's statement "On the Education of Hindu Females" (1846): "She must be refined, reorganized, recast, regenerated."

7 See H. Bannerji: "The project of the creation of a new social identity or a new common sense is only partially a planned one. Its complex nature is not accounted for by the correspondence theory of base and superstructure, but rather it is various, disparate and *ad hoc*, and often in the colonial case, one of an acute and quick response. Imitation, reaction, absorption and recreation were all ingredients in this social response" (1989: 1042). See also P. Chatterjee (1986) and P. Addy and I. Azzad (1973: 71–112).

8 See the Introduction to K. Sangari and S. Vaid (eds) for a discussion of the class agenda of social reform: "Middle-class reforms undertaken on behalf of women are tied up with the self-definition of the class, with a new division of the public from the private sphere, and of course with a cultural nationalism" (1989: 9). See also H. Bannerji (1992).

9 The plethora of literature on women's social subjectivity and the family is too large for selective citation, but from Bankim Chandra Chattopadhyay, the conservative thinker on women, to Rabindranath Tagore, a liberal, the same preoccupation is shared. The names of a few 'improving' texts are cited below: Chandranath Basu, *Hindutwa* [Hinduism] (1892) and *Stridiger prati upadesh* [Advice to Women] (1901); Iswarchandra Basu, *Nariniti* [Woman's Conduct] (1884); Manomohan Basu, *Hindur Achar Vyavahar* [Hindu Customs] (1887); *Garhasthya* [Domesticity] (1884); Taraknath Biswas, *Bangya Mahila* [The Bengali Woman] (1886); Girija Prasanna Raychoudhury, *Grihalaxmi* [The Goddess Laxmi of the Hearth] (1884).

10 This is also noted in the European colonial racist–sexist context. For example, Sander Gilman's essay, "Black Bodies, White Bodies: Toward an Iconography of Female Sexuality in Late Nineteenth Century Art, Medicine and Literature" (in H.L. Gates Jr [ed.] 1985: 223–61) remarks on the nature of the body—both female and black—as a signifier for colonial

and other forms of domination and an ideological repository or representation, as well as a site of moral hegemony.

[11] Meredith Borthwick, in her *Changing Role of Women in Bengal, 1849–1905* (1984), gives us an overview of the world of middle-class Bengali women, especially with regard to their educational project, as put forward in women's magazines of the time. She lists the women's maga- zines and approximates their circulation, claiming a large readership in Dhaka, in Calcutta and its suburbs, in small towns and even villages, both among men and women.

[12] For example, autobiographies of women printed in the last century or reprinted more recently such as Rashasundari Dasi's *Amar Jiban* [My Life] (1860).

[13] In this essay the idea of animality is securely linked by Hiranmayee Debi with children and savages and associated with any kind of physicality among adult men and women. It marks stages in the development of civi- lization through social stages and life stages, the goals of both being the suppression of the physical or the 'natural/emotional', and elevation of the non-physical/rational. Social Darwinism's 'scientific' support for misogyny remains a field to be explored in the Bengali colonial context.

[14] For the notion of the effeminate *babu* and his female counterpart, see Sumanta Bannerji, *Keyabat Meye* [Bravo, Woman!] (1988) or *The Par- lour and the Streets: Elite and Popular Culture in Nineteenth Century Calcutta* (1989), and nineteenth-century satirical journalism such as Kaliprasanna Sinha, *Hutom Penchar Naksha* [The Owl's Skits] (1856) or Tekshand Thakur, *Akaler Gharer Dulal* [Spoilt Darling of the Worthless Rich] (1841). See also M. Sinha where she states: "The suspicion against the Bengali middle class found expression in the popularity of the racial and cultural stereotype of the 'effeminate Bengali Babu'" (1995: 6), and "The Victorian Anglo-Indian generally considered Bengali society to be steeped in sensuality. They were constantly apalled by open discussion of sexual matters in the Hindu household. The *Pioneer* found the talk of sex 'too odious for description in a newspaper read in respectable house- holds'" (1995: 21).

[15] This makes us rethink the whole notion of motherhood as found in Ben- gal, which seems to function as an antidote to women's sexual being. This may have been a way to redeem the physical and the reproductive with- out any overt or implied reference to sexuality—all allusions to mother- hood are posed antithetically to female sexuality. See Jasodhara Bagchi (1990) and Maithriyee Krishnaraj (1995).

[16] On this theme, see D. Sayer (1991), and also R. Inden (1990) who traces the emergence of these concepts and applies them to the European con- struction of India.

[17] Articles in the magazines allude to the common presence of large num- bers of upper- and lower-class women in public spaces for reasons of pil- grimage and other religious activities as well as social rituals, or for prac- tical reasons such as bathing, washing clothes or fetching water, long before the 'emergence'.

[18] It is not an accident that much of the satire against 'modern women' was levelled at 'educated' women, who were very well covered in an asexual

and virtuous manner. These women, as 'disguised prostitutes' and home-breaking 'masculine' viragos, attracted more ridicule and venom from the satirists than prostitutes,

[19] See satires against 'educated' women, who are seen as 'masculine', and their husbands as 'feminine'. This 'unnatural' social presence was carica-tured and castigated in images and written texts. The thesis about this inversion indicating the end of an aeon, going through a fallen stage, is expressed in the notion of *Kali Yuga*, the age of Kali.

[20] Regarding *griha*, see H. Bannerji (1992).

[21] It is obvious that Bengali men and women lived with each other with the kind of clothing that they later repudiated as 'savage' or 'uncivilized' without any violation of ethics and aesthetics. In her popular journalism about Indian women's clothes and ornaments, Chitra Deb, for example, brings out a basic change in erotic aesthetics and ethics between pre- and early colonial times and the later nineteenth century among the proper-tied classes; see C. Deb (1989). Two English women visitors in India, Eliza Fay and Fanny Burney, also leave us with descriptions which do not show any negativity among the Bengali households as to what women or men wore; see Sumanta Banerjee (1989).

[22] In "The Queen's Daughters: Prostitutes as Outcast Group in Colonial India", Ratnabali Chattopadhyay discusses the iconography of the 'bad woman' or the prostitute and the referential relationship between this construct and that of *sati*, the chaste good woman, or the *bhadramahila* with her refined moral purity: "In a number of moral tracts the chaste wife (*patibrata stree*) and the prostitute (*beshya*) are constructed into visi-ble signs" (1992: 29). Chattopadhyay also quotes a few lines from an anonymous tract entitled *Stridiger Prati Upadesh* (Advice to Women): "The good wife, *patibrata*, is shy, silent, does her duty and is totally un-demanding, stays away from men, keeps her whole body covered and does not wear flashy clothes", while the "*beshya* is loudmouthed, always restless, bares special parts of her body, falls on men, demands jewelry and continuously wears revealing clothes" (1874: 29). This distinction was so widely touted, and morally organized, that it is not surprising that it formed a part of the consciousness of middle-class educated women who were particularly sensitive regarding their respectability or *bhadrata* and wanted no confusion between their own project of emancipation and the 'freeness' of 'bad/loose' *itar* women.

[23] Many authors, both Indian and western, have commented on the British preoccupation with Indian moral degeneracy and savagery, particularly with regard to sexual morality and women. For example, Major C.A. McMohan writes: "Native public opinion would not go with us in an attempt to put a stop to professional prostitution. The mind of a native is no more shocked at the thought that a girl should be born to be a pros-titute than that a man should be born to be blacksmiths and carpenters. Prostitution is an institution the history of which in India at all events is lost in the mist of ages. Prostitutes danced before Yudishthir and Rama and in the guise of dancing girls and singers. They are a necessary part of most domestic ceremonies today" (Home Judicial File No. 48.P.1143, 7th June 1872, to C.M. Riwarzi Esq., Officiating Undersecretary to the

Government of Punjab). See also T. Niranjana (1990) as well as Shibaji
Bandyopadhyay (1991).

24 See K. Ballhatchet (1980) and also R. Chattopadhyay, who writes: "The
main focus of the missionary narrative rested on recreating the atmosphere of vice. This was done to show the exact division of space that
existed between the rulers and the ruled" (1991: 17).

25 See the account of Rev. James Ward, excerpted by Sumanta Bannerji:
"Before two o'clock the place was cleared . . . when the doors of the area
were thrown open, and a vast crowd of natives rushed in, almost tread-
ing one upon another, among whom were the vocal singers . . . who
entertained their guests with filthy songs and danced in indecent attitudes
before the goddess, holding up their hands, turning around, putting
forward their heads towards the image, every now and then bending
their bodies and almost tearing their throats with their vociferations"
(1989: 54).

26 See, among numerous sources, A.C. Dasgupta (ed.) (1959); J.R. Martin
(1837); Rev. J. Long (1974); J.C. Marshman (1864); Mary Carpenter
(1868).

27 See R. Inden (1990).

28 Sukumari Bhattacharji, a scholar on ancient India, as well as Uma
Chakravarti have done much work on the status of women in ancient
India, challenging the Aryan myth. The physical status of women is evident, according to Bhattacharji, from the settled agricultural period by
her deprivation of education and control over her body (and its fruits) by
men: "The wife had no property rights, nor had she any right over her
body (*Satapatha Brahmana* IV 4: 2: 13). If she refused to oblige the husband sexually she should first be coaxed and cajoled, then bribed and
'brought over' (cf. *avakriniyat*) with gifts; if she still refused, he should
beat her with his palm or with a rod into submission (*Brhadaranyaka
Upanishad* VI 4: 7)'" (S. Battacharji 1989: 30).

29 Fanon points out the physicality/body status attributed to the colonized
and the rationalist essentialism of the European colonizer's 'self'. This
shares the same ground with patriarchy in so far as women are seen as
'nature' or 'body' and equated with a reproductive self, qualitatively a
different consciousness, and incapable of rationality.

30 For the myth of the Aryan woman and its implications for nationalism,
and nationalism's influence on social reform for women, see Uma
Chakravarti (1989).

31 On this notion of divided subjectivity of women caught in the interpellation of class and patriarchy, see H. Bannerji, "Fashioning a Self"
(this volume: 138–39): "it can be said that women class members were
'summoned' both by Bengal's urban propertied classes' formative agenda
and Bengali nationalism's 'emancipatory' calls to become 'social actors',
and hence their presence in the stage of education. This amounts to
'dominant ideology' interpellating women to function as class subjects,
while that subjectivity itself is sought to be contained, managed, truncated and inauthenticated by the repression of their full social being
through patriarchy."

Fashioning a Self

Educational Proposals for and by Women in Popular Magazines in Colonial Bengal

Woman was not created to be the ignorant slave or the plaything of man. As it is the purpose of a woman's life to do good to others, and to live for them, so does a woman live for herself. And the serious responsibilities that are entrusted to her demand not only a sympathetic heart, but also a cultivated head.

Krishnabhabini Das, "The Educated Woman", *Sahitya* (1891c)

We call this *moral regulation*: a project of normalizing, rendering natural, taken for granted, in a word 'obvious' what are in fact ontological and epistemological premises of a particular and historical form of social order.

Philip Corrigan and Derek Sayer, *The Great Arch* (1985)

Introduction

Nineteenth-century Bengal is characterized by its preoccupation with social reform, much of which concentrated on women. Immediately meant for bettering the lot of women, it also aimed at reorganizing fundamental social relations and forms of consciousness structuring the family and lives of women among the middle classes.[1] A reconstructive contestation resulted between the colonial state and the Bengali male intelligentsia whose object was 'the new Bengali woman'. But from the last decades of the century women themselves sought to contribute to this formative process of their social subjectivities and agencies. The issue of education

This essay was first published in *Economic and Political Weekly*, Vol. 26, No. 43, 1991, pp. 50–62.

attracted much attention, being the most well articulated and definitively ideological area within the scope of social reform. Controversies raging around women's education and 'the educated woman', alias *bhadramahila* (the gentlewoman), signalled far beyond the immediate social problems of women and served as a complex signifier of the composition of social subjectivities (that is, 'common sense') of the middle classes.[2] Seen thus, the various social reform projects of the century could be interpreted as marking moments in a battle for hegemony in which a class, or a class fraction, elaborates an ideological stance in its bid to become morally, culturally and politically a dominant force within the civil society or everyday life. That is, it is a stage in what Gramsci has called "the passive revolution",[3] amounting to attempts at transforming the common sense of classes by persons within the ruling relations prior to, or concurrently with, assuming a directly political role. The important question for us, then, while dealing with social reform, is what role women themselves, of their own volition, play in this "passive revolution", which involves being drawn into the hegemonic fold, and the role of women themselves as agents in this hegemonic process (Gramsci 1971: 105–20).[4] We need to know, as with all studies in the subjective–cultural dimensions of class formation and politics, how women fared in the 'self-making' of their classes, and of themselves, and what modes they adopted in this necessary task of fashioning selves and society.

Although most public facilities were not available to women in their self-defining project, the print media, creating a bridge between the public and the private, offered them a wide communicative space. These women were already 'educated', far beyond the literacy stage, the older ones mostly at home, and many of the younger ones in girls' schools. Magazines such as *Bama-bodhini* established by the male reforming intelligentsia held space for women writers under the heading of *Bama Racana* ("Women's Writings"). But there were also other magazines, such as *Bharati* (edited by such eminent women as Swarnakumari Debi), along with *Antahpur, Sahitya, Mukul, Sakha, Pradip* and others, all of which created an extensive sphere of social influence and a field of participation for the rudimentary women intelligentsia of the time.[5] It is through an exploration of the content and quality of this influence and participation that we can arrive at some understanding of the type of social subjectivity and agency that these women created for themselves. This does not require an extensive media study, but more an exercise in historical sociology using representative material.

In the pages of these magazines, the women writers and their women readers build up an extensive network and a general fund of communicative competence. They work on 'women's issues', 'women's approaches', and invite pieces on new themes or hold essay competitions among the readers. Thus it is difficult to see them as solely male-identified and as an isolated mimic intelligentsia, as Sumanta Banerji seems to suggest in his book *The Parlour and the Street*.[6] Even though the loss of an *andarmahal* (inner/women's quarters) makes for a substantial change and losses in a certain type of popular and women's culture, as he claims, what follows cannot simply be seen as a destruction of 'women's culture and community' and the emergence of a class of women thoroughly absorbed in the male moral–intellectual space with women isolated from one another. Rather, the attempt seems to be to introduce new communicative modes, availing of a certain kind of facility such as the journal or magazine, with the purpose of creating another social, moral and cultural space for and by women, with different mediations and signifiers. Thus the situation is not one of complete cooption by sexism of their male counterparts, as women of the *andarmahal* also were not fully coopted by the general patriarchal social organization within which they lived. Obviously both the society of women in the *andarmahal* culture and that of the magazine culture shared forms of patriarchal consciousness with their male counterparts, but what is interesting is that beyond, and through, their particular educational 'women's agenda' they sought a guidance role within society as a whole, as 'women' members of propertied classes. As Krishnabhabini Das put it, "It is unjust to say that only men should cultivate that intelligence, that God has given both men and women. God could never have imparted such a great gift without a noble end in view" (Krishnabhabini Das 1891c). From this step of universality she deduces the "noble end in view":

> Especially, since the education of male kind [*purush jati*] depends
> essentially on women's education and sense of morality, and since
> we can directly see how a man's character depends on his home
> life, especially on his mother's example, then who can deny that
> higher and quality education for women, lies at the root of
> national progress and morality? (1891c. This and all subsequent
> translations from Bengali are mine.).

This sentiment and argument, expanding in concentric circles, from the mother, the home, to the nation—from the self-
improvement of the woman, through her son, to the nation—are
found consistently and centrally in the works of all the women
writers who provide material for this essay. They are Swarnakumari Debi, Gyanadanandini Debi, Sarala Debi, Hironmoyee
Debi and Krishnabhabini Das. In order to explore the ideological
dimensions of their thought, I seek to locate their educational proposals within a larger problematic of mediatory and constitutive
relations between the social relations and cultural forms of gender,
class and colonialism. The ideological dimension is particularly
explored with regard to the nature of social subjectivity and agency
assumed and recommended by these articles, and their implications
for the hegemonic aspirations of their class or class fraction. In this
process, it is hoped that it will become clear how 'cultural', in the
broadest sense, 'class' is, and how deeply gendered is the agenda of
'class', and how 'classified' is the construction of gender relations
within it.

The special type of subjectivity that women have within a
class topography can be captured conceptually by adapting Louis
Althusser's notion of ideological interpellation (1984: 44–51).[7]
This allows for the conception of a social agency for a divided and
yet unified purpose. That is, it allows for problematizing women's
relationship to the patriarchal and gendered norms and forms of
their own class. This has to be thought through as a situation for
women of all classes, but especially for women of propertied classes
who are simultaneously empowered by their social location and
subordinated to the class's patriarchal, gendered organization.
From this perspective it can be said that women class members
were 'summoned' both by the Bengal's urban propertied classes'

formative agenda and Bengali nationalism's 'emancipatory' calls[8] to become 'social actors', and hence their presence on the stage of education. This amounts to the 'dominant ideology' interpellating women to function as class subjects while that subjectivity itself is sought to be contained, managed, truncated and unauthenticated by the repression of their full social being through patriarchy. The women intelligentsia of the time are themselves not unaware of this double-edged situation. Their texts are therefore structured through complicity and antagonism, convergence and contradiction, making them simultaneously objects and subjects of their own discourse.[9]

Studying an ideological process so woven with complex mediations of unequal relations of power, we need to be specially attentive to the processes of conceptual negotiation and moral syncretism which involve various adaptive, cooptive, exclusive and innovative strategies. We have to note traces of 'collaboration' which are highlighted by the very marks of 'resistance'. We need to look both for values and symbols, interpretive devices and epistemologies, which share gendered patriarchal (local and colonial) class terms, and for those which they fashion through an 'inner struggle' against patriarchy within the same class space.

Finally, at the end of this introduction, we must stress what has been noted by many scholars of hegemonic formation and alluded to by myself, that the ideological agenda, or the hegemonic agenda, is invariably an agenda of morality, of values expressed through both ideas and practices. This is to say, as do Philip Corrigan and Derek Sayer (1985), or Judith Walkowitz (1980) and others studying Victorian reformation, that the hegemonic agenda, among other things, is a *moral agenda*. It is through the creation, recreation and diffusion of a set of norms and forms that the necessary 'consent' can be built which is essential for hegemony's fullest expression. Gauri Visvanathan uncovers the hegemonic (moral) design, the shaping force of values and world views in something seemingly so innocuous as the teaching of 'English Literature' in India (1990: 8–9). In our case we do not examine the doings of a colonial state but rather those of a social group who hold a subordinate and/or collaborative position within classes which are ruled (by English colonialism) and ruling (of the indigenous productive classes), and who wish to throw off the yoke of colonial subjection. One of their main moral ideological tools, as with colonialism, is also 'education', and we look at the informal aspect of education in examining non-institutional ideas and content for and by women in these magazines.

Framing a Method

As noted by scholars of women's education such as Meredith Borthwick (1984), women's education in the nineteenth century and well into the twentieth had little to do with economic functions, needs, or development of professional expertise among women: "Whereas education for males was directly related to the pursuit of employment, female education had no economic function" (Visvanathan 1990: 61). In the period that the present study covers, from about 1880 to 1910, the magazines make it clear that the main public use of women's education lies in its very nature as a private acquirement. Its ability to meet social needs to create appropriate personalities, familial–social relations and households, and to offer a moral basis for the everyday life of the *bhadralok* or the gentry, provides the ground for its justification. Women's educational projects are thus always phrased in terms of both social and moral 'betterment', and the totality of this 'betterment' is consistently expressed as the welfare of the family. 'Proper' child-raising, character-building and conjugality as the core of the familial life supply the occasion and the legitimation for a non-institutional, home-based education among the women of urban propertied households, especially in the households of professionals and bureaucrats (Visvanathan 1990: 68). Even when 'schooling' is considered later it is not in terms of acquisition of knowledge, profitable or otherwise, but rather in terms of the attitudes of family members or the lifestyle of the family. The general sentiment is phrased by Krishnabhabini Das herself:

> There are some who raise objection to women's education on the ground that women lose their womanly virtues through the influence of education. They compete in everything with men and pay no attention to housework, etc. But if they [those who object] were to open their eyes they could see that this belief is wholly

erroneous. In spite of the great amount of progress made in women's education in America, women there are neither inattentive to their homes, nor ignorant of child-care. In fact they are able to do both child-care and housework with great regulation and discipline, thus increasing happiness within the home, and facilitating the progress of their nation. Of course a few women, wearing men's clothing, abuse their independence and higher education, but does it make any sense to be outraged about women's education and independence in general by the examples of a few? (Krishnabhabini Das 1891a)

Even though her own examples of the ideal results of education come from America, it is clear that she uses these to make a point supporting her demand in the Bengali context. In her essay "Jatya Jiban o Hindu Nari" ("Life and Hindu Women"), Krishnabhabini Das (1901) reiterates the nation's dependence for its future improvement on women and their organization of family life.

The cluster of women, education and the family around which the social reform agenda is organized points to fundamental ways in which to rethink the social and cultural dimensions of 'class.' The centrality of the family as a site for social construction becomes explicit when we realize that norms and forms, the moral and cultural life of this institution, are not static, ahistorical and 'natural'. Writers such as Philip Ariès in *Centuries of Childhood* (1962) or Eli Zaretsky in *Capitalism, The Family and Personal Life* (1976) bring home to us the fact that the word 'family' signifies a dynamic organization of social reproduction which is both grounded in, and mediates, the general social relations of production.

It is important to realize that the concern for educational social reform which alters family mores indicates the need to devise new forms of social reproduction. If a society needs to develop new forms of 'class consciousness', subjectivities, ways of being and seeing, this can only be done in its most fundamental form by reworking the family form. The family is after all an institution which is equally grounded in the unregulated life of the civil society and the institutional life of polity, law, etc. The sexual–social division of labour that characterizes the family at different stages, or of different social classes, are of a piece with the gender organization and division of labour that mediate the mode of production as a whole. Therefore, what we concretely understand as 'class', its subjective, cultural moment, is vitally expressed and constructed through familial gender relations, for example, socialization to masculinity and femininity, mothering, and so on. It is not surprising that these form the very topics for the new educational project outlined by the women intelligentsia.

Education is always a moral proposal and the concept of morality allows us to be social and personal at the same time. It is only fitting that the educational proposals for and by women are primarily conceptualized in moral terms—of 'educing' or cultivating moral sentiments of the woman and her family. This agenda is not simply a spontaneous expression of common sense, but rather of a well thought-out ideological position which has substantially reconstructed and rearticulated its prior elements. This elaborates 'appropriate' social norms and forms for inhabitants of a particular section of the social space and creates 'social' individuals, identities and subjectivities within historically constructed relations (P. Corrigan and D. Sayer 1985: 4).

Before we can proceed to an examination of the material at hand we must also note that this two-way relationship between common sense—the everyday world—and ideology is central to hegemony. Ideology (as a conscious, unified and organized system of ideas)[10] results from attempts at a conscious and coherent discursive construction, through selectively interpreting and putting together elements from common sense and articulating it to ontological and epistemological premises of a particular and historical form of social order and social class or classes. But its articulated unity is continuously fractured in the process of social circulation among other relations of everyday life, and crumbles or diffuses back into common sense. This fracturing itself is provided by the multiple significational nature of common sense and prevailing contradictions in social relations. The social location of the significational aspect of ideology supplies the multiplicity of meanings, fissures, the openings and closures (always semiotically signalling out) which even the most thought-out ideological formulation cannot escape. This process of continuous widening (drawing into common sense) and narrowing (being 'shaped' into 'ideology') has been remarked upon by all scholars dealing with history of consciousness. Partha Chatterjee, for example, in his *Nationalist Thought: A Derivative Discourse?* (1986) phrases it in terms of a wider "problematic" and a narrower "thematic", one as a realm of possibilities and the other as a narrower zone of "intentionality" marked by a "subject matter".[11]

An examination of the women's texts must be attentive to this two-way relation between common sense and ideology. While we trace the determinate direction of the ideological proposal, we have to remember the continuous process of negotiation that is involved in an ideological effort—between different aspects of common sense—and the tension between and within ideology (fractured or whole) and lived experience. In fact it is the ability to mediate, manage and contain these divergent elements that makes or mars the success of an ideology, and charts the direction and the political cultural form of hegemony. This fluidity in ideological formation clearly indicates the difficulty of demarcating forms of consciousness "residual, dominant and emergent" with any precision, and exposes the fallacy in a 'reflective' view of culture. Writers on ideological formations in nineteenth-century Bengal are therefore, not surprisingly, preoccupied in dealing with 'shifts and slides', 'liminality' and so on—pointing to a multidimensionality within one ideological position or its class articulation.[12]

In the middle of such fluidity what we can speak of, however, is only a claim, a contested claim at that, by certain ideological positions as candidates for hegemonic ascendancy. The ephemeral (non-classic) texts that we are concerned with, no less than others with well-defined and developed ideological positions, must also be read within the same analytical framework that has usually been advanced for such macro-formulations, such as the ideology of 'nationalism'. The enterprise put forward by these women reformers advances claims on two levels: that of ethics—implying an epistemology; and that of practical management—purporting to create a 'better social life' both in the realm of ideas and practically at that of social reproduction. These 'claims' all rest on the legitimacy of a universal good but do not actually transcend the particularities of class and gender interests; they are an essentialist

way of speaking about the 'is' and 'oughts' of the social life of
women and men of propertied classes. The generalizations on what
women 'are', their nature and so forth, build on or reflect an empirical knowledge of experiences and material conditions of those
who are producers of the ideology. It is with this proviso in mind
that we can appreciate the thesis of this paper, that by studying the
educational writings of the women reformers/intelligentsia at the
turn of the century we can come to an understanding of the advocated gender relations (within urban propertied classes in Bengal)
in terms of one of the hegemonic agendas advanced by competing
agents for their roles and places within nationalist politics. Within
the purview of this ideological formation, to quote Corrigan and
Sayer: "Certain forms of activities are given the official seal of
approval, others are situated beyond the pale. This has cumulative,
and enormous, cultural consequences for how people identify . . .
themselves and their place in the world" (P. Chatterjee 1986: 6).

The Matter at Hand

The language of social reform in the nineteenth century,
and the early years of the twentieth, is inscribed with the discourse
of 'crisis'. Allusions to 'continuity and change', 'tradition and
modernity', all involve the management of gender roles and division of labour outside and within the family in terms of the needs
of the new times. For example, Tapan Raychaudhury, in *Europe
Reconsidered: Perceptions of the West in Nineteenth Century Bengal* (1988), makes this idea of "new times" and "encounter" between 'the east' and 'the west', the point of departure for his whole
interpretive and historical exercise. The "encounter", he points
out, means "a change". "It is a part of modernization", "the revolution in their world view". He also notes that the "changes occurred"—not just through "influence"—not just through the "adoption of cultural artifacts, like specific elements in western life habits
and belief systems. . . . The contact was a catalyst. . . . It induced
mutations in inherited ways" (T. Raychaudhury 1988: ix–x).

Though not in terms of 'the catalyst' and 'mutation', the
same emphasis on 'change' (rather than on continuity) comes out
in the works of many scholars in the area, for example, that of
Tanika Sarkar. In her essay on "Hindu Conjugality and National-

ism in Late Nineteenth Century Bengal", she remarks on the extreme and unprecedented nature of this 'change' brought about by the colonial encounter in the following terms: "For the first time, since Manu perhaps, and in a very different sense from him, family life and womanhood directly and explicitly emerges as a central area of problematization" (T. Sarkar 1995a: 98–99). A few pages later she points out "a compulsive, almost obsessive probing of tension spots . . . all the traumas of a woman's life were brought out and examined, nothing was taken for granted" (1995a: 102).

Whereas Tanika Sarkar puts her finger on the concrete as well as ideational nature of the change in historical–sociological terms, Tapan Raychaudhury, in spite of the suggestive notions of 'the catalyst' and 'mutation' of 'inherited ways', leaves us solely at the level of the history of ideas. The ideas, such as they were, are left unproblematized in terms of actual social relations and politics, whereas Tanika Sarkar's essay, though not speaking exactly in these terms, can be drawn upon to explore the meaning of this change in terms of social reproduction or in terms of forming political ideologies. Raychaudhury does not connect the 'ideal constructs' with anything as concrete as social reproduction or formation. Contentions between different conceptual or symbolic forms in terms of hegemonic contradictions within the complex parameters of gender, class and colonialism, are not reflected in his pool of history of ideas.

But if we were to read between the lines in all this talk of 'change and continuity', 'tradition and modernity', 'crisis' and 'the new times', watch the prolific world of ideas in its frantic exuberance of proposals searching eclectically, adapting and innovating the past and the present, the local and foreign forms and norms of consciousness—we might come to the conclusion that most fundamental social formations, involving social identity and political subjectivity, lay at stake in this change. We would also realize that the fact that 'education' is both practical and a conceptual and a moral aspect makes it a wide entry point into social reformation and creation of ideology. Understandably, the century reverberates with thoughts on education, especially women's education. This search for the right conduct, right epistemology fitted to, produced from, a particular social ontology does not, unlike Sumit Sarkar's

(1985) or Partha Chatterjee's (1990) or Gulam Murshid's (1983) observations (though otherwise they vastly differ from each other), decline with the rise and consolidation of nationalism and hindu revivalism,[13] nor does it come to a contained and managed stage through the same nationalist development.[14] The 'crisis of Bengal renaissance' (of values and projects represented by Rammohan Roy, Vidyasagar, Derozio, Young Bengal, etc.) did not really put a halt to the urge for social reform, including a search for the solution of 'the woman question'. 'Reform' and 'revival', enlightenment and nationalism, sought exclusive or negotiatory paths with each other and sometimes, especially in the voices of women such as Krishnabhabini Das, utilitarianism spoke with a 'difference' from the vantagepoint of gender inhabited by middle-class women.

By the later part of the last century there was a fuller development of the middle classes, of new modes of mediation and culture, a clearer political agenda, and new negotiatory terms leading to divergent formulations of the relations between nationalism (male, upper class/caste) and class formation on the one hand, and the needs of women on the other. Positive and negative valorizations of women's active role in society and concern with the symbolically feminine and feminized symbols coexisted with furious or calmly reflective thoughts and projects on women's education, for example, or the family. It is true that the more exalted (male) writers did not feel positive about 'the educated woman' in all her dimensions (though some agreed about the need of some education for women), but less exalted ones, more pervasive because they were writers of magazine and occasional literature, both men and women, wrote a vast number of pamphlets, books and articles on women, the family and education.

The educational content of the magazines under investigation assumes a miscellaneous air unless we thematize them to establish a focus. This thematization revolves around the family, involving a desire for reconstruction of forms and relations of social reproduction embodied by it. This is inclusive not only of a sexual division of labour but also of a cultural–moral dimension. The two central themes in this context are the familial social space designated as *andarmahal/antahpur* (inner quarters) and *griha* (home/household); the main creator–organizer of this space is named in the latter half of the century as *grihini* (the mistress of the home/homemaker), especially in her incarnation of *bhadramahila* as the mother. This typology of 'sentimental, morally-educative motherhood' subsumes social relations peculiar to the ideal social space of the *griha*. These two notions, of *griha* and the *bhadramahila* mother–homemaker, an educator and a nurturer, involve much more than a domestic labourer or a biological reproducer and a physical dwelling space. The aim of education, as propounded in the magazines, is to enunciate and elaborate on these concepts, to construct the typologies, and to socialize them through various practical advices and know-hows.

The model of the ideal home or *griha* which emerges from the magazines' pages, and to which the concept of the *bhadramahila* is integral, offers a critical insight into the changes in conceptual and actual organization of the social space in nineteenth-century Bengal. The usual use of the words *andar/antahpur* and *griha* is non-discursive, that is, descriptive, and interchangeable. They are used to designate a 'private' social space as opposed to the 'public' one, and to neutrally demarcate a physical, architectural and social inferiority with no indication of their 'essential' difference. But as women reflect in these magazines on the changes in their social space and construct the ideal home, the newness of the concept of *griha* (now) and its difference from *andar* (then) stare us in the face. Sharing many of the social functions, they yet mark or represent different moments of social reproduction and ways of thinking about society. They also indicate a very different relationship to *bahir* (the public/the outside world). This *andar/antahpur*, which indicates a social domain in women's care and which is the constant habitat of women, children, domestic servants and the nocturnal habitat of adult males, can only be understood in its specificity when contrasted to *griha*, 'the home', which forms the central project of thoughts on women's education.

The main difference between *andar* and *griha*, treated discursively, consists of the fact that while the former indicates a separate physical domain for women, appropriate to a more differentiated type of sexual division of labour with very little indication of any direct normativeness or emotionality inscribed in the concept, the latter is a concept of morality and affect. It speaks less

articulately to a strongly differentiated division of labour, and more
to the moral, emotional social relations appropriate to a distinctly
narrower social space presided over, created by, a central female
figure. It is conceived more in terms of an emotional and moral privatization than of a physical privatization. Lacking an architectural
correlate (which forbids adult kin males much participation, and
non-kin males [non-servants] of any), *griha* represents a state of
mind, an ideological venture propounding a conscious moral and
social being, rather than a functional place on earth. It is here that
self-consciously advanced moral (and social) projects of 'mothering' and 'conjugality' bloom, and it has to be 'achieved' through a
process of ideological clarifications, and conscious, practical socialization. *Griha* encapsulates the ideal type of moral harmony embedded in the lifestyle of the *bhadralok* (the western educated
urban gentry).

What these magazines bring out is the fact that this master
concept of the home, implying familial life surrounded by ideological clusters of a new social design and moral imperatives, provides the main destination of women's education. In Swarnakumari
Debi's reminiscences in "Sekele Katha" ("The Story of Yesterday"
or "Old Times") (1916), for example, we find a description of a
gradually vanishing *antahpur* being replaced by a more 'modern'
form. Concerned with women's education in premodern days,
Swarnakumari Debi offers us a view of life in the women's quarters
where even the selective nature of the topic does not shut out a
sense of everyday life. We catch a glimpse of a whole social domain
when she says:

> In our *antahpur*, in those days, reading and writing, like eating,
> resting and worshipping, were daily rituals among women. Just
> as every morning the milkmaid brought the milk, the flower-
> women supplied the flowers, and Deben Thakur came with his
> almanac and rolls of astrological charts, to foretell the daily aus-
> picious and inauspicious details, just so a bathed and purified,
> white-robed and fairskinned Baishnabi Thakurani appeared
> within the interior of the household radiant with the light of
> knowledge. She was no mean scholar. (Swarnakumari Debi 1916:
> 1114–24)

Or:

> I remember the days when the flower woman came to sell
> books—what a commotion it created in the women's quarter! She
> brought a few new books published in *Battala*—poetry, novels,
> tales of fantasy—and increased the size of sister's library. As in
> every room there were dolls, other toys, clothes, so there were
> books in trunks. When I grew up I thumbed through them.
> (1916: 1114–24)

This *andar* or *antahpur* simultaneously expanded and contracted and was focussed through the moral design of social reform
whose object was women. Swarnakumari Debi herself describes
this transition and links it to the return of her father Debendranath
Thakur, from the foothills of the Himalayas. Both the narrowing,
the centralization of the household from a social domain to a moral
design, as well as its expansion in breaking the segregation of the
inner/the outer, male and female world, become clear from her following statements. She begins by drawing the reader's attention to
Debendranath's stature as a "social reformer", not to be encom-
passed within the conventional view of him as a 'religious reformer': "We can testify to the fact that it is through him that women's
higher education received its foundation [in Bengal]. He was the
first to reform the custom of child marriage, and carefully attended
to the project of creating civilized clothing for women" (Swarnakumari Debi 1916: 1114–24).

Not content with that, he discarded the stone *shalagram*
and initiated everyone into the Brahmo religion, and:

> He also removed mean female rituals, prevalent through India,
> one by one from women's quarters. He invented a mature age of
> marriage . . . and put together a marriage ritual. From my mid-
> dle sister on all weddings in this household are performed in that
> way. When his infant daughters reached the proper age he started
> their education by using an improved method. He hired a *pandit*
> for us. After completing the second primer we began to learn San-
> skrit. 'Mems' [white women] started coming into the women's
> quarter.
>
> At the time when our household was being thus
> improved, Keshab Babu became my father's disciple. For the first

time, a non-kin male entered from the outside world, into the
women's quarter, unpenetrated by even the rays of the sun.
(1916: 1114–24)

It is evident that this evolution in the ideological–moral
dimension of the familial social space, as described by Swarnakumari Debi in its pre- and post- social reform phase, serves to
illustrate the difference put forward above between *andar* and
griha. It also spells out a new social division of labour, for example, in the male reformers' involvement with women's daily lives
and rituals, and an equally new relationship to *bahir*, which comes
into the house as adult kin and non-kin family members and white
women.

It is in a piece by Gyanadanandini Debi entitled "Stri Shiksha" (Women's Education), written in 1882, that we get the manifesto for women's education.[15] This advocates and displays the
good results of the desegregation of the sexes, that is, of a rigid
sexual division of labour, and shows how education is both the
cause and the result of this process. It elaborates an educational
content which incorporates affective–moral functions into
women's household tasks. Like Krishnabhabini Das, she also re-
defines and recodes the conventions of gender. In the extreme practicality of Gyanadanandini's itemization of education, we see the
construction of the home of the *bhadramahila* linen by linen, and
relation by relation. The principle of organization of the text,
which may seem rather eccentric because household chores and
conjugality are put on the same plane, becomes evident if we see
these chores also as moral/sentimental codes. Thus it is that she can
speak of the necessary companionship of the husband and wife, of
pleasing the husband with musical skills and child-rearing, in one
breath with tailoring, recipes, clothing and ornaments, nursing and
healthcare involving a knowledge of anatomy, physiology, hygiene,
chemistry, accounting and so on. This goes with Krishnabhabini's
previously quoted statement that women will not be worse home-
makers, mothers and wives, but rather much better, if they are
educated.

This construct of the *griha*, 'the home' (practically 'the
hearth'), is centred around, or radiates from, the construct of the

sentimental, educative mother who is one of the mother figures thrown up at this time. Her traits are those of the *bhadramahila*. She is not the *bibi*, the caricature of the educated/modern woman, but rather her reversal; a self-consciously fashioned figure from all the benefits of an education and cultural exposure, available in the new social context. Not diabolic or inverted, an image of the leaden times of *kali yuga*, masculinized through overstepping her 'women's domain' as depicted, for example, by Kalighat painters, she is instead sweet, moral, capable of reason and learning—a creator rather than a destroyer of homes. Through the new mode advocated by women themselves rises, in conjunction with their reforming male counterparts, an individual nurturer of the body and the sentiments. She builds 'character' on postulates of personal morality and psychology rather than, for example, a directly collective conduct of caste and class. In this scheme of motherhood, physical reproduction is socialized in a particular way, through a philosophy compounded of notions of sentimental education from England and Europe, theories of the German kindergarten education of Froebel, utilitarianism, and social darwinism, compounded by indigenous and foreign notions of the innate motherhood of women.

Along with this sentimental–educator mother is born 'the sentimental child' which subsequently becomes the basis of a whole literary genre of reminiscences, for example, Rabindranath Tagore's *Chhelebela* (Childhood) (1961). This construct of the child, individually nurtured by mother and mother nature, provides the basis of personal *bildungsroman*, of autobiographies. This child construct is male, and every female child is typed on 'the mother'. The required educational content for women (and girls) is directed at *his* developmental process. Krishnabhabini Das' essay on "Kindergarten" captures the essence of this mother–child relation and its educative content and mode. As she puts it, "mothers are the natural teachers" of (male) children, the real education of children begins at her knee (Krishnabhabini Das 1891b). The process begins from birth, and the distinction between education and socialization is obliterated:

> A child has an inkling of his mother's love or her nature through

his senses, and this love slowly enters into the child's half asleep soul as mother holds him to her bosom or puts him into his cradle with great care, and breast feeds him as soon as he wakes. In this way a mother's selfless love, joy and gratitude enters the child's soul and lays the foundation for a sacred, noble and exalted human nature. It is through this affectionate interchange of mother and son that a sense of the spiritual first awakens in the human [male] heart. (1891b)

Both Krishnabhabini and Gyanadanandini speak of the mother's educational role in terms of teaching to play, to sing and so on:

In mother's sweet and simple songs and games of house keeping are spent the child's three years. At four the child should go to a kindergarten. But of course where boys learn from their mother all of what the kindergarten could teach, for them their home is their school, they need not go anywhere else. (Krishnabhabini Das 1891b)

The above passages should be explored with regard to changes in the mode of physical and social reproduction as conceived in *griha* and its contrast with the ways of *antahpur* or *andarmahal*. To begin with, it speaks to a single female nurturing figure, a biological parent, personally, daily, engaged full-time in child-raising. This individually-based duo of mother and child is remote from child-raising in the context of a joint family where the care of children is done by different female kin figures—grandmothers and aunts, older female siblings and cousins of various sorts. It is interesting that no allusion is made here to these sources of nurture and socialization which actually existed in everyday life. They also do not refer to the fact that childhood in Bengali upperclass/caste homes is also highly dependent on female and male servants. The construct does not have any space for these extra actors on its ideological stage. It is the triad of mother, father (that is, wife and husband) and the child that is the icon of this 'holy family'. And of course all interactions are individualized.

In Sarala Debi's short autobiographical sketch of her childhood, we find this same approach to childhood, a time of growth read through the construction of individual nurturing and sentimental care, all embodied in the presence or absence of the mother (Sarala Debi 1906). Rabindranath speaks of a childhood spent in the domination of male servants and other male mentors as though it was his personal fate. But the text gives evidence of an ordinary daily life where not just he but all male children routinely grew up being fed, bathed and clothed in the inner quarters, returning there at night to sleep, while being inducted into a male life and conduct by older men. It would appear from his account of sufferings that there were other male co-sufferers. But Rabindranath, like Sarala Debi, read the workings of the division of labour between *antahpur* and *bahir* through the ideological lens of *griha*, a sentimental small unit, where a woman, the very same woman, is always involved in caring for (male) children. The interesting thing about Sarala Debi's account is that she also read her life among her siblings, the joint family nurture that she was provided with, through the same frame of missing a 'sentimental mother-care'. And she was unusual in that she demanded this care, the realization of the ideal type of nurture, which was put in place to raise boys. She, in that sense, was not the nurturer of the model, but the nurtured. And the most important thing from the point of view of social reproduction is precisely the fact that what these authors wanted and missed, and their actual experiences, indicate the difference between *andar/ antahpur* and *griha*, both in terms of ideology and practice. In fact, the concept of *griha* might have anticipated an embryonic form of nuclearization of urban middle-class families and its moral regulation, and captured a tendency of change in the pattern of social reproduction among the urban propertied classes. The *andarmahal/antahpur*, on the other hand, has no particular reference to the individual, in terms of his/her psychic, moral life. Rather, it comes across mainly as a 'domain', a physical/architectural correlate of women's social location within a general patriarchal mansion.

Since the organization of *andarmahal* and *griha* is both gendered and patriarchal, it is not surprising that the women writers display an ambivalence, bordering sometimes on antagonism, regarding both. On the one hand they deplore the segregation and what they consider to be the social unimportance of women in the former; on the other, they resent the Pygmalion-like role that men play in shaping the *griha* and its regulatory form, *garhastha*. In Gyanadanandini's "Stri Shiksha" (Women's Education) (1882), Swarnakumari Debi's "Strishiksha o Bethune School" (Women's Education and Bathune School) (1888) and "Sekele Katha" (1916), Krishnabhabini Das' "Striloker Kaj o Kajer Mahatya" ("Women's Work and its Value") (1892) , and articles submitted for essay competitions by women for *Bamabodhini* under the title of "What Advantages May Accrue Should Women's Education Become Common in this Country and What Disadvantages Result from Its Absence",[16] we find much evidence of this ambivalence regarding the segregated social space of the older division of labour and the new relatively fused one. In their constant reflection on 'then' (as *andarmahal* social organization seems a vanishing form) and 'now' (the '*griha*' of the new *bhadramahila*) they are at times nostalgic, or downright angry, about the loss of a domain for women which, they felt, held a relative autonomy of male non-interference. In an essay entitled "Amader Hobe Ki?" ("What Will Happen to Us?") Krishnabhabini Das projects such a resentment when she says:

> Even in terms of freedom our mothers and grandmothers lived in a better state. As everyone knows, Hindu women were in enclosure for a long time, but even so they had a full right to pilgrimages, worshipping at holy sites, and other religious rituals of religion, and travelling. But on account of this 'little or half education' we are about to lose this pleasure of our distinct [or separate] lives. Now Bengali young men are furious at the very mention of women's pilgrimages, they don't believe in worshipping 'dolls'. Well then, explain to them [women] why such things are bad, and what religion really means, and take them elsewhere and show them nature's beauty, and you will see in what a short space of time they rid themselves of superstition. (Krishnabhabini Das 1890a)

Her essay on "Swadhin o Paradhin Nari Jiban" ("Independent and Subjected Lives of Women"), Krishnabhabini Das (1888) repeats her accusations about male encroachments in all areas of 'modern' life as instructors and judges of women. Swarnakumari Debi's "*Shekele Katha*", while hailing the reforms

introduced by her father in the women's quarters, actually evokes
a nostalgia about the happy bustling women's world in her description of the bygone days.

But the other pole of this ambivalence is the forward-
looking overall thrust of their work. Upon scrutiny it begins to
become clear that this ambivalence comes from holding a subordinate location within both social/familial forms and regrets, not the
loss of the segregation but the loss of control/power women may
have over their own lives. In fact, the underlying standpoint of
women, along with an evolving class social/moral agenda, is that of
a quest for influence and power. In the final analysis they are not
positive about the little special power that women had in their
antahpur lives. Having once broken the older barriers, they do not
wish to be put back into a new form of male control. Thus education becomes the rallying cry—which coincides with the reforming
male demand—but women go beyond the prescribed male agenda
in demanding for women the full right to higher education, not just
the 'little learning' to serve the male purpose which is handed out
to women. Noticing the threat of the loss of 'self' that the new reorganization of social reproduction holds in the context of a steady
male redefinition of woman's life and work, Krishnabhabini wrote
about how a male-defined or patriarchal morality is being 'nor-
malized' and how women had to be content with the little learning
that they were permitted and faced continuous male criticism of
their unwitting ignorance. She pleaded for a higher, 'useful' education that would end women's *paranirbharata* (dependence on
others) and spoke thus about the male judges, censors and experts:

> Lately Bengali men have become completely puffed up in the
> arrogance of their education and civilization. They lecture every-
> where about *swatantrata* (independence/freedom/self-distinction)
> but, even in their dreams, they cannot conceive of the fact that
> the bud of national independence and civilization must first
> quicken in characters of that nation's individuals. How each par-
> ent treats his/her children, or young men their mothers, sisters
> and wives, tells us about that nation's civilization and progress.
> But if any other nation looks into our lives what will it say about
> the shameful things that exist in Hindu families, such as quarrels

between fathers and sons, between brothers, the general degradation of wives, all sorts of tensions within families? What will
happen to the young men's arrogance about their civilization and
education? (Krishnabhabini Das 1890b)

She echoes the sentiment of many of her peers when she says:

Whenever there is the talk of righting the wrongs of Hindu
women, and establishing their equality with men, many [men]
refer to the scriptures and speak of their status as the goddess
[Devi]. But where do we see any respect for this goddess?

No other young male of India shows such hatred (contempt), neglect, distrust, towards mothers, wives or sisters, as
does the Bengali. (1890b)

This ambivalence about emancipation, about women
'coming out' and men 'coming in', is not from our point of view a
case of the 'reluctant debutante'. As mentioned before, not only
Krishnabhabini, in the essays mentioned above, or in "Karjya
Mulak Shiksha o Jatya Unnati" ("Useful Education and National
Progress"), but also Hiranmoyee Debi in her various social scientific articles and observations of Newnham College, where she studied, put forward a strong stress on making women's education a
'real' social and personal achievement, not simply an expression of
the new gentry's lifestyle—the aim being 'real emancipation', that
is, a degree of self-definition and social–familial control. Even
Swarnakumari Debi, while describing 'those days' so nostalgically,
in the end falls on the side of 'serious education', of philosophy,
spiritual thought, literature of the classic kind and so forth, which
came in with the new social mode and women's education. Women
such as these repeatedly stressed the need to go further rather than
retreat. But within their general class position, the gender struggle
continued.

All the women writers agree that this loss of domain is to
be recouped by extending to women 'real educational' facilities
which would provide them with the required information, morality and cultural practices to create an informed self, a good son and
a good home. The loss of the previous domain is to be counteracted
by women taking on some of what was considered the male part in

the division of labour, as mental producers. Neither *jenana* education nor *jenana* living are advocated as solutions for women's lack
of viability. It is also their genuine concern for women's intellect,
morality and authority which make them deplore these customs,
not just a submission to the patriarchal mode. And finally, not only
do women feel that they should have the right to 'come out' and
live in 'mixed company', but they also do not wish to do so in the
older feminine terms; rather, they set new terms and conditions for
their emergence and emancipation. The hearth-centric education
therefore held in itself this double-edge of containment and emancipation of women, typified by the mother figure, which contains
in itself simultaneously the sternness of moral authority and sweet
sentimentality.

These contrary dimensions of power and submission, of
sentimentality and moral education, intuition and rational investigation into the laws of nature (senses) are revealed at their best in
the essays on child education and child-rearing. They contain an
injunction for unqualified dedication to and love for the child, but
also forms of guidance and discipline. Texts such as Gyanadanandini's "Kindergarten" or Krishnabhabini Das' essay by the
same name, or her essay "Sansare Shishu" ("Child in the Family")
(1893), for example, are organized around the apt metaphor of the
gardener and her garden. Plant imageries, imageries of natural
growth, are accompanied by the image of a gardener that knows
and loves the nature of the plan, and cooperates with it intelligent-
ly 'for its own good' by pruning and otherwise gently directing it.
The mother is thus the first teacher to the child—who must know
better than the child what his real emotional and moral nature is,
and thus produce the finally desired result.

These essays on the mother's role in child-raising and education, while stressing sentiments, are materialist in their emphasis.
Discussing principles of human nature and reason, with the help of
Rousseau, Froebel, Helvetins and others, they posit a clear relationship between body and mind, senses and intellect, thus connecting physical reproduction with social, moral and intellectual
education. They discuss how knowledge arises in the first instance
from sensory impressions. Putting forward the proposition that
"whatever enters the mind is through the senses", they go into

details of toys, "to suspend a coloured ball or rattle over the child's cradle", to a series of games observed in detail which teach children while they delight and express the needs of the senses (Krishnabhabini Das 1893). Throughout, of course, the mother learns about the child and can trace in his developing lineaments the physiognomy of adulthood. Science combines with the intuition of sentimental education, and we find statements such as the following to that effect:

> As the embryo of a fully grown tree lies hidden in the seed, which in time becomes a huge tree with roots, as the seed of life within an egg matures into a bird with wonderful limbs and wings in the due course of time, so in the child or the infant lies the possibility of a whole human being. (Krishnabhabini Das 1893)

Though no one can go against this natural law and all that it implies, and here we see why social Darwinism attracts the highly educated Hironmoyee Debi, these laws of emotions, morality and intellect (of the whole human nature and the individual nature of the child) can be learnt about. Kindergarten philosophy and social Darwinism are both attractive because both theoretically and practically they offer the mother instructions in knowledge for child-rearing. Here, in the notion of instruction to the mother, we see a superaddition to the theme of maternal love and intuition. Though her 'natural' predisposition makes her the best teacher, she herself needs to be educated in moral philosophy and practical sciences for her precise job. While discussing kindergarten education at home, it is thought that: "A woman can effortlessly learn [Froebel's philosophy] and use this knowledge in a short time, and show great results. A child is the dearest treasure of the mother, who will be more attentive to and successful in his education?" (Krishnabhabini Das 1893). And, the thought continues in a peculiar blend of a naturalist and practical argument, it is in fact better to teach it all to her, because she shows a greater proficiency than "a most learned man". And "for a woman to be simultaneously a nurturer and an educator, she absolutely needs to acquire knowledge, which is produced by the type of mental cultivation that give her strength and help in this matter" (1893). This kind of logic that connects the natural with the moral/ intellectual, and places women centrally in the realm of social construction, is stated succinctly (and repeatedly) in the following statement:

> Nature has vested in women the responsibility for people's health, and their moral and mental health lie hidden within their physical condition. Therefore, it is only by understanding the laws or dictates of nature and following them that one can devise a design for children's physical, moral and mental health. (1893)

In this construct of motherhood, intuitional mothering combines with the attributes of a teacher, thus reworking a patriarchal service ideology into a still gendered but relatively autonomous and stern form. If loving is the attribute of a mother, then moral authority and discipline marks the teacher. This implies a permission for emotionality for both the mother and the child, as well as the practice of emotional discipline, which lies at the heart of morality. The pruning process of the gardener curbs excesses, develops the emotional life of the duo with discretion and judgment. The new education deplores corporal punishment, harshness and so forth, but achieves a restraining effect through a sustained and reasoned appeal to conscience and personal love. Gyanadanandini in "Stri Shiksha" offers an example of how to discipline a child, and points out in her discussion about 'children's games' (devised as a part of the educational plan by the instructors) the end in view, namely, social adjustment/norm induction (i.e. control) and discipline. The randomness of play is undercut by the fact that it is the parent or the school who decides when a game begins and ends, or what rules to follow: "Children must have much joy in these games, but they must obey the rules of the game and the school" (Gyanadanandini Debi 1882). Thus, "No one can join or break the game at will". Through this training process they are inducted into a 'gentleman's conduct'. Good manners, politeness, obedience, rule maintenance, thrift and so on, all fall within this province of the 'feminine' method of schooling. And of course this ideological venture of personal–moral education itself rests on another new ideological notion, that of the 'individual'. It presupposes a private realm of conscience, though in harmony with a social or a collective conduct.

The novelty and daring implied in this type of motherhood

(where women both consent to a gendered/patriarchal service role and turn it around to gain social control) and its attempt to recoup and expand a lost domain, while seeking to embody a moral authority, does not become fully evident unless we examine accounts of actual lives of women presented by various reformers as the point of departure for reform. Rammohan Roy's description of women as a physically abused household drudge,[17] Vidyasagar's portrayal of women's lives of continuous male repression, Rasasundari Dasi's (1868) description of her daily life and secret attempts at education, among many, show how radical an emphasis this insistence upon a teaching role provided.

But, of course, as with all ideologically interpellated agents, it was a *radical*, not a *revolutionary*, proposal. The women intelligentsia undercut their submission through reform, but the same gestures of reform further entrenched the conditions for their submission. This becomes clear when we remember that not only do women gain power by being delegated agents of class socialization as a whole, but they are engaged in a more ambiguous scheme in gender terms. While the mother–child figure can be expanded to include all men and women in an affective and educative relation, thus conferring on to the woman an adulthood and the man an infantilization, it is in the long run not as empowering to women as it may initially appear. In so far as such an ideology calls for women to be active participants, they gain an agency and a degree of self-definition of a socially regulatory role. But the tyranny of being governed by the needs of the child to be educated and moral to nurture the *bhadralok*, or heroic in order to nurture the heroic sons of Indian nationalism, all go to show the double-edged nature of such an ideologically interpellated form of subjectivity. In this connection, Sarala Debi's essays on women's conduct in the political context of nationalism provide the best examples of heroic subordinated selves of women. Gender controversies put forward by 'less political' women writers offer a far more radical stand than she, who accepts the male typologies of Bengali cultural nationalism (and of other Indian provinces), and seriously sets about promoting the myth of aryan hindu heroism, inventing and advocating hero-creating rituals for women. The ritual of *Virashtami* was mainly a support and morale-boosting for males rather than for women to be 'heroes' in their own right. But again, as with the educative role of women, this was also partially empowering to women, since a direct gesture to power is partly a gesture of power. This dilemma is emphasized in a negative form in an essay by Jasodhara Bagchi entitled "Representing Nationalism: Ideology of Motherhood in Colonial Bengal" (1990). In it, speaking of the construct of the mother goddess and the feminized ideology of Bengali nationalism, and their impact on the status of women in Bengal, she is forced to come to the conclusion that "it was ultimately a way of reinforcing of a social philosophy of deprivation for women. It was a signal for women to sacrifice everything for their menfolks" (Bagchi 1990: 70). She goes on to say: "The nationalist ideology, therefore, simply appropriated this orthodox bind on women's lives by glorifying it. This renewed ideological legitimacy made it even more difficult for women to exercise their choice or autonomy in the matter" (1990:70). Though the construct of the sentimental educative mother, unlike the goddess *Devi* or *Bangamata* typology, has more of an agency space for women in offering them a critical and active role of reason and moral authority, this statement holds some truth for it as well. Though the self-improvement and dedication of a highly educated mother does not call for self-sacrificing in any direct and explicit manner (which is why this is probably the most favorite typology for middle-class women), the boundaries between dedication and sacrifice are blurry in many cases.

Where these boundaries are most clearly drawn, among the women writers I explore, is in the works of Krishnabhabini Das. Sharing with others, male and female, a general urbanity and emphasis on the practical, daily dimension of this motherhood and mothercraft, her ideological position leaves room for an ego for women, a right to develop a 'self'. In this, she makes an efficient use of the openings that are to be found in the concept of a moral, educative mother, to escape from the first circle of patriarchal containment. In fact, it is the morality of complete self-abnegation preached to women, and the consequent male exploitation, that she deplores in the essay "Amader Hobe Ki?" ("What Will Happen to Us?") (1890a). Discussing *matrittwa* and *satittwa* (motherhood and wifehood) and their destructive use by the contemporary

middle-class Bengali young men, she comments: "But as the beautiful flower when put into a child's hand lies immediately torn in the
dust, as jewels are grounded to dust in the hands of a mad man, so
does that great virtue [woman's selflessness] lie trodden underfoot
when put into 'unworthy [man's] care'" (Krishnabhabini Das
1890a). She notes a growing misogyny among the males of urban
propertied classes, and a great hypocrisy among male reformers
who preach various virtues to Bengali women, including the forti-
tude and courage of Roman mothers. But she notes with sarcasm:
"Many Roman mothers such as Cornelia, pass in front of our eyes
among Hindu women, but how many Caiuses, or Tiberiuses, appear
in the midst of Bengali families?" (1890a) She attributes women's
selflessness to a forced submission to patriarchal ideology and economic dependence, and mentions the ease with which men gain control over, or possession of, women in Bengali society. After all:

> She [the wife] knows that the husband is the only recourse for a
> Hindu woman. Whether that husband is honest or dishonest,
> kind or cruel, he remains the object of a Hindu wife's worship.
> Following him is the foremost religious conduct enjoined to her.
> Probably just for that very reason ignorant, churlish young men
> return that bottomless love, devotion and faith, with such cruel
> arbitrariness. (1890a)

She turns the patriarchal notion of women as 'natural mothers' on
its head and uses it as the reason for the upliftment of women's
education: "That nature has given women the higher role of being
the 'mother of the world' is a notion that has to be understood in
its real meaning. To make it come true, so they truly live up to that
high calling, requires an equally advanced education." (1890a)

   This slide between self-sacrifice, self-dedication and self-
improvement is the range within which the various constructs of
nineteenth-century motherhood can be situated. Arguments, such
as those of the women educators and reformers (in tandem with
their male counterparts) or their antagonists, for or against a greater incorporation into a patriarchal mode, lean more towards one
pole than the other. But underlying this controversy is a basic difference, or manipulation, of an epistemology. We are confronted in
this with the classic mode of arguing by nature and reason, and

secondarily, with arguments relatedly based on the 'nature of women' and 'women as nature'. Educational philosophy for women was constructed on the basis of these initial epistemological convictions. The notion of the self-sacrificing mother rests on the premise of the 'natural motherhood' of women and an intrinsic, essentially feminine nature of the female psyche. This equation between women and nature, women as creatures of instincts, emotions and intuitions—rather than of rationality—was both positively and negatively valorized.[18] This created an ambivalence about women as both weak (frail and feminine) and strong (primal power). What kind of feelings or instincts women actually have, what their 'femininity' essentially consists of, and other related speculations filled the world of social thought. But what is apparent on the whole is that both pro- and anti-reform schools shared much in common by subscribing to some sort of a notion of argument by nature and the innateness of a gender-coded consciousness. Thus, reform and reaction shared a similar epistemology, though their different manipulation of the nature–reason binary determined their views on women's education. The special view of the 'feminine', with its core of motherhood, overdetermined whether women were educable or otherwise. Wherever the 'feminine' indicated the entire absence of the rational intellect, any principle of enlightenment was not super-added to emotions in order to create educational possibilities. But much of the argument for education of women came from simultaneously assuming their potential for reason and the notion of the instinctually feminine. It advocated a 'knowledge' which would both augment and correct the traits of femininity, namely, 'educe' their basic nurturing instincts. Often, there was a belief in a gender differential in the content and purpose of women's education which, however, was not universally or wholly accepted by all women educationists. Their social subjectivity took on here a double agency whereby they criticized and accepted, reinterpreted and added to a patriarchal epistemology.

The women reformers' epistemological participation in the themes of reason and nature shows that even though they share the basic premise of an essential femininity or the naturalness of women, they strongly hark back to the principle of reason as an

attribute of their general humanity. In fact, they perform a recon-
ciliatory gesture by implanting reason in nature, the intellect in the
senses, as is evident in the way they conceptualize the educational
growth of the child. They claim that women are 'natural' but that
'reason' is a sex-neutral 'natural' gift for both men and women.
Krishnabhabini Das, for example, develops this approach in her
polemic with an anonymous male critic who wrote in *Sadhana*
against her essay "Shikshita Nari" ("The Educated Woman"). In
"Shikshita Nari" she begins by addressing a pseudo-scientific biological argument for barring women from education, namely, that
women have a smaller brain. While her complicity with 'scientific
education' makes her unable to challenge the initial thesis, she
introduces a critical dimension from her interest in social psychology. She believes that social and mental activities have an effect on
the body:

> The smaller brain size among women is caused by the absence of
> education from primitive times to now. There is no doubt that if
> women received the same education as men, from the time of the
> creation to the present time, then their brains would have devel-
> oped equally with men. (Krishnabhabini Das 1891c)

She claims that the same would have happened to men had they
undergone the same experience.

In her reply to her critic she introduces the theme of nature
in a way that is advantageous to women, succeeding in denatural-
izing the arguments against women's education by giving once
more a critical social dimension to the position. She concedes the
value of 'feminine virtues' advocated by her male critic but goes on
to make her point:

> No thinking person can deny that woman's gentleness, inno-
> cence, modesty, etc. are admired everywhere. But no one respects
> a woman's ignorance. For this reason, a true education can only
> improve these virtues of women, rather than degrade them. . . .
> Therefore, when the critic of *Sadhana* says that nature has par-
> ticularly vested woman with a special function, an instinct and a
> drive, and made her "a denizen of home"—who would disagree
> with him? But, on the other hand, who would deny that though

nature has made woman a home-dweller, she has not endowed her with the instincts of a cage-dweller, or made her a creature who is permanently incarcerated? Therefore, when everywhere in the world, using this excuse of natural weakness, men wholly rob and control women, and continue to argue whenever the topic of women's education and independence is raised, then it does not require much intelligence to recognize the male selfishness and tyranny that lie at the bottom of women's incarceration. Since it is possible to torture people by inflicting on them both starvation or physical force, by preventing the natural exercise of their physical faculties or by repressing their emotional needs, a powerful group or a race can oppress another in both ways. (1891c)

From this position that she representatively held along with other women, Krishnabhabini wrote other essays, such as "Strilok o Purush" ("Women and Men"), "Karyamulak Shiksha o Jatya Unnati", "Sansare Shishu", and so on, wherein she claimed that whereas there are some special additions to be made for women, the fundamental educational basis for both sexes should be the same. She claims that: "Education is equally healthy for both sexes. Knowledge, and its pursuit, which fill a man's mind with good thoughts and intentions, is equally healthy for women" (1891c). Swarnakumari Debi's positive view of the educational changes introduced by her father corroborates Krishnabhabini's position. She points out the fact that Baishnabi Thakurani "was no mean scholar", and that:

> She even excelled in Sanskrit, and needless to say, knew excellent Bengali. Above all, she had a wonderful ability to describe, and charmed everyone by her recitations. . . . Young newly weds, married daughters learnt from the Baishnabi, but the unmarried girls went together to the gurumahashay's *pathshala*. It may not have done much else, but laid the foundations for learning for girls and boys on the same principle. (Swarnakumari Debi 1916)

She speaks with great admiration of one of her mother's aunts for her interest in serious, philosophical and classical education (along with readings in lighter literature—novels and fantasies), and of the education introduced by her "esteemed" father, who brought male

and classical education into their *antahpur* and who, not content
with the *jenana* education imparted by *pandits* and white govern-
esses, sent his daughters to Bethune School. She particularly prized
the fact that he "enriched his family's store of learning, especially
by polishing the intelligence, knowledge, and religiosity, of the
inhabitants of the women's quarters, by advising them on 'true'
religion, spirituality, conduct, and at times by speaking about
science in a simple language" (1916).

These details argue for a reliance on the universality of
reason while showing how women can use reason for self-develop-
ment and definition, and use it, as in the following quotation, to
make a practical, domestic contribution. This passage argues that
an education meant for males and economic viability is also needed
for the home. The formulation pushes motherhood and the home
to the border of the public domain.

> Many are unwilling for women to learn affairs of administration.
> According to them, habits of work are needed only for shop-
> keeping and running offices. There is [supposedly] no need for
> that kind of education in the little lives of women in their little
> homes. But if we pause a while, we see that management, habits
> of accounting, etc., are indispensable in smaller and larger affairs
> of life. . . . In this there is no difference between running a home
> or an office or shop. This cannot be done with little knowledge
> and intelligence. Like all other serious responsibilities running a
> home requires controlling family affairs, maintaining order and
> accuracy—hard work, thrift, frugality, skill and judgement.
> (Krishnabhabini Das 1891c)

This reinterpretive enterprise concerning the concepts of
motherhood and the home, in the first place, expands women's
work of humanizing (*manush kara*) their children to themselves on
a basis of universalism. Then it is pushed by Krishnabhabini, for
example, to introduce the concept of 'women's freedom' (*stri
swadhinata*) and economic freedom as integral to humanization.
Though, as mentioned at the outset, the great injunction of the
Bengali primer which warns that only "Those who study will ride
in carriages or horses [or 'horse-drawn carriages']" does not wholly
apply to middle-class women, writers such as Krishnabhabini deem

it important for a woman's and a mother's dignity to be self-supportive in times of penury. Economic viability is recommended in the name of a moral and social independence and as a display of women's capacity rather than of poverty. Thus Hiranmayee Debi in "Newnham College" (1891b) and Krishnabhabini in *"Ingraj Mahilar Shiksha o Swadhinatar Gati"* ("English Women's Progress in Education and Independence") (Krishnabhabini Das 1891a) speak about women's career development. Of course, they are careful to link this achievement with a better motherhood and better home.

It is easy to see, then, in their negotiatory and adaptive ideological strategies, why the women educators or reformers did not find much use in even the powerful figure of the mother goddess. Since their project was both practically ethical and social, they could not look to this symbolism of an asocial, unpractical, mythic nature for any direction in concrete terms of social reproduction. Nor is this 'mother figure' a 'mothering' one in terms of her association with weapons and war rather than with a child in arms. It is understandable that a writer such as Sarala Debi, with her concern about national politics rather than the politics of reproduction, found the heroic, aryan version of the 'mother goddess' congenial, while the others in these magazines hardly allude to her in any important way. This abstinence cannot be read so simply in terms of a Brahmo influence, as it is the convention to do, since women of non-Brahmo background refrained from using it, while Sarala Debi, who used it herself, came from one of the oldest Brahmo families in Bengal. It is the fact that their central concern is the family, the home and motherhood, in a daily practical or reproductional rather than a symbolic or metaphoric way, which should be looked into for a credible explanation of the non-occurrence of this phenomenon which swept the world of male cultural nationalism. The domesticated, quasi-hindu, aestheticized version of this mother goddess, in the figure of *Bharatmata* (Mother India), did not fare any better in the negotiatory scheme. It is perhaps the urban–folk symbol of *Bangamata* (Mother Bengal) that to some extent shared the affect base with the new Bengali mother. But the critical educative and practical elements introduced by the typology of the sentimental educative mother only allow for a partial convergence. The basic construct of womanhood that underlies this notion of motherhood is, therefore, non-mythical, non-aestheticized or non-symbolic. It is, rather, a signifier, a configuration of a set of mundane, secular, urban and domestic social codes. The ideal woman type, the mother, is of the same world as the creator of the typology. The typology combines in one construct the woman, 'feminine' intuitions or insights, and principles of utilitarianism in her pursuit of practicality, with shadows of universal reason or enlightenment. She is 'feminine' but with a difference.

Looking for reasons that make this difference between a fully patriarchal view of motherhood and the view of writers such as Krishnabhabini Das, we cannot avoid realizing the presence of a gendered Victorian femininity and an equally Victorian utilitarian reform tradition which I have alluded to before. The cultural inflexions of Victorian England in the world of consciousness of the middle classes of Bengal constitute too expected and obvious a reality to deserve much attention. Many of the themes mentioned so far—'the individual', 'the child', 'sentimental education', 'mother educator' and so on—are to be commonly found in English literature and social thought, beginning from the late eighteenth century through the Victorian era; various developments of romanticism are expressed as continuous but unsettled relations between reason or rationality and emotions or intuition. Dickens' *Hard Times* is a powerful statement of this, while Mill expatiated on his total ethics by adding Coleridge (emotion/intuition/imagination) to Bentham (rationality/utility/practicality) (J.S. Mill 1966). To what extent these modes of thought influenced or created new thoughts among the colonial intelligentsia cannot be precisely indicated, but Gauri Visvanathan's *Masks of Conquest*, for example, or readings from contemporary literature, official documents and the growth of publishing, all indicate a diffusion and absorption of romantic and Victorian sentimental discourse and forms in Bengal. So, perhaps it is not an overstatement to say that educational projects in Bengal at this time were promulgated on the terrain of colonial discourse. "The gestures of enlightenment and reform", to quote Gauri Visvanathan, "co-existed or existed through colonial forms" (Visvanathan 1990: 69). As Bengali women expressed themselves often through the patriarchal Bengali mode, so they relied on certain 'colonial' concepts as well: their ethos at times was Victorian.

But to simply brand these women as colonial or creatures of patriarchy reveals neither the real complexities and contradictions implied in their ideological position nor indicates clearly the nature of class formation in Bengal. It is after all the case that class consciousness anywhere forms from available cultural symbolic presences in the environment and the social relations that they mediate. It is hard to think what else it could be if consciousness is socially produced and materially organized. Thus it is far more interesting to sidestep the notion of colonial discourse, which works so well to read the administrator but not the administered, and to instead show it as a common cultural element to which the women intelligentsia also hold an interpellative relation. As we found in the case of their relation to the male-stream social thought of the local male intelligentsia, so are they ambivalent with regard to the wisdom of the patriarchal Victorian world view: they are both moulded by it and resist it.

The figures of the Victorian lady and that of the Victorian woman reformer, the successful, economically viable, good homemaker American woman, the female intelligentsia of different colleges in prestigious English centres of learning, scores of emerging women white-collar workers and professionals, all these work as examples and mobilizing signifiers in the writings of these educationists. They allow for imaging the woman face of the new social relations of production. These images concretize the women intelligentsia's own role as both active agents and colonized interpreters. Their use of these as reference points and as inspiring anecdotes of the freedom of other women elsewhere is both a venue of expression of their own freedom and desire as women as well as being an acknowledgment of 'our' inferiority, of being organized as the 'other' while the frame is searching for the 'self'.

Thus, Victorian womanhood was adapted and absorbed with a double edge to it. There was that 'feminine' sensibility combined with refinement and sentimental predilections, but this was simultaneously undercut, most vigorously by women themselves, with utilitarian reformism—through the practical homemaker and the figure of an asexual, moral, forthright female educator for whom conjugality or mothering is less a pleasure than a duty. It is in fact in this depreciation of female sexuality, the insistence on constructing a manageable conjugal form which serves mainly men and male children and 'the home', in trading off intensity or passion as a woman for a sweet sexless and moral motherhood, that the Victorian influence is most effective. This sentimental utilitarian familial mode does not allow for any excess, especially for women, so deprived is it of any passionate or 'heroic' gesture and so full of emotional/sexual repression for both men and women. Domesticity, the hallmark of the little affective home, is its typical social form with which the women intelligentsia seem to be in a constant struggle, creating it as an extension of themselves while seeking to go beyond it in their arguments for women's independence and reason. In this matter, they use the utilitarian/enlightenment discourse and pick up their western examples less as a colonial self-castigation, but more as ways in which to undercut both local and colonial forms of patriarchy. In essays on the progress of European women there is no hint of any inherent inferiority or disability of Bengali or Indian women. The western educated woman stands as a realized example of the capabilities of all women.

Where women are criticized for being dependent on colonialism for their concept of 'freedom' as women, that is, by being seen to function as an anti-nationalist force, one can only point out the basically orientalist and colonially patriarchal nature of Bengali cultural nationalism. Though it engaged in various transferences and inversions, it grounded itself discursively in colonial discourse. Historians such as Uma Chakravarti and Sumit Sarkar remark on various aspects of this phenomenon, for example, the hinduization and aryanization of this nationalism.[19] And yet the colonial nature and orientalism of this discursive space does not create much trouble for men, whereas the use of European ideas and attitudes by women earn the epithets 'anti-national', 'anti-patriotic' and 'imitators of the west' for women. It is here that nationalism cannot wholly contain the implications of social reform for women even where it supports some formal education for them. The point of conflict rages not around the fact that women 'come out', or that they are literate and so on, but against the very terms and conditions for their own emancipation that women such as Krishnabhabini present. The fragile masculinity of Bengali middle-class males, 'feminized' by the colonial relations and discourse, felt fundamentally threatened by the epistemologies, social views and demands of such women, and saw them as emasculators.[20]

This threatened response is in the end quite predictable, given that women use European material with a principle of selection and, as such, choose anti-patriarchal ideas and practices and as often as not point out the gender struggle in the colonizer's society. Their admiration for the Victorian code of chivalry and social refinement never constitutes the very core of their adaptation of utilitarian or enlightenment ideas of education, self-improvement and homemaking. The resentment against the misogyny and private gender malpractices of male nationalist figures or reformers is not only a proof of admiration of a colonized nation for customs of their foreign masters and mistresses.

One cannot end a discussion about the relationship between women's emancipation, education and nationalism without pointing out the same ambivalent relation here as in other areas of social subjectivity of women. Here too there is a tension between becoming a subject in and through an ideology which is both inspirational and circumscribing. *Stri swadhinata* (women's emancipation) is an accompanying part of the call for national emancipation, for the conceptual space of the discourse of *swadhinata–paradhinata* (subjugation) underlies the women's gender struggle as well. To respond to the call of the nation [male], to be socially and nationally useful, to be the 'mother of the hero', the 'mother of the race', coincides with women's need for an active social agency. And yet, as the word 'freedom' is increasingly foregrounded, it becomes apparent to women how concepts such as *satittwa* and *matrittwa* can bring women back into the patriarchal fold. There remains always a tension between achieving full subjectivity as women and as class members. Nationalism, with its gender codes and patriarchal relations, though newly configurated, activates the moral–cultural code of class hegemony.

Conclusion

From the twists and turns of adaptive and negotiatory strategies sketched above, it should be obvious that we can come to no conclusion regarding the ideological position of the writers explored without stating, first and last, the impossibility of establishing one, single, unified, monolithic consciousness for each class. Not only is it impossible because mental spaces are constructed from invisible but powerful, uncountable sources, recreated and created in such various forms and contents, but also because a class itself is never, even objectively speaking, a solid, one-piece entity. It is a fragmented entity from within. Whereas each fraction within the class may hold the same relation to the means of production, or a place in the ruling apparatus, its subjective and objective social existence is fractionalized and fractured. Antonio Gramsci's "Notes on Italian History" (1971), for example, outlines one possible political formation on the basis of such fractionalized existence, and shows some of the ways and needs for homogenization or unification in the course of Italian bourgeois development. Marx's discussion in *The Eighteenth Brumaire* (1963) also speaks of fragmentation, fissures, ruptures and attempts to eliminate and/or negotiate them, which is the sum of a political process. As pointed out by writers such as Asok Sen, Partha Chatterjee and others, Bengali nationalism shows numerous fragmentations and negotiatory containment and formative strategies.[21] It is worth remembering that the same or similar relations to the means of production, and the same or similar existence in the terrain of colonial capitalism, did not produce an invariant, solid ideological position. The ideological range extends from secular economic and utilitarian liberalism to hindu revivalism, wherein secularists can coexist with or participate in religious cultural forms and the hindu revivalists can support economic liberalism and use positivism for their argument's presentation.

The difficulty of pinning down the elements of any ideological mode is further complicated for Bengal because of the type of class formation or lack of clear differentiation which colonialism dictated. In the world of post-1793 (Permanent Settlement) Bengal, class fusions, their general retardation, the fusion and distinction between the country and the city, the colonial and local, popular and elite, the cultural interface, all go towards the making of the most divergent class subjectivities within which there are formations that compete and seek to dominate each other. As a corollary to this indeterminacy there is the peculiar nature of the propertied classes in Bengal which are, like Janus, two-faced—ruled and ruling. Whereas the coercive aspect of the colonial discourse is remarked upon, one should also note that in a society with such a highly developed hierarchy in mental and manual labour, the local elite discourse also *voluntarily* took to a foreign elite discourse. There was a convergence of aims and views which were not simply 'imposed' on the colonized. A society that was hierarchical (caste/ class), patriarchal and familiar to empires and the military, with developed forms of commercial capital, with an organized elite (both hindu and muslim), did not exactly need to be inducted into 'the command of language and the language of command'.

These notes about the general formation of ideology or the Bengali colonial context are important for us in our assessment of the position of the women writers. Their consciousness is elaborated in the same terrain and shares the same common sense of both absorption and submission, resistance and subversion. We see in the above discussion how they share a base with both reformers and revivalists, working within a colonial, and a local, patriarchal social mode. But what is significant about them is this added double-edged dimension of resistance to patriarchy while sharing at the same time a colonized space with their male counterparts and putting the middle class's homes in order. It is the 'difference' that marks their acceptance of 'motherhood' and 'femininity', while their experience as colonized people marks the way they manipulate colonial cultural elements. This double relation stamps their social agency and textures the organization of their thought. There is obviously no denying the 'westernization' of their consciousness. It may also be remarked that the strand of thought we have examined here is peculiar to a Brahmo–Victorian combined ethos. And it is also inferred, as it was by members of the male nationalist intelligentsia of the time, that it is wholly anti-nationalist. But again Gyanadanandini in "Ingraj Ninda" (Blaming the English) or Krishnabhabini in "Bilat Bhelki" (The English Trick) perform an interesting feat when they point out that there is no need to blacken all of the western civilization and to valorize all aspects of ours, but rather to search eclectically for what we can take from 'them' in order to develop our own culture and economy and get on with the main business of moving towards a 'genuine independence'. This is an example of the adaptive strategy which is to be found in the case of the main theorists of Bengal's cultural nationalism as well. Such an attitude is a product of, and holds a project for, the here and now, allowing for an overall 'modernity' along with a reinterpreted 'tradition' and a reworking of English and European rationalist thought.

In the cases of both the male and female intelligentsia we see the birth of social subjectivities which have absorbed into their own making many indigenous cultural forms as cultural lineaments of the colonizers. Of course, the values, symbols and epistemologies that are thus culled and reorganized do not fuse perfectly. Signifiers continue to have their lives in the domain from which they were culled unless undercut and mixed thoroughly in the new project. They can, and do, often pull away into unintended directions. The Victorian woman, at times, can and does overdetermine the construct of the Bengali *bhadramahila*. But what is of greater importance to us is the general direction through (not to) which this educational ideological venture moves. It keeps a balance, a fine tension between speaking as and for a (gendered) class, as well as 'women'. It seeks to redefine gender codes, expressing new relations of social reproduction while striving towards a relative autonomy by using the concept of 'individual freedom' as a sub-set of 'national freedom'. Finally, it appeals to the notion of 'humanity' as a form of legitimation and destination for the whole project.

In this interpellated ideological form neither patriarchy nor the gender division of labour is discarded but is rather redefined and displaced in such ways as to mediate the emerging new social relations and to form a new ideological cluster. As class agents, the summoned subjects, the women intelligentsia are active 'modernizers' and inventors of 'tradition'. Their domain, however, is social reproduction rather than social production, and they help to crystallize an ideology of 'home', womanhood and a type of motherhood, all of which serve as complex social and emotional signifiers working with desire and practical needs. Even to this day, and especially now, it is this cultural–symbolic cluster to which domestic capital and consumer advertising cater in a promise to make a dream come true. Both the exhortatory and practical articles testify to this concern and the ability of women to transform and organize social mediation through the family form. The transformation of the *andarmahal/antahpur* into *griha*, the emergence of the *bhadramahila* as a mother and a conjugal partner, even when captured at a conceptual level through an organization of the common sense of the propertied classes into an ideology, both anticipate and mark the moment of advent of a 'modern' society where women and men can overstep the older sexual division of labour. In this new construct and proposed mediation women can 'come out' and be 'public' and men can 'go in', and yet the psyches and social relations become increasingly more individualized—that is, privatized and personal.

Lest we substitute a history of ideas and glimpses of social life for the real history of how people actually live, and forget how grey is 'the twilight zone' of their common sense, we can only remind ourselves that what we are dealing with is a *construct*, a *category* for interpreting reality, 'trimming off an epoch in history'. We have attempted to merely highlight an aspect of class formation in terms of consciousness and social reproduction with an emphasis on the hegemonic. We have tried to show the formation of a normative agenda put together selectively from the common sense of the urban propertied classes of colonial Bengal, and sought to illustrate how they are cathected to their social ontologies, concretely put forward as reform projects.

Marx in *The Communist Manifesto* introduced a notion that he did not elaborate upon. It is that of the "hidden struggle" of classes (Marx and Engels 1984: 15). In *The Civil War in France* (Marx 1933) or *The Eighteenth Brumaire* (Marx 1963) we see its elaboration and historicization through the depiction of class struggle that happens 'within' and not just 'between' classes. In the language of Gramsci and the Gramscians this could be understood as hegemonic fractionalism. This fractionalism is as much an 'objective' aspect of class formation (for example, different stages or aspects of capital) as it is the subjective foundation for how people make their history. In this sense the realms of ideology or common sense, that is, the cultural dimension of social reproduction, are as much a site for class politics as is the world of social–economic production. The conquest of civil society, as Gramsci points out, is the conquest of the hearts and minds of the people. This is the formation of consensus on which ruling rests. It is this that provides the 'moral regulation' that is institutionally and daily elaborated and sought to be implemented. Social agencies arise from within this 'moral regulation' and work with and against it. If we reconsider what the women's magazines have to say in this light, then what we have to say about the social subjectivity and agency of women in the context of education (social reform) points to a whole range of possibilities of cooperation and antagonism. Possibilities open and close at the same time. In fact, the dynamic is such that one might say that often they open in order to close, to take in seemingly disparate elements, whose absorption offers bonding possibilities with others of different positions. They are the communicative competence of the central ideological position—as, for example, the different typologies of motherhood, their submissive and subversive elements, signal to each other. But it is equally impossible to see this ideological enterprise as fully intentional, with a blueprint from its birth. All we can say is that in their ventures of self-creation, which involves discovery and compromise, writers such as Swarnakumari Debi, Gyanadanandini Debi and Krishnabhabini Das, in particular, bring to the fore social topics structured in such current symbolic, conceptual terms, that wider and wider circles of women can speak to each other in at least partially meaningful ways. An example of this is surely the overlapping discursive worlds of the middle-class hindu and muslim women. Writers such as Begam Rokeya, for example, in the magazine *Nabankur*, speak of the same topics, though with a specific concern for the realities of muslim women's lives, and share a very similar discursive space.

The ideological success that this social reform enterprise initiated a long time ago, in terms of hegemonizing the consciousness of the present-day Bengali middle-class women, can perhaps be guessed if we look at the current epistemological and ideological substructure of welfare policies and practices regarding women. Much of what structures even today the paraphernalia and attitudes towards education, social work, and even some aspects of feminist politics and thought, derives from the typology, subjectivity and form of agency constructed in the pages of these eminently perishable magazines a long time ago.

Notes and References

[1] K. Sangari and S. Vaid say something similar: "Middle-class reforms undertaken on behalf of women are tied up with the self-definition of class, with a new division of the public from the private sphere and of course with a cultural nationalism" (1989: 9).

[2] Here the term 'common sense' is used in the sense in which Antonio Gramsci formulates it in *The Prison Notebooks*; see, e.g., his use in "The Study of Philosophy" (1971: 323–33). Gramsci considers this as the general state of consciousness in the everyday sense—pre-scientific, pre-ideological. It is a kind of 'political unconscious'.

[3] Gramsci (1971: 105–20).This speaks to the development of what Gramsci calls "the equilibrium of political forces" where the ground is moving towards a readiness for a politico–military hegemony by transforming the cultural–social domain.

[4] This concept is ubiquitous in Gramsci's work. The whole of *The Prison Notebooks* (1971) may be read in terms of the definition, refinement, complication and assumption of hegemony. Gramsci's use of this Machiavellian (and older) concept is marked by his understanding of ruling or power that lies in building 'consent' which provides 'legitimation' at a moral and social level.

[5] See M. Borthwick (1984: 60–108) on women's education and the role of magazines in this process. Borthwick gives statistics and tables showing the extensive spread of female education (1984: 76–80).

[6] See especially the chapter on "Elite Culture in Nineteenth Century Calcutta" (1989: 147–48).

[7] While presenting how ideology interpellates individuals as subjects, Althusser states: "I shall then suggest that ideology 'acts' or 'functions' in such a way that it 'recruits' subjects among individuals (it recruits them all), or transforms the individuals into subjects (it transforms them all) by that very precise operation I have called interpellation or hailing and which can be imagined along the lines of the most commonplace everyday police (or other) hailing, 'Hey, you there!'" (1984: 48).

[8] See P. Chatterjee 1990.

[9] See P. Corrigan and D. Sayer (1985). This book offers an extremely useful demonstration of the moral dimension to the study of state formation. This same approach is also very useful for aspirations to hegemony as well.

[10] See the chapter on ideology in R. Williams (1979).

[11] See chapter 2, "The Thematic and the Problematic," in P. Chatterjee (1986).

[12] "It is in the shifts, slides, discontinuities, and unintended moves, what is suppressed as such as what is asserted, that one can get a glimpse of this complex movement, not as so many accidental disturbing factors but as constitutive of the very historical rationality of its [nationalism's]

process" (P. Chatterjee 1986: viii). See also S. Kaviraj's discussion on 'liminality' in the works of Bankim Chandra Chattopadhyay (1995).

[13] 'Hindu revivalism' should be considered as another orientalist inflexion of nationalism, another construct, which means something very particular by the word 'Hindu', and certainly the concept of 'revivalism' screens the fact that this is an 'invention of tradition' (E. Hobsbawm and T. Ranger 1983). With this awareness in mind, I use this expression simply as a conventional code word signifying the selective use of 'Hinduism' as a part of the nationalist ideology.

[14] See P. Chatterjee 1990. The abeyance of the women's question is not a failure of liberal thought for this author, but "nationalism had in fact resolved 'the women's question' in complete accordance with its preferred goals" (237).

[15] See also Gyanadanandini Debi (1884).

[16] See *Bama Racana Competition*, "Edeshe Stri Shiksha Samyak Prachalit Na Howatai ba kiki apakar haitechhe?" *Bamabodhini* (1866) (B.S. 1292).

[17] "At marriage the wife is recognized as half of her husband, but in after-conduct they are treated worse than inferior animals. For the woman is employed to do the work of a slave in the house, such as, in her turn, to clean the place very early in the morning, whether cold or wet, to scour the dishes, to wash the floor, to cook night and day, to prepare and serve food for her husband, father, mother-in-law, sister-in-law, and friends and connections" (R. Roy 1820: 126).

[18] A discussion of these different aspects of 'motherhood' and their ideological implications is presented in J. Bagchi's article (1990). She notices an invention and continuity in this tradition of symbolization through constructs of motherhood of different kinds. She also points out something which is equally tenable for the construct I deal with, namely, that these are 'public' politico-symbolic enterprises, not 'private' existing realities.

[19] Here we need to look at U. Chakravarti's essay, where she speaks about identity formation for "the nationalist cause", and the difficulty of constructing an "alternative identity" for women "given the need for a different kind of regeneration that was necessary in her case" (1989: 50). There was no "single or coherent model", hence the 'Spiritual Maitreyee' 'Superwoman' aryan construct.

[20] See T. Sarkar on this threat to masculinity. Sarkar shows how hindu men perceived the hindu marriage (and by extension the family) as the "last unconquered space" and also how "sensitive and fragile this structure was" (1995a: 1).

[21] See Sen (1977) on class formation and forms of consciousness and ideology, and also V.C. Joshi (ed.) (1975).

Re-Generation
Mothers and Daughters
in Bengal's Literary Space

My marriage occurred at the age of twelve. I knew nothing of this matter until now. One day I had gone to bathe at the pond, and there were many people there. Upon seeing me one of them said, "Whoever gets this girl will be really gratified, they [may] have wished for [such a girl] for a long time." Another said, "Lots of people are coming to take her [away], if [she] is given they will take her away instantly. [But] her mother does not [give her]." Then another added, "It will not do to not give [her away]. She has to be given to someone. [Otherwise] it is useless to be a woman."

Hearing these things I began to feel very sad and upset. I was utterly bewildered. Afterwards, I went home and said to my mother, "Mother, if someone wants me will you give me away?" My mother said, "Bless you! Whoever told you that I will give you away? Where did you hear all this? How can I give you away?" Saying this my mother went into her room, wiping her tears. The moment I saw that my mother was crying, my soul flew away. Then I knew for certain that my mother would give me away to someone. Then it was that my heart broke into pieces. I thought, what has happened? Where will my mother put [send] me?

Rasasundari Dasi, *Amar Jiban* (My Life) 1868

This essay was first published in *Proceedings of 'The World My Mother Gave Me' Conference*, ed. Mandakranta Bose, University of British Columbia, 1999.

Introduction

The legacy of our mothers is an ambiguous and elusive one since, generally speaking, our mothers are or were not in a position to give us much of the world which mostly lay beyond their reach. And yet they did give us something of that out-of-reach world in the shape of an intense longing for it. And they gave us the local everyday world, of homes and interiors, a world of women and children. But it is this out-there elusive world which drew us as it drew them, since we came out of their womb, inscribed with the same longing for space, activity and movement in time (history) and for an effective, transformative presence.[1] Our inheritance from our mothers, then, is not of property, the physical–economic ownership of any part of the world, since only the patriarch can provide a patrimony. Instead, it is a longing for becoming, for a creation of ourselves, and an entitlement to discover, to recreate what surrounds us. This inheritance is a desire for sculpting a woman through the creative efforts of successive generations. This woman is sculpted by many lives of mothers and daughters, one taking up the task from the last one. This does not have to be, often is not, a conscious decision, but lived movements of and through history, of women designing, rewriting their 'selves', embodying the stories of being and becoming.

Since our mothers' gift of the world is so ambiguous and unsettling, given through both limitations and strivings, how can we relate to this mother and her gift? Do we resent or blame her for not having much by way of property to give us, for the struggles that lie in store in seeking to become, for passing on these unsettling longings? Do we also not love her with an undying love, for both what she does give us and could not, as we carry this longing for our selves and the world, all our life, in our very being?

How can we not, as we are 'of woman born' and not Athenas springing forth fully armed from the brow of a male god (Rich 1976)? Even Freud knew of this ambiguity and of the ambivalence of emotions in the mother–daughter relationship, but he caught hold of only one end of the equation. Even for him it was evident that lying sideways, as this relationship does, to the potentially resolvable oedipus complex, the female psycho-sexual development into adulthood carries the mother in us through our lives in one form or another.² She remains our point of departure, as a bedrock of sorts, of our being. Our own trajectory of becoming both shapes her and distances us from her. Thus we remain all our lives in a complex formative relationship with our mothers, and also with ourselves as actual and potential mothers of daughters.

The everyday world of women, of mothers and daughters, even of the propertied classes, has been everywhere largely outside of written history.³ It is an embedded world where nature and nurture blur. It is an ephemeral, ever-changing world of spoken words and lived lives, as with peasants and others who live a daily, physical/manual life of social production and reproduction. Thus women too have been 'a people without history' until recently.⁴ Like the inside of the earth with its innumerable layers, colours and hardnesses, with its own evolutions and revolutions, it needs a geologist of a historian to tell the stories of women's worlds. Or maybe our writers are archaeologists who reconstruct women's history from buried artefacts and other traces of living, from objects made and consumed—a history of material life. Thus folklorists, ethnomusicologists, historians of handicrafts and so on have traced the presence of women in history, their world. It would seem that this humble world of daily life, of orality, continues when and where we least expect it, appearing in this or that practice, form and meaning. It is only in the last few decades that women are taking their place in official history, mostly through the labour of feminist historians doing their work in areas of histories of families, sensibilities, moral regulation and sexuality, private lives, and limitedly, through work on social and political movements.

In this situation of late and slow revelation in the realm of history, where can we look for and find our mothers? In this bifurcated world that we still inhabit with male visibility and female invisibility, the best place so far is to be found in the realm of the arts. Literature, extended to include other forms of textualities than fiction, drama and poetry, including letters, memoirs, autobiographies and biographies, offers the richest resource so far. It is in the literary space that women narrate, fictionalize, project their complex and contradictory reality.⁵ Unbounded by factuality, having the room to use the symbolic at its fullest, extending its domain through the polysemiosis of metaphors, dipping into orality, literature has provided us the richest source for exploring the world our mothers gave us.

In this chapter I examine five literary texts by three Bengali women for the purpose of exploring both the mother–daughter relationship and the self-making of women. These include an auto-biography and four autobiographical novels, all of which have characteristics of *bildungsroman* or growing-up stories. The texts are *Amar Jiban* (My Life) by Rasasundari Dasi (1868); a trilogy by Ashapurna Devi comprised of *Pratham Pratisruti* (The First Pledge) (1964), *Subarnalata* (1966) and *Bokul Katha* (Bokul's Story) (1973); and *Nabankur* (The Seedling) by Sulekha Sanyal (1956). These are inter-generational stories in which women, both mothers and daughters, engage in their promised undertaking of fashioning themselves as adult subjects who are effective to some extent in changing their own lives and society. They mark a journey from the inner quarters of daily and biological reproduction to the outside world. They speak of generation and re-generation.

A World Apart: Sexual/Social Division of Labour and Interiorization/Incarceration of Women

The texts which I explore range from the nineteenth cen-tury to the 1960s. It would be interesting to know which of the social norms and forms pertaining to women, family lives and households of the propertied classes of Bengal which are depicted in them date back from precolonial times, and which are colonial constructions. Very little, in fact, is written about the continuation or reconstruction of precolonial social forms, creating the impre-ssion that colonialism radically changed most of the social mores of the propertied classes in Bengal. In the related areas of social subjectivities and cultural production, gender identities and social organization of families and households, colonialism is said to have introduced major renovations, if not even an absolute break with the past (Chatterjee 1990).[6]

Precolonial social organization and moral regulation are most often spoken about in terms of the reform–(hindu) revivalist controversy where the older, 'traditional' mores or social organiza-tion were pitted against each other as better or worse for 'the nation', that is, for the families of the gentry of Bengal. The 'new woman' typology (*nabina*) and the older, precolonial one (*prachina*) respectively signify households where women were in the inner quarters or present outside of them. But that question of what was good for the family or 'the nation' has now been surpassed by contemporary scholars and rephrased as what was 'good' for women themselves. Several Bengali scholars, mostly male, have offered the thesis that a greater or better social space existed for women themselves in precolonial Bengali society, which colonialism/modernity curtailed or distorted. These scholars have advanced the possibility that precolonial feudalism held greater social freedom and cultural autonomy for women.[7] To what extent is this a feasible view?

My reading of these women's texts puts a large question mark around the claims of these critics. Though it is difficult at the present stage of social history writing to fully recover an actual way of life from older times or from autobiographical–fictional narratives, some recovery is still possible. A continuity of older social forms and norms may be discerned in their pages, along with changes brought about by responses to the new times which seem to call for their adaptation or rejection.[8] The older norms which are in question do not seem to be particularly positive for women when they are depicted by women themselves. A good example is a book such as Rasasundari Dasi's *Amar Jiban* (1868), whose life covers a long period, between 1806–1900. Colonial or modernist reform projects or nationalist responses to them are singularly marginal factors for her. Well into her middle age when she writes the autobiography, she seems to inhabit an undisrupted familial–social world, and whatever changes for women seep into her world are portrayed as tenuous. She herself extends approval to them and some envy regarding the reform projects for girls' education, including wearing of shorter veils and being allowed into "mixed company" or the public.

Written much later, Ashapurna Devi's trilogy extends over three generations of women and begins its narrative in the very last part of the nineteenth century. The novels organize themselves temporally and also spatially through a movement from the countryside to the city of Calcutta. Having arrived, they mostly stay in the city, with occasional detours. In spite of the difference in time,

Ashapurna's rural and urban social and family settings and mores
are remarkably similar to Rasasundari's. That this was not just a
literary convention is verifiable from other biographies of women
and literary/historical sources. Ashapurna Devi, born more than
100 years after Rasasundari, depicted a similar kind of social life in
the first two parts of her trilogy as that described by her predece-
ssor regarding Bengal's propertied classes. The patriarchal, hierarchical, intensive gender organization of the family, the condition of
widows, relationships of power among family members, and a rigid
division of the worlds of production and reproduction construct
her narrative world. Sulekha Sanyal, who was born even later,
shares this same space with her, with some modifications. This is
the world of women that reformers sought to change and which
did change to some extent as India moved through various socio-
economic and political stages, from a colonized country to a capitalist democracy after 1947. Serving as a baseline from which
women's journey into self/personhood must be measured, the older
world which kept women and men in their separate domains continued to be carried forward into the new one that was emerging.
Sulekha Sanyal's *Nabankur* is no different from Ashapurna's trilogy in this respect. The journey is again from segregation and inte-
riorization to the outside world, and perhaps to a new moral space
which is a fusion of both.

Themes of sexual–social segregation and of a rigid sexual
division of labour in all their ramifications are perhaps the core of
all the texts that I have studied. This severely binary organization
of every aspect of social–moral life, of households and family lives
into masculine and feminine, encompasses all levels, from the economic to the personal. This binary social organization is simultaneously a complex of structural relations as well as the ground for
female (or male) subjectivities and agencies. It is important to note
that this organization of the social into the public and the private,
the world and the home, indicating separate spheres of conduct
and activities for men and women, is considered by subaltern historians and scholars, such as Partha Chatterjee, as a nationalist 'resolution' of not only 'the woman question', but of nationalist male
elites coming to terms with colonialism.[9] In this view the binary
arrangement of the home and the world provides a mechanism for

creating a protected space where colonialism cannot enter. This unconquered and thus non-violated world of women and children is the nationalist male's sphere of rule. This, according to Chatterjee and others, gave rise to the new middle-class males' strategies of management and moral regulation of family life in the nationalist context. What they forget to mention is that this is the conduct proposed even by those males who otherwise served the colonial system. That is, being anti-reform was no guarantee of being 'nationalist'.

This observation regarding the nineteenth-century family form in the colonial context seems convenient and plausible, except that the same severely binary form is alluded to as a basic condition of women's lives by Raja Rammohan Roy in his arguments against *satidaha*.[10] The time he speaks of is before the emergence of the colonial gentry with their colonially emasculated selves (see Sinha 1995). The *andarmahal* or *antahpur*, also known as the *zenana*, the inner quarters of women of propertied–feudal classes, seems to have been an entrenched formation just as much as the *bahir*, or the public, was the domain of men, of the economy, of political and overarching religious–moral dictates. This social division was also embodied by architectural designs indicating segregation of both sexes, and containment or domination of women in the form of interiorization/incarceration. These feudal enclosures continue to express the new semifeudal–colonial bourgeois sense of family 'honour' where wealth is present and adapted to middle-class, less affluent lives. In this world of 'honour' a woman's public presence continues to be an inversion of the norm, just as a male presence would be in the kitchen, in childbirth or in child-rearing. In fact, in the late nineteenth century, when the domains are relatively collapsed into each other at the imperatives of capitalist colonialism and urbanization, the social environment is loud with censures and satires against masculine women and feminine men for inverting stable norms.[11] This is the world where our mothers lived and which they bequeathed to us in turn. In the literary works we study it is this world that had to be reformed, that is, reorganized within the umbrella of an enlightened patriarchy. *Amar Jiban* is replete with complaints against women's incarceration, the twin brutalization by housework and the deprivation of the exercise of reason.

In *Pratham Pratisruti* and *Nabankur* we see constant and violent censorship of young girls who are spirited and intelligent and who thus attempt to be both seen and heard in public. In *Subarnalata* this longing for the outside is expressed by the heroine's pathetic appeal for a balcony from which she could see the street. Needless to say, she is not only denied, but also ridiculed.

From its ubiquitous presence in these and other Bengali texts, its vestiges lingering among us today, decried by reformers and praised by the hindu revivalists then and now, it is impossible to believe that 'the home and the world' is only a nineteenth-century nationalist invention. It is more likely that this feudal social life of the propertied classes of Bengal/India lent itself to manipulations and adaptation by elite male proposals for the construction of the 'nation'. This arrangement, however, was never satisfactory, nor fully accomplished or conclusive. Rabindranath Tagore's novel of the same name, *Ghare Baire* (The Home and The Outside/ World), speaks to the ultimate impossibility of such a division. Thus, hindu revivalists harking back to the feudal segregation of the sexes and spaces in all senses seems to have served more as an ideological anti-reform slogan since this older social form was already there producing a constant challenge of disruption. In fact our texts here mark different moments of this disruption or over-coming as well as a persistence of the old structures and emotions.

Even though both women and men of the nineteenth century struggled to end this sexual division of labour and its morally gendered identities in favour of humanist equality, recent cultural critics of Bengal have found a way to glorify an adapted traditional social arrangement as a critique of modernity and an upholding of difference. They have found in the *andarmahal* or women's quarters an autonomous domain of happy women's culture and separate female morality/consciousness. It is interesting to explore the process whereby they have combined the hindu nationalist glorification of an interior world of women with what they understand to be a liberatory vindication of sexual difference. But the deep structure of this theorization relies on the tired capitalist colonial/ imperialist paradigm of 'tradition and modernity'. All that they do in their simplistic, difference-oriented anti-colonialism is to reverse the colonial or imperialist values—and thus glorify 'tradition', no matter in what 'classicized' or 'modernized' form, as a positive, contributory challenge to women. This is similar to what the hindu notables once did in their criticism of the Age of Consent Act.[12] What is more, they can present this gesture as one of postcolonial critique, since any 'reform' or challenge to this so-called nationalist 'resolution' may be seen as colonial/modernist. This new and radical conservatism among cultural theorists and historians has attempted to occlude women's own voices and confused issues of subjectivity and agency. Women's writings show a deep-seated rejection of this subjugated subjectivity proposed by the nationalist resolution, and of attempts to overcome this life in a social–spatial enclosure with a derivative agency. Their voices and accounts have been as usual drowned out by the patriarchal critics. These 'subaltern' critics, in order to be read right, have to be read against the kinds of texts by women under examination here.

Themes of segregation, spinning into women's incarceration achieved through physical restraint and moral means, reverberate in Bengali literature. Conservative novelists, such as Bankim Chandra Chattopadhyay, may find this 'natural' and good, while others might militate against them, but all agree on their presence both at the level of discourse and actuality. This incarceration is maintained by severe punishment for transgression, combining physical coercion with structural and moral coercion. The creation of consent or moral hegemony among women themselves is a most powerful weapon. Moral regulations through guilt and shame, of which I will say more later, help to provide psychological restraint and an environment of violence. These novels and Rasasundari's autobiography speak of girls as young as eight to ten years of age (often married) being barred from any active physical life or play. Any and every expressive and extrovertive behaviour, of body or speech, is negatively sanctioned. This includes sanctions against women/girls eating with a healthy appetite, asking for a second helping or better quality of food. Sulekha Sanyal in *Nabankur* portrays an amazing moment of disciplining a girl into proper femininity while her heroine eats with her brothers:

> Chhabi, too, holds out her bowl. "You're giving the others more—give me some more too, Grandma. I'm still hungry."

"There's no more. Look." Purnasashi holds out the empty bowl for her to inspect.

All of a sudden, Chhabi's head burns with rage, and she screams sharp and shrill, "You gave everyone two helpings, and me just one, and so little too. When Poltuda or Monida ask for more, you never say it's gone!"

"Well, I never!" Purnasashi is struck dumb for a second, and then she lets off, "Teach her to read and write, and look what happens next! The girl imagines she's as good as these darling boys of mine! Ridiculous! Will you be earning like the boys? All you'll ever be is a shackle on your father's neck. Yes, those days are coming, and pretty soon, when we won't be able to get food down his throat for worrying over how to get you married off. . . ." (Sanyal 1956: 293)

Rasasundari speaks of the days when, as a married woman, as mother, she went without food, while for the widows eating turns out to be a privilege rather than a need. This is how Rasasundari tells her story, only a part of which I translate here:

One day after making sure that everyone else had eaten, as I sat down to eat a man came as guest. The man was from the scheduled caste, he did not want to cook, nor did he agree to eat other things. He said, "I would eat some rice if I could have that." There was no time to cook then, so what could I do, but give to the guest the rice that was for me. I thought, I could eat when cooking is done for the night. Afterwards, completing all the tasks for the afternoon, I went to cook. I was terribly hungry then, and I was by myself, with no other person in the room. There were many edible things in the room, I could have eaten them, who could have prohibited me? In fact they would have been contented to see me eat. But I could not serve myself anything else to eat than rice. For this reason many kinds of food were not eaten by me. . . .

Having cooked a lot I waited until late into the night. The *kachari* [meeting] in the outer part of the house just did not break up, and the master never showed up. Then I gave their meal to everyone else, more or less completed my task, and sat waiting with the master's meal, and kept thinking, the master hasn't come yet, and in a while the kids [boys] will wake up. Then I won't be able to eat today. As I kept thinking this way, my thoughts turned out to be true. Just as the master came into the house, one of the boys woke up and started crying. I served the master his rice and fetched the boy. I thought that by the time the master finishes the boy will fall asleep, maybe I could eat with him in my lap. But no sooner did he finish eating, than another boy woke up and started to cry. Then I thought, maybe I could eat with both of them, and so saying, fetched that boy as well. I started to eat, with both of these boys. In the meanwhile a rain-storm started, and the lamp in the room went out. (Rasasundari Dasi 1860: 35–36)

This theme of women's life-long imprisonment in the 'home', ensnared in reproductivity and feminine conduct, and under-nourished, is a life sentence. It is hard to imagine in the face of such negative evidence, how anyone could read a happy and an auto-nomous women's culture or a 'new-found freedom', a 'new social responsibility' and challenge, in the *andarmahal* (P. Chatterjee 1989: 248). But obviously there is such a thing as ideological reading where a patriarchal, especially male, reader could perform a feat which would erase from the written pages of women most of what is on them, and substitute a patriarchal script in their place.

This gendered segregation and identity based on feminine conduct is painful for women in their denial of the exercise of reason and intellect, even though not all women demanded to exer-cise it in public, for intellectual debates or economic independence. 'Good women' of 'respectable' families were strictly enjoined against any form of learning, including literacy. The texts refer to superstitions, such as that an educated woman causes her hus-band's death or becomes blind herself. Oblivious of the fact that the deity of learning is herself a woman (*Pratham Pratisruti*), women are relegated to an instinctual–emotional life, considered as nothing but the body, for which they are both blamed and praised.[13] The exercise of the intellect is seen as a quintessentially public act, even when conducted in private for the purpose of read-ing sacred texts or literary pleasure. It signals an act of transcen-dence, encroachment into realms of reason and imagination.

Enclosed as she is, with a book in her hand, a woman may still escape her enclosure and bridge the gap between the mind and the body, the public and the private. Women seeking knowledge, therefore, became outlaws and guerrillas of their familial world by initially secret, and later defiantly open, pursuit of knowledge, including that of formal education. They reached out to reason and spiritua-lity, philosophy and ethics on wider humanist principles rather than obey the injunction of a patriarchally approved conduct based on feminine difference. The texts at hand centre on these emotional struggles and causes of passion as women fight to gain access to this forbidden world of knowledge and public space for themselves and their daughters. This is the motivating force of the plot and tra-jectory of their narratives.

In all of these texts, which cover over 150 years of Bengal's changing history, we see direct and indirect violence against women for aspiring to knowledge in any formal sense. Their attempts do not gain gradual legitimacy solely because women rebel, leave home and cover themselves in ignominy. This subjective movement, their agency, is aided by social and political formations within Bengal which weaken the colonially inflected feudalist patriarchy among the upper classes enough to support in the end, for example, the mother in *Nabankur*, who sends her daughter away to educa-tion, not marriage. This is distinctly different from Rasasundari's secretive attempts at learning to read the scriptures. Satyabati's loss of her married life and her daughter Subarnalata to betrayals by husband and mother-in-law, or Subarnalata's tragic unfulfilled life and death, yield to some social changes. Satyabati's promise to herself and her younger female generation of a life of knowledge and ethical judgements, in short, the emergence of women with greater social agency, is thus a generational project. The project of reason and creativity is finally realized by a woman, in the third generation, in *Bokul Katha*, through Bokul, who is the writer of the stories of the previous generations, of their transgressive desires and their punishments. Women's desire for learning, the trials and tribulations they underwent before they could tell their own stories, comes out at its purest in Rasasundari's account. It is this story that lies at the base of all Bengali women's aspirations to and achievement of knowledge and public literary creativity. I translate some passages from her own text.

> Then my desire for learning to read these [scriptural] texts became intense. I began to be angry with myself. What a terrible annoyance was this! No woman learns to read and write, so how can I? I began to wonder what I should do. Not all the customs of our country were bad in those days, but they were certainly bad in this regard, that they kept women deprived of knowledge. Women of that time were most unfortunate, to be counted among animals. But there is no point in complaining against others, our own luck is to be blamed! Old ladies [of our time] were most displeased if they saw paper in the hands of girls or women as signs of being against custom. How was I to learn reading and writing? But my mind was not to be placated by these thoughts, it was always craving to learn. I began to remember that in childhood I sat in the school and learnt a little just by hearing the boy students. Couldn't I recall even a little of that? Ruminating this way I began to recall the thirty-four letters of the alphabet, joint letters and some spellings. But even in those days I could barely read, and not write. I wondered what I should do. In all honesty [it must be admitted that] without a teacher, no one can learn. Particularly as I was a woman, and a married one at that, I could not speak to anybody. If anyone were to speak harshly to me [for doing this] I would die! In fear I spoke of this [desire to learn] to nobody. I would pray day and night to our great Lord!: "Lord, teach me to read and write. I must absolutely learn. If you don't teach me, who will?" This is what I would always say to myself. Days passed in this way. (Rasasundari Dasi 1993: 40–41)

Then began her self-instruction:

> When the book was kept in the room I opened it and took out a leaf, which I hid. Where was I to hide that leaf? I was very afraid that someone would find it. I thought if anyone ever saw it in my hand there would be no end to criticism, perhaps I would even be severely reprimanded. To incur displeasure of people or tolerate harsh words is not easy. I have been always afraid of that and those days women lived entirely subordinated . . . I was deeply

troubled about that leaf. I held it in my hand and thought, what should I do? . . . I came to the conclusion that I should keep it in a place where only I could find it. So where should I put it but under the firewood in the kitchen . . . but there was no let up in the household's daily chores. I had no time to study that page. At night it got too late by the time the cooking was finished. And no sooner were the chores all done than the children woke up. Is it possible to do anything else then? One would say, Ma, I want to pee; the other, Ma, I am hungry; the other, Ma, hold me; and another would wake and start crying. One had to console and look after them. And as night progressed sleep overcame [me] and there was no time left to study. I saw no way for me to learn. . . . So when I cooked I kept the page in my left hand, and once in a while sneaked it within my veil to look at it. But what could mere glancing accomplish? I could not even recognize the full alphabet.

In those days my eldest son used to write on palm leaves. I hid a palm leaf as well. I would look at this palm leaf first and then the page from the book, and refer to my mental image of the alphabet. And then again I would try to compare this with how people talk. Some days passed in this way. I would occasionally take out the book's page, and then hide it under the logs lest anyone should see it! (1860: 40–41)

Throughout this superhuman project of acquiring the simple tools for knowledge she continued to comment on her own predicament as that of all women:

Especially if one wants to write one needs equipment—paper, pen and a bottle of ink. You have to lay them out publicly as you sit down to write. I was a woman, and a married one at that, and a woman must never learn to read and write. That has been considered as a great transgression for the woman-kind. In this state of affairs what would people say if they saw me all decked out in this way preparing to write? (1860: 46)

Heroines of these novels compare to the vedic women Maitreyi and Gargi—the 'truth-seekers' and 'truth-speakers'—but not to the submissive mother/wife ideals of Sita, Sati and Savitri.[14]

They are not lauded, however, for being social critics and reformers, as ethical teachers. Their fate is not consecration by Bengal's
nationalist thought, but rather marginality, exclusion and ex-
communication. Through their transgressions by reaching out from
an interiorized and physicalized existence into the open space of
knowledge and public life, they become shamed outsiders both in
life and in Bengal's moral discourse for women. Even their own
daughters, as in Ashapurna Devi's novel, would be happier if they
were not alive. The conduct in pursuit of truth, knowledge and
courage which would have earned a man his highest accolade earns
them the reputation of whores and harpies. As we read through
these and other texts, it becomes apparent that this brahminical
patriarchy, which once condemned women and low castes to ignorance and severe physical punishment for aspiring to knowledge of
the sacred and the scripted, would mete them out again if the times
permitted.[15] But burnt in the fire of patriarchal violence, a woman
is forged over time who is not an exception, as were the vedic
women sages, who has the capacity to be learned, creative, upstan-
ding and uncompromisingly human. This is a woman made with
the history of many mothers and daughters.

The topics of humanity and humanism bring us to social
and political notions such as personhood, citizenship and the individual with reference to women. These notions imply a social subject who is in possession of herself, attributed with a socially recognized and personal will. Mothers and daughters of these texts are
clearly not accorded this self-possession and volition. They do not
own themselves—either in terms of their bodies or their labour
power. Without a bill of sale, but like serfs, they belong to males in
a social organization of patriarchal kinship. They come with the reproductive domain as serfs did once. Therefore, they cannot alienate their labour power or their bodies voluntarily and do not hold
the authority for arriving at forms of consent or contract, and this
in a world organized for men in the nineteenth and twentieth centuries on the basis of contract, voluntary agreement and self-
possession. This lack of a legitimated will and ownership of their
own person both in law and social morality is both the result and
cause of their subordinated segregation. Women's status as social
and legal persons, moral beings and citizens is still being debated

internationally. And not accidentally, this situation is connected with the issue of property, and not only in economic terms, as women are property themselves, rather than self-possessors with an economic independence.[16]

The family as an institution and stages of women's lives

The narrative organization of these texts, and other texts by women, is most often one of a journey through segregated spaces from the inner to the outer, entailing discoveries and dangers. This journey pattern assumes its concreteness by depicting various stages of a woman's life in the institution of the family and the relationship to the public domain. The life of these inhabitants of the inner quarters is divided into the stages of a short childhood or girlhood, succeeded by wife and motherhood, and often by widowhood, as women were frequently married to much older men. The familial kinship structure is governed by marriage and motherhood. A woman is primarily defined in these marital terms and only subordinately as her father's daughter, a role in which she is relatively free. Defined, then, as a man's wife and a mother of sons (woe to her if she wasn't!), her marriage is akin to a life sentence, beginning early—sometimes as young as seven or eight. It is not surprising, therefore, that at the level of popular culture, a sense of tragedy overhangs the marriage, or even the birth, of girls. Not only the brides themselves but also others close to her suffer from acute fear and anxiety regarding the fate of a girl being 'given away'.[17] This fear to this day drives up the amount paid out in dowry. Once 'given away' she enters into another clan, another household, and so on. No longer entitled to full funeral rights for her parents, she may not have even the permission to visit their deathbed. A woman's subjectivity and social agency, then, derives wholly in relation to the institutions of marriage and (a son's) motherhood. The crucial importance of marriage in determining a woman's life status is best revealed in the degradation of widows in Bengal or elsewhere among the upper-caste/class Hindus. Doomed to sexlessness, deprived of food and nutrition, bondaged to unending housework, the widow is the darkest shadow of the married woman. The horror of this existence is somewhat mitigated if she has mothered sons who have, and through whom she has, a degree of economic control.[18]

Patriarchy, within the confines of these feudal, colonial, petty-bourgeois homes, assumes a specific and highly mediated form. It articulates women in its hegemonic cause, in administrative and ideological services. Not only is there an overt and explicit overarching male domination, but also a patriarchal moral regulation and social organization within which women themselves engage in socializing, policing and punishing women within hierarchies of male-centred kinship structures. The husband's mother and his sisters are specially privileged in this context, a husband's sister appearing in the eye of the terrified bride as a 'royal tigress'. As the key source of female power lies in husbands and sons, a woman as mother *may* command some obedience from her sons, while demanding absolute obedience from her daughters-in-law. This world of women also holds a threat of violence, physical and otherwise, since older kin women could punish the younger physically, while husbands hold this power as a general prerogative. Altogether, this enclosed domain of women implodes within while violence also stalks its outside. All this is reflected in the architecture of enclosure of women's living quarters (see Borthwick 1984).

Male violence towards women as depicted in these texts is mainly of two kinds. There is of course the overt physical abuse, or humiliations, such as being locked out of the bedroom, put out in the street, or returned to the parents in disgrace. Ashapurna's and Sulekha's novels speak extensively of these and other forms. But they also speak of secret sexual violence, of marriage as the beginning of child sexual abuse by adult husbands and often continuing as unending marital rape, resulting in unwanted pregnancy. If a husband chooses to be 'good', that is, to not exert his 'rights', the gratefulness generated in women by this gesture is overwhelming. Kindness of fathers to daughters is noted with great love and reverence by women—this being the best face of men that women ever see. While older sons are often objects of fear, the young son holds no terror for the mother. At this stage the relationship is one of great indulgence and devotion, while daughters are also disciplining as young apprentices in caring roles. For the rest, a woman's world is one of overt and covert force.

In view of this, women hold a complex and ambivalent relationship to 'motherhood' and their children, particularly if they are male. On the one hand, having successful sons does give a woman social power and viability; on the other, as an ideology of sacrifice, as moral regulation, motherhood mainly serves to oppress her. Feminist cultural critics, such as Jasodhara Bagchi, have discussed the oppressive role of the motherhood ideology and shown its particularly problematic deployment by hindu nationalists (Bagchi 1990: 20–27). Through this ideology, which constantly enjoins her to sacrifice, devotion and nurture, especially for her male children, women are denied a substantive sense of self and an agency for an effective presence in the world. This saintly, sacrificing and weeping mother is of course by definition not in reciprocal relationships, and this one-directional, inhumanly devoted, enjoined subjectivity is elevated to the level of goddess.

Other than the pedestals of motherhood or goddesshood, there are various moral mechanisms to ensure female submission and subjection. These notions are equally hegemonic and extend to honour, propriety, shame and guilt. Giving powerless women the responsibility of upholding the family's honour is another way of relegating them to their assigned space and station within the overall social organization. This 'honour', which is not of the woman but that of the family, of a patriarchal kinship, requires them to act as the plinths of the women's quarters or as the core of the hindu upper-caste/class familial morality. Honour and its related notion, 'propriety', serve both as a means of pacification and interpellation of women in the patriarchal cause. The texts I use elaborate on the human cost of such notions (H. Bannerji 1994).

On the reverse side of honour and propriety stand guilt and shame. Enforcing or practicalizing them into social relations and prescribed or proscribed practices also creates the requisite patriarchal, property-owning class's hegemonic psychic forms. One should remember in this context the old Bengali saying that '[a sense of] shame [shyness] is a woman's most precious ornament'. In the tightly organized, highly patrolled women's world, any active, assertive, outreaching gesture is supposed to produce shame and guilt. The transgressions range all across daily life. Speaking out, arguing, using a loud voice, wanting education, any desire for self-pleasing such as good food, romantic love, or active sexuality—all call for guilt, shame and punishment. A woman's 'goodness', then, is a negative thing, it consists of what she does not, rather than does, do. And the trial for proof extends life-long. Hence the Bengali proverb, "*purlo meye urlo chhai/ tabe meyer gun gai!*" ("a woman is burnt, her ashes are thrown to the wind / not until then can we sing her praise").

This guilt/shame dynamic is deeply explored and complexly described in these five texts. The central characters, all women, spend the earlier phase of the development of their subjectivities in an oscillation between anger, guilt and shame. Most often their anger is directed towards themselves and their children, but they also hate their patriarchal world, their violent or gutless husbands, calling all this their 'fate'. 'Hysteria', that momentary uncontrollable acting out, also marks some moments here. The theme of madness is always in sight, and suicide a pending threat. When a woman actually does die, her 'husband god' speedily mounts the marriage platform. This is captured by a Bengali proverb, "*abhagar ghora mare, bhagyabaner bou mare*" ("an unfortunate man loses his horse, the fortunate one his wife"). It is also said that there is no lack of 'serving maidens' in the country. This is not patriarchy of an ordinary kind, but rather misogyny in its diffused social form.

A scrutiny of attitudes towards sexuality provides the best entry-point to assess the situation of women, both as social subjects and objects. Women are not to have any independent sexuality outside of the context of marriage. Thus, their childhood is not a deterring factor in marrying young girls to much older males who are sometimes fifteen to twenty years older. As the age of marriage rises through time, even one hundred years later, the general pattern is to arrange marriages with little regard to the real consent of women. These novels speak of marriages solemnized and consummated, without consent, very early in life. This decides the girl's or woman's fate in life, both as a wife and a widow. It magnifies the lack of right to her own will and consent. Thus, she is typologically without any sexual self or control over her body. Possibilities of marital rape, unwanted pregnancy and children, other physical and mental indignities and brutality, are the social parameter within which the rights of husbands are demonstrated. This is true even when men do not exert these 'rights'.

Sexuality, then, is the bane of a woman's life. As we see in the character of Subarnalata, who is beautiful and vibrant, she must have sexuality only for her husband and not for herself. But in her 'chaste wife' role she should be attractive, and always ready, for his pleasure. It is not surprising, then, that our literature rebounds with women's distaste for sex, often disguised in a moral or spiritual discourse.[19] Both physical invasion/submission and the dread of pregnancy combine to create a sense of aversion. And yet this indiscriminate, often violent use of a woman's body is presented in the ideologically reversed patriarchal moral regulation of *satittwa* or 'wife's chastity'. As a complementary part of the ideology of motherhood, her readiness is enjoined as the highest form of moral conduct, and it may extend into her next life. This readiness to give up *everything* to and for him finds its logical and actual extension in the practice of *satidaha* (the burning of widowed women on their husbands' funeral pyre). As she is 'his', her willing submission to sexual/social unfreedom is presented to her as her field of glory. This is where she is to show her prowess. Her pleasure must therefore be always tinged with a masochism, and marriage is the altar on which she is sacrificed to this male god called 'husband'. When we look at the list of *satis* (mythic chaste figures) —Behula, Chintamoni, Savitri and so on—we see that 'wife' and 'motherhood', these deeply patriarchal moral regulations, are considered a woman's true religion. This she can practice without any direct knowledge of the scriptures, or even a sense of god. Exquisite forms of self-destruction become the proof of her religious life.

Women, then, display direct or indirect, overt, muted or displaced disgust for sex, and adopt ways of avoiding contact with their husbands. Falling in love, which is mostly an extramarital matter, leads them to grief—prostitution, madness or suicide. It is not surprising that women frequently try to use the ideology of motherhood to their own advantage. As she is only sexual 'for', rather than 'in' herself, motherhood becomes a woman's preferred vocation in which a physicality of a direct but different sort with young children gives her some satisfaction and keeps the husband at bay within socially approved sanctions. She uses patriarchy's major ideology, that the 'mother' is not a sexual being, in order to accomplish this. She takes to sleeping in the children's bed.[20] The space shortage endemic to Bengali middle-class joint families facilitates this. As her children grow up she divests herself of the responsibilities of feminine attractiveness. General neglect, repeated childbirth and hard work in any case take their toll. But perhaps she can then have some relief from constant sexual availability.

Women also practise religion at different levels—of rituals or *bratas* and spirituality—the latter having a philosophical/contemplative element to it. This spirituality presupposes a transcendence from the immediately practical and the pragmatic. The *bratas*, or women's rituals, in keeping with assigned feminine conduct in everyday life, fall somewhere between sympathetic magic and prayer. Their prayer may be directed to the main hindu pantheon deities, or to the quasi-demonic goddess of cholera or smallpox, or angry planets such as Saturn. These *bratas* are a woman's preserve, participated in also by children, and they are ways of controlling an otherwise (for her) uncontrollable social organization and relations of power. Prayers are in the nature of pledges or vows for ensuring success. In fact, these women's rituals are magical attempts to realize in their lives and fates what patriarchy requires. They also entreat self-protection and centre around such issues as securing a good husband and mother-in-law, male progeny, children's health, averting polygamy and the pain of a co-wife, avoiding widowhood—and finally, the husband's prosperity.[21] They morally inscribe and socialize girls and women into all aspects of their patriarchally organized lives.

It is important to note that all of the authors of these five texts are averse to or sceptical of these rituals. They attend them, if at all, as social obligation, and asides in the texts hold their criticism. What they want is spirituality, a contemplative/reflective existence—a form of religion usually seen as a male preserve. Women occasionally encroach into this, especially when they are widowed. Spirituality requires a knowledge of the sacred texts, of a philosophy of transcendence, and involves meditation and so on. Since this is a forbidden zone for most women, like Prometheus they steal fire for themselves and other women, including their daughters. They begin to lay claims on metaphysics, forge a morality rather than social propriety, and call upon universal equality of souls and notions such as 'truth' and 'justice'. This pits them against the laws of the father.

Need for spirituality among women derives directly and negatively from their oppressed lives. It is not surprising that they want to transcend their everyday world and be in communication with a divine being who sees a soul beyond gender, and thereby escape the claustrophobia of domesticity and intellectual and imaginative starvation. They reach out to a knowledge which expands their consciousness and unifies it with the universe. But along with these aspects, women's relationship to god is like one to a surrogate human companion who can really understand them in a caring way. This idea of god as a wise and compassionate presence is an inner higher court of appeal for a morality based on justice. For Rasasundari, this presence of the Divine, the All-Merciful (a name her mother taught her) lies under the quotidian phenomenal world. This is the way she narrates it:

> As soon as I was put into the palanquin the carriers started to move. I had no friend or relation with me, I fell at once into a sea of dangers. But since I saw no other recourse I kept saying in my mind, "Lord, you be with me." I said this to myself and continued crying. What a terrible state of mind was I in then! When they take a little goat to be sacrificed for the worship of Durga or Shyama, and that goat gives up its hope of life, and calls for its mother in a state of unconsciousness, my state of mind at that time was just like that. I continued to cry, calling my mother's name since I could not see any member of my family near me, and also kept calling on God with great concentration. And I kept thinking, my mother said if you are frightened, call for God. (1868: 20)

For Satyabati in *Pratham Pratisruti*, this sense of the divine is supplanted by the secular moral categories of truth and justice. The god of reason has now become a conduct of reason, based on a social criticism of what is true or false, right and wrong. When Satya leaves the world of the family to go to Benares, she is not looking for salvation but to live out her life in her chosen occupation of teaching children. It is interesting that as we progress in urbani-zation and general development of colonial capitalism and political resistance, women authors appeal to secular morality more so than to spirituality, divine mercy or forgiveness. In *Nabankur* the ques-tion of morality becomes one of economic and political justice, and the protagonist Chhabi comes under the influence of communism and takes part in peasant struggles.

While we are on this topic, we also need to mention the curious transference from her mother to god which engenders and informs Rasasundari's poetic and scholarly spirituality. Implanted with the idea of god as her protector by her mother, god becomes her mother's emissary and emanation which stays with her right through her life. For children snatched from their mothers and their childhood, their world of play, and entering as brides into strangers' homes, it makes sense to have a god of their own. It is also this forced and foundational estrangement, combined with the life we have already discussed, which produces in women's lives and literature their spiritual bent. The most frightening and dis-figured form of religion is manifested in the lives of young widows which are depicted in detail in the novels. For them religion, often deprived of spirituality, provides the only point of reference and validation in a life of severe austerity and denial. It does not serve as a source of solace or transcendence but of discipline or mania, as a means of self-flagellation. Their lives serve as a condemnation of a society that has thrown women into a pit of brutality.

Female spirituality is the other face of fear which domi-nates women's lives. Fear, as young Satyabati remarks in *Pratham Pratisruti*, has already killed women at their birth. It is everywhere and ranges from the fear of individual relatives to the fear of society at large. Woman's economic dependence, lack of education, sexual autonomy and lack of social resources in general, and an obsessive concern for reputation—all coalesce into an overall ethos. The ultimate fear, of course, is of her own self, of acting out or behaving in ways that could lead to being cast out and thereby becoming a prey of the male world as a domestic servant-cum-prostitute, and of a solitary unholy death. It is not surprising, then, that rituals, god and spirituality are such consistent themes in women's writings, appearing as talismanic and contemplative forms of self-protection. And perhaps by posing the ideal standard of the divine next to the fallen world in which they are forced to live, women make their idea of god their criticism of man's world.

Conclusion

The world our mothers gave us, then, is not one which is full of joys of mind and body, and of openness, freedom and dynamism. It is, however, in its mode of negation of what actually exists in society, incisively indicative of what is lacking and needed for a fuller subjectivity and agency. By looking at this world with a cold eye, these women authors tell us the meaning of the word 'human' in its social sense and offer a challenge to the dualism of the private and the public, the body and the mind. They call into searing question the gendered equation of a whole half of humanity as having a mindless body, while the other half has the prerogatives of both body and intellect.

Our mothers' worlds, into which we came as daughters, called upon us to right this wrong in every generation. In each generation of women there have been attempts, punishments meted out, and prices paid for breaking the barriers between the body and the mind, the home and the world, the public and the private. In each generation there has been a call for justice, for social reform. From nineteenth-century Bengal or India have resonated cries for justice for women by both women and male social critics and reformers. It is currently fashionable to decry all of these in the name of anti-colonialism. Students of nationalism who seek to provide a critique of colonial discourse have found in our 'social reformers', collaborators of the colonial project who compromise our authentic national identity. Nothing can be more blind, tendentious and collaborative with the project of colonization in its deepest sense than to take this anti-critical stance. This leads us to pretend that all was well for women in precolonial societies, or that women's bodies and minds must be sacrificed to the altar of a patriarchal anti-colonial/nationalist cause. This theoretical and ideological–political position is a reworking of the old colonial imperialist paradigm of 'tradition and modernity', 'barbarism and civilization', in which the national/anti-colonial stance amounts to no more than a simple inversion of values given to each notion. It is sublimely unaware of difference based on social relations of power and basic questions of justice in both pre and postcolonial social formations. Contemptuous of rational/critical projects, this anti-reformism hides deformations of societies based on property and its suitable forms of propriety, especially within the ex-colonized countries of the world.

The world that our mothers gave us, then, is this world that our women authors describe, which cries out to be both enjoyed and changed. By their lives, struggles, imagination and words they gifted us with an ongoing creative and political project. A woman is still in the making, in a task of ongoing generation in which we make ourselves and re-make our world. This is a project of justice, of creativity, of re-form and revolution in social relations and ethics, to be taken up from the woman's standpoint.

Notes and References

1 For women's efforts in this direction and participation in politics, see R. Kumar (1995), and also C. Ghosh (1991).

2 For Freud on female sexual development, see Freud (1966).

3 See S. Rowbotham (1977), and also L. Davidoff and C. Hall (1987).

4 The phrase is Eric Wolf's; see Wolf (1982).

5 See the two volumes of anthology of women's writing edited by S. Tharu and K. Lalitha (1991); see also P. Chatterjee's seventh chapter, "Women and the Nation", in Chatterjee (1994).

6 P. Chatterjee, "The nationalist resolution of the women's question", in Kumkum Sangari and Sudesh Vaid (eds) (1990).

7 See S. Banerjee (1990); also other anti-modernist/reformist writings on domesticity and women, such as D. Chakrabarty (1993) and the work of Ashis Nandy.

8 See T. Sarkar (1993b); also P. Chatterjee (1994).

9 This view of an accomplished 'resolution' of 'the women's question' and the creation of a hegemonic 'nationalist thought' indicative of a successful 'passive revolution' at the level of civil society is advanced most elaborately by Partha Chatterjee. This view is developed piece by piece in "The Nation and its Fragments" (1986).Though referential to colonial discourse, and responsive to demands of modernity, in the public aspects of life nationalist discourse is for Chatterjee a formidable force at the cultural/domestic level. Sudipto Kaviraj's *The Unhappy Consciousness* (1995) echoes the same position, offering a romantic hindu nationalist thought as *the* anti-colonial cultural–political thought. The same view is also shared by Dipesh Chakrabarty (1993). Such a stance suppresses other nationalisms, such as that of a reformist/liberal or secular variety. Uma Chakravarti in her essay "The myth of 'patriots' and 'traitors'" (1996) offers a powerful argument against this patriarchal mythic 'resolution'. Her stance and exposition not only rejects the patriarchy of

the nationalist thinkers (which borders on misogyny), but provides us with a basis for questioning and exposing the complicity of the 'subaltern school' in this social and epistemic violence against women—all in the name of the civil society and 'the nation'. For a complicit stance with patriarchy in the name of anti-colonial discourse and 'tradition', see also Ashis Nandy's *At the Edge of Psychology* (1980) and his other writings.

[10] See especially the tracts by Raja Rammohan Roy, "Translation of a Conference between an advocate for, and an opponent of, the practice of Burning widows, Alive; from the original Bangla" (1818); "A second conference. . ." (1820); "Abstract of the Arguments regarding the burning of widows considered as a religious rite" (1830); and his "Anti-Suttee petition to the House of Commons", all in R.R. Roy (1947).

[11] On this issue of satire against educated, outwardly-oriented women, see P. Chatterjee (1992), and also chapter three, "The Nationalist Elite", and chapter six, "The Nation and Its Women", in P. Chatterjee (1994).

[12] See H. Bannerji, "Age of Consent and Hegemonic Social Reform", in this volume; also Tanika Sarkar, "The Hindu Wife and Hindu Nation" (1992a).

[13] See G. Lloyd (1993). Controversies surrounding the Widow Remarriage Act of 1856 or the Age of Consent Act of 1891 show in the most blatant way how women amounted to no more than a body, both in terms of social and biological reproduction. See also J. Bagchi (1993: 2214–20).

[14] For use of mythic ideals for inculcating an ideology of pure womanhood, see Uma Chakravarti (1996) and T. Sarkar (1995b).

[15] See Kumkum Roy (1995) and also Sukumari Bhattacharji (1995).

[16] Lucy Carroll (1989); see also Zoya Hasan (ed.) (1994).

[17] As expressed by Rasasundari Dasi (1868) in the passage that serves as my epigram.

[18] See Kalyani Dutta (1994); also Uma Chakravarti (1993: 130–58) and Dagmar Engels (1996).

[19] Women and spirituality in Bengal has not yet captured as much scholarly and feminist attention as it should. But see the excellent article by Tanika Sarkar, "A Book of Her Own. A Life of Her Own" (1993b).

[20] Sulekha Sanyal's *Nabankur* (1956) opens with a child waking and looking at all the people sleeping in the room, and situating herself among them.

[21] Satyabati in *Pratham Pratisruti* (A. Devi 1964) reveals the nature of *brata* as women's sympathetic magic when she recites a verse to her father, enjoining suffering and an early death to a co-wife.

References

There are some inconsistencies in the citation pattern of the Bengali nineteenth-century magazine articles. These were hand-copied by several people, some of whom took down page numbers and publication details while others did not. There was also inconsistency in the methods of pagination used by various copyists, making it impossible to arrive at a uniform, accurate mode of citation for quotations from the articles. Therefore, I have not given individual page numbers for quotations, but rather have cited the page numbers of the entire text. Over the years, much of this very fragile material has perished. I have made use of these articles even with their inconsistencies, because this at least preserves some part of them, rather than lose them in entirety for the future. The names of the magazines and authors give an indication of where they may be found, if indeed they should exist any more.

In addition, some of the nineteenth-century publications from Calcutta appeared as pamphlets and tracts, many of which did not include the publisher's name, but only the place of publication.

Abrams, Philip (1982), *Historical Sociology*, Ithaca: Cornell University Press.
Addy, P. and I. Azzad (1973), "Politics and Culture in Bengal", *New Left Review*, 79: 71–112.
Alloula, Malek (1986), *The Colonial Harem*, Minneapolis: University of Minnesota Press.
Althusser, Louis (1984), *Essays on Ideology*, London: Verso.
Anonymous (1869), "Sindur" [Vermillion], *Bamabodhini Patrika*, 4 (63) (B.S. Kartik 1275).
——— (1870), "Strilokganer Snan Pranali" [Women's Bathing Customs], *Bamabodhini Patrika*, 72 (5) (B.S. Sraban 1276).
——— (1872), "Meyether Poshak" [Attire of Women of Bengal], *Bamabodhini*, 99 (8) (B.S. Kartik 1278).
——— (1891), "Shikshita Narir Pratibader Uttar" [Reply to Educated Woman's Protest], *Sadhana*.
Archer, Mildred and Toby Falk (1989), *India Revealed: The Art and Adventure of James and William Fraser, 1801–35*, London: Cassell.
Aries, Philip (1962), *Centuries of Childhood*, trans. Robert Balrick, New York: Vintage.

Arnold, D. (1993), *Colonizing the Body: State Medicine and Epidemic Disease in Nineteenth Century India*, Berkeley: University of California Press.

Bagchi, Jasodhara (1985), "Positivism and Nationalism: Womanhood and Crisis in Nationalist Fiction—Bankimchandra's *Anandmath*", *Economic and Political Weekly*, 20 (43): WS 58–62.

——— (1990), "Representing Nationalism: Ideology of Motherhood in Colonial Bengal", *Economic and Political Weekly*, 25 (42–43): WS 65–71.

——— (1993), "Socializing the Girl Child in Colonial Bengal", *Economic and Political Weekly*, 28 (41): 2214–20.

Ballhatchet, Kenneth (1980), *Race, Sex and Class under the Raj: Imperial Attitudes and Politics and their Critics, 1793–1905*, London: Weidenfeld and Nicolson.

Bandyopadhyay, Shibaji (1991), *Gopal-Rakhal Dwanda Samas: Upanibeshbad o Bangla Shishu Sahitya* [An Elision of *Gopal-Rakhal: Colonialism and Bengali Children's Literature*], Calcutta: Papyrus.

Banerjee, Sumanta (1988), *Keyabat Meye* [Bravo, Woman!], Calcutta.

——— (1989), *The Parlour and the Streets: Elite and Popular Culture in Nineteenth Century Calcutta*, Calcutta: Seagull.

——— (1990), "Marginalization of Women's Popular Culture in Nineteenth Century Bengal", in Sangari and Vaid (1990).

Bannerji, Himani (1989), "The Mirror of Class: Class Subjectivity and Politics in Nineteenth Century Bengal", *Economic and Political Weekly*, 24 (19): 1041–51.

——— (1992), "Mothers and Teachers: Gender and Class in Educational Proposals for and by Women in Colonial Bengal", *Journal of Historical Sociology*, 5 (1).

——— (1994), "Textile Prison: Discourse on Shame (*lajja*) in the Attire of the Gentlewoman (*bhadramahila*) in Colonial Bengal", *Studies in Moral Regulation*, ed. M. Valverde, Toronto: Centre of Criminology and Canadian Journal of Sociology.

——— (1995), "The Passion of Naming: Identity, Difference and Politics of Class", in H. Bannerji, *Thinking Through: Essays on Feminism, Marxism and Anti-Racism*, Toronto: Women's Press.

——— (1998), *The Mirror of Class: Political Theatre in West Bengal*, Calcuta: Papyrus.

Barthes, Roland (1973), *Mythologies*, trans. Annette Lavers, London: Paladin.

Basu, Chandranath (1892), *Hindutwa* [Hinduism], Calcutta.

——— (1901), *Stridiger prati Upadesh* [Advice to Women], Calcutta.

Basu, Ishwarchandra (1884), *Nariniti* [Woman's Conduct], Calcutta.

Basu, Manomohan (1884), *Garhasthya* [Domesticity], Calcutta.

——— (1887), *Hindur Achar Vyavahar* [Hindu Customs], Calcutta.

Bernal, Martin (1993), "Black Athena: Hostilities to Egypt in the Eighteenth Century", in *The "Racial" Economy of Science: Toward a Democratic Future*, ed. Sandra Harding, Bloomington: Indiana University Press.

Bhattacharji, Sukumari (1995), "Laws on Women: Judaism, Christianity and Hinduism", in *Indian Women: Myth and Reality*, ed. Jasodhara Bagchi, Hyderabad: Sangam: 24–33.

Biswas, Taraknath (1886), *Bangya Mahila* [The Bengali Woman], Calcutta.

Borthwick, Meredith (1984), *The Changing Role of Women in Bengal 1849–1905*, Princeton: Princeton University Press.

Burton, Antoinette (1994), *Burdens of History: British Feminists, Indian Women and Imperial Culture, 1865–1915*, Chapel Hill: University of North Carolina Press.

Carpenter, Mary (1868), *Six Months in India*, London: Longmans.

Carr, Edward Hallet (1964), *What is History?* Middlesex: Penguin.

Carroll, Lucy (1989), "Law, Custom and Statutory Social Reform: The Hindu Widow's Remarriage Act of 1856", in *Women in Colonial India: Essays on Survival, Work and the State*, ed. J. Krishnamurty, New Delhi: Oxford University Press: 1–26.

Chakrabarty, Dipesh (1993), "The Difference–Deferral of (A) Colonial Modernity: Public Debates on Domesticity in British Bengal", *History Workshop*, 36 (Autumn): 1–33.

Chakravarti, Uma (1989), "Whatever Happened to the Vedic Dasi?" in *Recasting Women: Essays in Colonial History*, eds Kumkum Sangari and Sudesh Vaid, New Delhi: Oxford University Press: 27–87.

———— (1993), "Social Pariahs and Domestic Drudges: Widowhood among Nineteenth Century Poona Brahmans", *Social Scientist*, 244–46 (Sept.–Nov.): 130–58.

———— (1996), "The Myth of 'Patriots' and 'Traitors': Pandita Ramabai, Brahmanical Patriarchy and Militant Hindu Nationalism", in *Embodied Violence: Communalising Women's Sexuality in South Asia*, Kumari Jayawardena and Malathi De Alwis, London: Zed Books.

Chatterjee, Partha (1986), *Nationalist Thought and the Colonial World: A Derivative Discourse*, London: Zed Books.

———— (1990), "The Nationalist Resolution of the Women's Question", in *Recasting Women: Essays in Colonial History*, eds Kumkum Sangari and Sudesh Vaid, New Brunswick: Rutgers University Press: 233–53.

———— (1992), "A Religion of Urban Domesticity: Sri Ramakrishna and the Calcutta Middle Class", *Subaltern Studies 7*, eds P. Chatterjee and Gyanendra Pandey, Delhi: Oxford University Press.

———— (1994), *The Nation and its Fragments: Colonial and Post-Colonial Histories*, Delhi: Oxford University Press.

Chattopadhyay, Ratnabali (1992), "The Queen's Daughters: Prostitutes as Outcaste Group in Colonial India", Occasional Paper, Christian Michelsen Institute, Bergen, Norway.

Choudhury, Hemantakumari (1901), "Striloker Paricchad" [Women's Attire], *Antapur*, Yr. 4 (6) (B.S. Ashad 1308): 137–40.

Cohn, Bernard (1983), "Representing Authority in Victorian India", in *The Invention of Tradition*, eds Eric Hobsbawm and Terrence Ranger, Cambridge: Cambridge University Press: 165–210.

———— (1985), "The Command of Language and the Language of Command", in *Subaltern Studies 4: Writings on South Asian History and Society*, ed. R. Guha, Delhi: Oxford University Press: 276–329.

Corrigan, Philip (1981), "On Moral Regulation: Some Preliminary Remarks", *Sociological Review*, 29 (2).

Corrigan, Philip and Derek Sayer (1985), *The Great Arch: English State Formation as Cultural Revolution*, Oxford: Basil Blackwell.

Das, Krishnabhabini (1888), "Swadhin o Paradhin Narijiban" [Free and Subjected Lives of Women], in *Pradip*.

———— (1890a), "Amader Hobe Ki?" [What Will Happen to Us?], in *Sahitya* (B.S. Kartik Chaitra 1296).

———— (1890b), "Samaj o Samaj Samskar" [Society and Social Reform], in *Bharati o Balak* (B.S. Poush, 1297, 14 yr.).

———— (1891a), "Ingraj Mahilar Shiksha o Swadhinatar Gati" [English Women's Progress in Education and Independence], in *Bharati o Balak* (B.S. Sraban, 1297, 14 yr): 286–91.

———— (1891b), "Kindergarten", in *Bharati o Balak* (B.S. Agrahayan, 1297).

———— (1891c), "Shikshita Nari" [The Educated Woman], in *Sahitya* (B.S. Magh, 1298, 2nd yr), No. 10: 474–78.

———— (1892), "Striloker Kaj o Kajer Mahatya" [Women's Work and Its Value], in *Pradip*.

———— (1893), "Sansare Shishu" [Child in the Family], in *Sahitya* (B.S. Ashad, 1299, 3rd yr).

———— (1901), "Jatiya Jiban o Hindu Nari" [National Life and Hindu Women].

Dasgupta, Anil Chandra (ed.) (1959), *The Days of John Company: Selections from Calcutta Gazette 1824–32*, Calcutta.

Dasi, Rasasundari (1868), *Amar Jiban* [My Life], reprint, Calcutta: Dey Bookstore, 1987.

Davidoff, Leonore and Catherine Hall (1987), *Family Fortunes: Men and Women of the English Middle Class, 1780–1850*, Chicago: University of Chicago Press.

Deb, Chitra (1989), *Abarane Abharane Bharatiya Nari* [Indian Women in their Clothes and Ornaments], Calcutta: Ananda.

Debi, Gyanadanandini (1882), "Stri Shiksha" [Women's Education], *Bharati*, (B.S. Asvin 1288).

———— (1884), "Samaj Samskar o Kusamskar" [Social Reform and Superstitions], *Bharati*, (B.S. Asad 1290, 7 yr).

Debi, Hiranmayee (1891a), "Sutikagrihey Banaratwa" [Apishness in the Nursery], in *Bharati o Balak* (B.S. Poush 1298): 483–91.

———— (1891b), "Newnham College", *Bharati o Balak* (B.S. Chaitra 1298): 612–23.

Debi, Sarala (1906), "Amar Balya Jiban" [My Childhood], *Bharati* (B.S. Baisakh 1312).

Debi, Sarojkumari (1923), "Krishnabhabini Das", *Bharati* (B.S. Agrahayan 1329 yr 46).

Debi, Swarnakumari (1888), "Strishiksha o Bethune School" [Women's Education and Bethune School], *Bharati o Balak* (B.S. 1294).

———— (1916), "Sekele Katha" [Story of Old Times], *Bharati* (B.S. Chaitra 1322): 1114–24, reprint of "Amader Griha Antahpur Shiksha O Tahar Samskar" [Domestic Education in Our Household and Its Tradition], *Pradip*, 1899.

Devi, Ashapurna (1964), *Pratham Pratisruti* [The First Pledge], Calcutta: Mitra and Ghosh.

———— (1966), *Subarnalata*, Calcutta: Mitra and Ghosh.

———— (1973), *Bokul Katha* [Bokul's Story], Calcutta: Mitra and Ghosh.

Derrida, Jacques (1978), *Writing and Difference*, Chicago: University of Chicago Press.

Dirks, Nicholas (ed.) (1992), *Colonialism and Culture*, Ann Arbor: University of Michigan Press.

Dutta, Kalyani (1994), *Khara, Bari, Thor*, Calcutta: Thema.

Engels, Dagmar (1996), *Beyond Purdah? Women in Bengal: 1890–1939*, Delhi: Oxford University Press.

Fanon, Frantz (1963), *The Wretched of the Earth*, trans. Constance Farrington, New York: Grove.

Forbes, Geraldine (1975), *Positivism in Bengal: A Case Study in the Transmission and Assimilation of an Ideology*, Calcutta: Minerva.

———— (1979), "Women and Modernity: The Issue of Child Marriage in India", *Women's Studies International Quarterly*, 2: 407–19.

Foucault, Michel (1980), *The History of Sexuality, Volume 1: An Introduction*, trans. R. Hurley, New York: Vintage.

Freud, Sigmund (1966), *The Complete Introductory Lectures on Psychoanalysis*, trans. and ed. James Strachey, New York: Norton.

Gangopadhyay, Jyotirmayee (1924), "Gown o Sari" [Gown or Sari], in *Bharati* (B.S. Aswin 1330).

Gates Jr., Henry L. (ed.) (1985), *"Race", Writing and Difference*, Chicago: University of Chicago Press.

Ghosh, Chitra (1991), *Women's Movement Politics in Bengal*, Calcutta: Chatterjee.

Gilman, Sander (1985), "Black Bodies, White Bodies: Toward an Iconography of Female Sexuality in Late Nineteenth-Century Art, Medicine and Literature", in Henry L. Gates Jr (ed.) (1985): 223–61.

Government of India, Legislative Department (1892), *Papers (Nos. 4, 11, 12) Relative to the Bill to Amend the Indian Penal Code and the Code of Criminal Procedure, 1882*.

Gramsci, Antonio (1971), *Selections from The Prison Notebooks*, trans. and ed. Quintin Hoare and Geoffrey Nowell Smith, London: Lawrence and Wishart.

Guha, Ranajit (1981), *A Rule of Property for Bengal*, New Delhi: Orient Longman.

Guha, Ranajit and Gayatri Chakravarty Spivak (eds) (1988), *Selected Subaltern Studies*, Oxford: Oxford University Press.

Harding, Sandra (ed.) (1993), *The Racial Economy of Science*, Bloomington: Indiana University Press.

Hasan, Zoya (ed.) (1994), *Forging Identities: Gender, Communities and the State*, Delhi: Kali for Women.

Hobsbawm, Eric and Terrence Ranger (eds) (1984), *The Invention of Tradition*, Cambridge: Cambridge University Press.

Hyam, Ronald (1992), *Empire and Sexuality: The British Experience*, Manchester: Manchester University Press.

Inden, Ronald (1990), *Imagining India*, Oxford: Basil Blackwell.

Jones, William (1799) *The Works of Sir William Jones*, ed. A.M. Jones, 6 vols, London: G.G. and J. Robinson, R.H. Evans.

———— (1970), *The Letters of William Jones*, ed. Garland Cannon, 2 vols, Oxford: Clarendon Press.

Joshi, Vijaya Chandra (ed.) (1975), *Rammohun Roy and the Process of Modernization in India*, New Delhi: Vikas.

Karlekar, Malavika (1991), *Voices from Within: Early Personal Narratives of Bengali Women*, New Delhi: Oxford University Press.

Kaviraj, Sudipta (1995), *The Unhappy Unconscious: Bankim Chandra Chattopadhyay and the Formation of Nationalist Discourse in India*, Delhi: Oxford University Press.

Khastagiri, Shrimati Soudamini (1872), "Strigoner Paricchad" [Women's Clothes], *Bamabodhini Patrika* 97 (8) (B.S. Bhadra 1278).

Kosambi, Meera (1991), "Girl-Brides and Socio-Legal Change: Age of Consent Bill (1891) Controversy", *Economic and Political Weekly*, August 3–10.

Krishnaraj, Maithreyi (1995), "Motherhood: Power and Powerlessness", in *Indian Women: Myth and Reality*, ed. Jasodhara Bagchi, Hyderabad: Sangam: 34–43.

Kumar, Radha (1995), *The History of Doing: An Illustrated Account of Movements for Women's Rights and Feminism in India, 1800–1990*, New Delhi: Kali for Women.

Kuznets, S. (1966), *Modern Economic Growth: Rate, Structure and Spread*, New Haven: Yale University Press.

Lloyd, Genevieve (1984), *The Man of Reason: "Male" and "Female" in Western Philosophy*, London: Methuen.

Long, Rev. J. (1974), *Calcutta in the Olden Times*, reprinted in *Nineteenth-Century Studies* 5, Calcutta.

Lutz, Catherine and Jane Collins (1993), *Reading National Geographic*, Chicago: University of Chicago Press.

Majeed, Javed (1992), *Ungoverned Imaginings: James Mill's The History of British India and Orientalism*, Oxford: Clarendon Press.

Mani, Lata (1989), "Continuous Traditions: The Debate on *Sati* in Colonial India", in *Recasting Women: Essays in Indian Colonial History*, eds Kumkum Sangari and Sudesh Vaid, New Brunswick: Rutgers University Press: 88–126.

———— (1992), "Cultural Theory, Colonial Texts: Eyewitness Accounts of Widow Burning", in *Cultural Studies*, eds L. Grossberg et. al, New York: Routledge: 392–405.

Martin, J.R. (1837), *Notes on the Medical Topography of Calcutta*, Calcutta.

Marshman, J.C. (1864), *Life and Times of Carey, Marshman and Ward*, London: Strahan.

Marx, Karl (1933), *The Civil War in France*, New York: International.

———— (1963), *The Eighteenth Brumaire of Louis Bonaparte*, New York: International.

———— (1977), *Grundrisse*, trans. Martin Nicolaus, Middlesex: Penguin.

Marx, Karl and Friedrich Engels (1973), *The German Ideology*, New York: International.

———— (1984), *The Communist Manifesto*, New York: Progress.

McMohan, Major C.A. (1872), Home Judicial File No. 48, p. 1143, 7th June 1872, to C.M. Riwarzi Esq., Officiating Undersecretary to the Government of Punjab.

Mill, James (1968), *The History of British India*, 2 vols, with notes by H.H. Wilson and introduction by John K. Galbraith, New York: Chelsea House, reprint of the 5th edition.

Mill, John Stuart (1966), "On Coleridge and Bentham", in *Selected Works*, ed. J.M. Robson, Toronto: Macmillan: 449–58.

———— (1972), "On Liberty", in *Utilitarianism, On Liberty and Considerations on Representative Government*, ed. H.B. Acton, London: J.M. Dent: 65–170.

Murshid, Ghulam (1983), *Reluctant Debutante: Response of Bengali Women to Modernization, 1849–1905*, Rajshahi: Rajshahi University Press.

Mustafi, Nagendrabala (1896), *Bamabodhini* (B.S. Vaisakh 1302).

Nandy, Ashis (1980), *At the Edge of Psychology: Essays in Politics and Culture*, Delhi: Oxford University Press.

Niranjana, Tejeshwari (1990), "Translation, Colonialism and the Rise of English", *Economic and Political Weekly*, 25 (15): 773–77.

Popper, Karl (1962), *Open Society and Its Enemies*, London: Routledge and Kegan Paul.

Pratt, Marie Louise (1992), *Imperial Eyes: Travel Writing and Transculturation*, London: Routledge.

Raychoudhury, G.P. (1884), *Grihalakshmi* [The Goddess Laxmi of the Hearth], Calcutta.

Raychaudhury, Tapan (1988), *Europe Reconsidered: Perceptions of the West in Nineteenth Century Bengal*, New Delhi: Oxford University Press.

Rich, Adrienne (1976), *Of Woman Born: Motherhood as Experience and Institution*, New York: Norton.

Rostow, W.W. (1985), *The Stages of Economic Growth: A Non-Communist Manifesto*, Cambridge: Cambridge University Press.

Rowbotham, Sheila (1977), *Hidden from History*, London: Pluto.

Roy, Kumkum (1995), "'Where Women are Worshipped, There the Gods Rejoice': The Mirage of the Ancestress of the Hindu Woman", in *Women and Right-Wing Movements: Indian Experiences*, eds Tanika Sarkar and Urvashi Butalia, London: Zed Books: 10–28.

Roy, Rammohan (1820), *A Second Conference between an Advocate for and an Opponent of the Practice of Burning Widows Alive*, Calcutta.

———— (1947), *The English Works of Raja Rammohun Roy*, eds Kalidas Nag and Debajyoti Burman, Calcutta: Sadharan Brahmo Samaj.

Said, Edward W. (1978), *Orientalism*, New York: Random House.

———— (1981), *Covering Islam*, New York: Pantheon Books.

Sangari, Kumkum and Sudesh Vaid (eds) (1990), "Introduction", in *Recasting Women: Essays in Colonial History*, New Brunswick, New Jersey: Rutgers University Press: 1–26.

Sanyal, Sulekha (1956), *Nabankur*, Calcutta: Manisha.

Sarkar, Sumit (1985a), *A Critique of Colonial India*, Calcutta: Papyrus.

———— (1985b), "The Women's Question in 19th Century Bengal", in *Women and Culture*, eds Kumkum Sangari and Sudesh Vaid, Bombay: SNDT Women's University: 157–72.

Sarkar, Susobhan Chandra (1979), *On the Bengal Renaissance*, Calcutta: Papyrus.

Sarkar, Tanika (1987), "Nationalist Iconography: Images of Women in Nineteenth Century Bengali Literature", *Economic and Political Weekly*, 22 (47): 2011–15.

———— (1992a), "The Hindu Wife and the Hindu Nation: Domesticity and

Nationalism in Nineteenth Century Bengal", *Studies in History*, 8 (2): 213–35.

——— (1993a), "Rhetoric against Age of Consent: Resisting Colonial Reason and Death of a Child-Wife", *Economic and Political Weekly,* 28 (36): 1869–78.

——— (1993b), "A Book of Her Own. A Life of Her Own: Autobiography of a Nineteenth Century Woman", *History Workshop Journal*, 36 (Autumn): 35–65.

——— (1995a), "Hindu Conjugality and Nationalism in the Late Nineteenth Century Bengal", in *Indian Women: Myth and Reality*, ed. Jasodhara Bagchi, Hyderabad: Sangam: 98–115.

——— (1995b), "Heroic Women, Mother Goddesses: Family Organization in Hindutva Politics", in *Women and Right-Wing Movements: Indian Experiences*, eds Tanika Sarkar and Urvashi Butalia, London: Zed.

Sayer, Derek (1991), *Capitalism and Modernity: An Excursus on Marx and Weber*, New York: Routledge.

Scott, Joan W. (1988), *Gender and the Politics of History*, New York: Columbia University Press.

Sears, L.J. (ed.) (1996), *Fantasizing the Feminine in Indonesia*, Durham: Duke University Press.

Sen, Asok (1977), *Ishwar Chandra Vidyasagar and the Elusive Milestones*, Calcutta: Riddhi-India.

Shanley, M.L. and C. Pateman (1991), "Introduction", in *Feminist Interpretations and Political Theory*, University Park: Pennsylvania State University Press: 1–10.

Sinha, Kaliprasanna (1856), *Hutom Penchar Naksha* [The Owl's Skits], Calcutta, reprint, 1992.

Sinha, Mrinalini (1995), *Colonial Masculinity: The "Manly Englishmen" and the "Effeminate Bengali" in the Late Nineteenth Century*, Manchester: Manchester University Press.

Smith, Dorothy E. (1987), *The Everyday World as Problematic: A Feminist Sociology*, Toronto: University of Toronto Press.

——— (1990), *The Conceptual Practices of Power: A Feminist Sociology of Knowledge*, Toronto: University of Toronto Press.

Soudamini, Kumari (1872), "Lajja" [Modesty], *Bamabodhini Patrika*, 95 (7) (B.S. Ashad 1278).

Spivak, G. Chakravorty (1988), "Can the Subaltern Speak?", in *Marxism and the Interpretations of Culture*, eds C. Nelson and L. Grossberg, Urbana: University of Illinois Press: 271–313.

Stokes, Eric (1969), *The English Utilitarians and India*, Oxford: Clarendon Press.

Stoler, Ann Laura (1989), "Rethinking Colonial Categories: European Communities and the Boundaries of Rule", *Comparative Studies in Society and History*, 31 (1): 134–201.

Taussig, Michael (1992), "Culture of Terror—Space of Death: Roger Casement's Putamayo Report and the Explanation of Torture", in *Colonialism and Culture*, ed. Nicholas Dirks, Ann Arbor: University of Michigan Press.

Tagore, Rabindranath (1961), *Chhelebela*, in *Racanabali* [Collected Works] 10, Calcutta: Visvabharati.

Thakur, Tekshand (1841), *Alaler Gharer Dulal* [Spoilt Darling of the Worthless Rich], Calcutta.

Tharu, Susie and K. Lalitha (1991), *Women Writing in India*, 2 vols, trans. Madhuchanda Karlekar, New York: The Feminist Press at the City University of New York.

Thompson, Edward P. (1966), *The Making of the English Working Class*, New York: Vintage.

Visvanathan, Gauri (1989), *Masks of Conquest: Literary Study and British Rule in India*, London: Faber and Faber.

Walkowitz, Judith R. (1980), *Prostitution in Victorian Society: Women, Class and the State*, Cambridge: Cambridge University Press.

Whitehead, J. (1995), "Modernizing the Motherhood Archetype: Public Health Models and the Child Marriage Restraint Act of 1929", *Contributions to Indian Sociology* (n.s.) 29 (1 and 2): 187–209.

Williams, Raymond (1979), *Marxism and Literature*, Oxford: Oxford University Press.

———— (1983), *Keywords*, London: Flamingo/Fontana.

Wolf, Eric R. (1982), *Europe and the People without History*, Berkeley: University of California Press.

Zaretsky, Eli (1976), *Capitalism, the Family and Personal Life*, New York: Harper and Row.

Index